MULK RAJ ANAND

UNTOUCHABLE

NANDINI BHATTACHARYA is Reader, Department of English, Bethune College, Kolkata, and guest faculty, Department of English, University of Calcutta. Her areas of interest are postcolonial theory and fiction and Indian writing in English. Her most recent books include *R.K. Narayan's* The Guide: *New Critical Perspectives* (2004); *A Lovesong to Our Mongrel Selves: Problematics of Identity in the Novels of Salman Rushdie* (2005). Her forthcoming book is entitled *Saratchandra Chattopadhaya and the Colonial Encounter*.

SAROS COWASJEE is Professor Emeritus of English at the University of Regina, Saskatchewan, Canada. Before moving to Canada in 1963, he was Assistant Editor with the *Times of India*, Mumbai, for two years. Educated in India and England, he has published several critical studies, novels and short stories. His important works include a seminal book on Mulk Raj Anand, *So Many Freedoms: A Study of Major Fiction of Mulk Raj Anand* (1977).

NILADRI RANJAN CHATTERJEE is Senior Lecturer, in the Department of English, University of Kalyani, West Bengal. His area of specialization is European Modernism and he has published several essays on writers such as E.M. Forster and Christopher Isherwood. He has an 'Entry on Mulk Raj Anand' in *The Readers Companion to Twentieth Century Writers,* edited by Peter Parker (1995); and is the co-editor of *The Muffled Heart: Stories of the Disempowered Male* (2005).

MULK RAJ ANAND
UNTOUCHABLE

Edited by

Nandini Bhattacharya

Untouchable published by Penguin Books India in 2001

ISBN 978-81-317-0725-8

First Impression, 2008
Fifteenth Impression, 2024
Sixteenth Impression, 2025

This edition is for sale in the Indian subcontinent only

Published by Pearson India Education Services Pvt. Ltd, CIN: U72200TN2005PTC057128

Head Office: 1st Floor, Berger Tower, Plot No. C-001A/2, Sector 16B, Noida – 201 301,Uttar Pradesh, India.

Registered Office: Featherlite, 'The Address' 5th Floor, Survey No 203/10B, 200 Ft MMRD Road, Zamin Pallavaram, Chennai - 600044

Website: in.pearson.com; Email:companysecretary.india@pearson.com

Digitally printed in India by Trinity Academy for Corporate Training Ltd, New Delhi in the year of 2025

CONTENTS

Acknowledgements

Strangely enough, it was my teaching of Raja Rao's *Kanthapura* in my graduate classes (Indian Writing in English Course, in the University of Calcutta) and the heated discussions with students in the classroom, regarding M.K. Gandhi's and B.R. Ambedkar's engagements with untouchability/caste prejudice in pre-Independence India that led to my interest in Mulk Raj Anand in general, and the text *Untouchable* in particular.

Subsequently, as one of the resource persons, I presented a paper and exchanged views on problems of untouchability and its literary and cultural representations in India with a group of teachers for an UGC-sponsored Refresher Course at the University of Calcutta. This went on to further enrich my perceptions about Anand's *Untouchable.*

Professors Janet and Steven Walker, both affiliated to the State University of New Jersey, Rutgers, Department of Comparative Literature, invited me to teach *Untouchable* as a part of their South Asia Studies Course to their graduate students. My interaction with the students of both North American, as well as Indian and Pakistani origins, went on to provide me with a vital perspective about the global relevance of the untouchability issue.

Finally, the lived reality of Dalit oppression in contemporary India, the complex matrix of caste politics in which the modern Indians like us are embedded, realities which continue to distort and disorient our 'modernity'—has rendered a 'reading' of Anand's *Untouchable* inevitable.

I acknowledge my debt of gratitude to Professors Janet Walker and Steven Walker, for giving me the opportunity to teach *Untouchable* in their university, exchanging many valuable ideas, and providing the intellectual stimulation, which only brilliant and dedicated teachers like them can.

ACKNOWLEDGEMENTS

I am grateful to my dear friend Professor Niladri Ranjan Chatterjee, affiliated to the Department of English, Kalyani University, for sharing many of the mundane problems of bringing out such a volume, while enriching its content with his knowledge of European Modernism, of which Anand was a part. His essay on the politics of the body in Mulk Raj Anand's *Untouchable* has been written exclusively for this volume.

My thanks to Urmila Dasgupta, for egging me on relentlessly to rework, rewrite and correct contents of this volume.

My sincere thanks to Saros Cowasjee, Professor Emeritus, University of Regina, Canada, an authority on Mulk Raj Anand, for kindly permitting me to reprint a part of his essay on *Untouchable*, originally a part of his book on Anand's fiction entitled *So Many Freedoms* (1977).

Finally, there are some personal debts, which cannot be repaid, but must be acknowledged. My husband Pradipta's love 'that looks on tempests and is never shaken'; my daughter Sunayani's jagged, restless pursuit of Plato's writings; and my son Pracheta's calm wisdom as well as his vital inputs on legal/constitutional ramification of caste politics in India has made this book possible.

Introduction

NANDINI BHATTACHARYA

Refusal to accept food cooked by dalit cooks on the part of students (as a part of mid-day meal scheme) in both Congress-governed Andhra Pradesh or Marxist-led West Bengal. Atrocities heaped on Dalits in Madhya Pradesh. Massacre of Dalits and destruction of Balmiki *bastis* (more than 50 homes torched) in Gohana of Harayana by Jats under the Congress-led Hooda government on 30 August 2005. On 3 September 2005, more than 25 dalit homes burnt down in Akola in Maharashtra. Mayavati, the Dalit leader of BSP waits for the tensions to boil over before rushing in with promises to extract maximum political benefit from the incident.

Similar incidents keep occurring throughout the nation periodically.

Introducing Mulk Raj Anand's *Untouchable* to the modern reader seemed the right time to present some randomly selected information from newspapers, news journals, and television reports. A comment by David Hardiman, summing up the condition of 'untouchables' in India today, would be in order:

> In contemporary India, the reality for most Dalits is a continuing routine discrimination in their daily life with acts of assertion being met by beatings, rape and murder. Although parliamentary and legislative assembly seats are reserved for Dalits, and they are given scholarships and reserved places in schools and colleges, only a small minority benefits from this, and even those who manage against the odds to obtain high qualifications are often denied employment. The large majority of Dalits continue to live in great poverty. The local police often fail to prevent attacks on Dalits, while covering up for the violence of the dominant classes. Politicians seek to win Dalit votes by claiming to abhor the practice of untouchability, but move to crush any acts that challenge

> Hinduism itself. In 2001, for example, some Dalits planned to stage mass conversion to Buddhism in Delhi.
>
> Hindutva activists promptly issued a threat that Dalits who attended would be attacked. Others who were not associated with the Hindu right added their voice to the anti-Dalit clamour, arguing that conversion would 'provoke communal tension.' The Bharatiya Janata Party (BJP) government used its power of office to prevent many Dalits from entering Delhi, so that the event turned out to be a damp squib.[1]

Imagining the Nation: The Alien Within

A reading of Mulk Raj Anand's *Untouchable* forces the reader to come to terms with, not only an extremely uncomfortable and painful aspect of Indian history but also to recognise the roots of several oppressive structures which flourish in contemporary India. It compels the reader to confront the paradoxes and contradictions at the heart of the Indian struggle for Independence as well as the contradictions that mire claims of a modern, egalitarian, equitable society. *Untouchable* is relevant because, even after seventy years of Indian Independence, far from fading out as a primitive/barbaric custom, caste prejudice is a rampant issue in contemporary India, and repeated atrocities heaped on Dalits across the country are a testimony to it. Scavengers (or *bhangis* as they are called in local parlance) are in many insidious ways still 'untouchables', even though untouchability has been recognised in the Indian constitution as a cognisable offence. In spite of giant leaps in technology in many spheres, modes of waste removal in large cosmopolitan cities (such as Mumbai) have still remained repulsively primitive and dependant on physical handling of waste material by members of the same community of scavengers (in the case of Mumbai, the Meghwars) who had been initiated as *safai karmacharis* (sanitation staff) by the colonial administration in the late nineteenth–early twentieth-century India.

Some questions that Mulk Raj Anand's *Untouchable* compels the reader to engage with are: how is the nation to be imagined at a critical juncture of history, when Indians were fighting for freedom from colonial stranglehold. On whose behalf is the new nation being imagined? Does this demand for independence and equality, this protest against British racism (which renders any person of colour as 'untouchable') have any relevance in a country where a large number of people are segregated, and systematically alienated from the mainstream because of the accident of their birth? Are these marginalized, desperately poor and reviled people, actually included in the act of imagining a new nation? The key to the relevance of the novel lies in the exploration of the word 'untouchable'.

Untouchable examines and interrogates this relentless process by which a majority community (and caste) systematically alienates certain groups of people apparently 'within' its fold, all in the name of 'religion' and 'tradition'. At the same time, the novel exposes the searing effects of such segregation so far as the very act of imagining a new and 'united' nation is considered. Bakha is the 'alien' within the nation, whose very touch is considered hateful and defiling. When Bakha is prevented from even coming near the precincts of a Hindu temple, and is consequently ignorant of even the names of Hindu gods, then how is he expected to imagine a nation, which has been conceived as a predominantly Hindu one? While the British picked up this one custom (of caste stratification) as an inevitable sign of Indian primitiveness, the nationalist leaders (almost inevitably coming from upper castes) found it as one of the most uncomfortable positions to defend. How could these very people—who had enslaved millions within their own fold, in the name of religion, and condemned them to live a life worse than animals—root for Independence? How could one speak of, or even 'imagine' one nation, where caste Hindus would not even touch a majority of their countrymen, let alone dine or have other social relations with them?

The novel explores this movement of its protagonist Bakha from a state of acute and searing alienation to a position of partial and tentative integration as well as an understanding of the 'imagined nation.'

For Bakha, this 'alienation' is two-fold as he is both a colonised subject, as well as an enslaved 'alien' within the system, which grades human beings on the basis of their caste-identity. Like most colonised Indians, he is alienated from his cultural roots as a result of systematic imperial desecration of indigenous cultural practices. He attempts to construct some sense of identity, some sense of belonging by imitating the fashions and manners of his British masters. In the case of Bakha, this adoration of British sartorial fashions almost assumes fetishistic proportions, as even a stray piece of European dress such as a hat, or a pair of trousers, assumes iconic status. For Bakha, however, this ridiculous as well as pathetic mimicry is also an attempt to lay claims on colonial modernity—a modernity that holds out hopes of a more egalitarian and democratic way of life for these 'aliens' within the nation. Paradoxically, he can establish some sense of identity with the so-called 'alien' British because they do not treat him with so much disdain, and because their daily customs appear to be far more egalitarian.

However, it is more than apparent that for Bakha, this effort to integrate, to find some point of correspondence with the British masters, can only be a far-fetched dream, as most Britishers, for all their professions of democratic brotherhood (as in the case of the Tommies) or altruism (as in the case of Colonel Hutchinson) ultimately consider a sweeper-boy to be mere dirt. Bakha himself realises that there is nothing 'British' in his life except for a pair of borrowed trousers, and a ridiculous (and eclectic) ensemble of clothes.

However, a far more intense and searing process of alienation awaits him closer home. After completion of his job of cleaning latrines, Bakha moves around the market in a state of relative happiness and peace of mind observing the sights, sounds and colours of what he considers, *his* locality, and *his* community. There are moments of disjuncture and alienation when he witnesses Hindu shopkeepers carefully avoiding his touch while receiving his payment for cigarettes and sweets, all the while sending out subtle but sure signals regarding his menial and 'alien' status:

> A number of packets of 'Red Lamp' and 'Scissors' cigarettes were arranged in boxes on his right … He halted suddenly, and facing the shopkeeper with great humility, joined his hands and begged to know where he could put a coin to pay for a packet of 'Red-Lamp.' The shopkeepr pointed to a spot on the board near him. Bakha put his anna there. The betel-leaf-seller dashed some water over it from the jug with which he sprinkled the leaves now and again. Having

> thus purified it he picked up the nickel piece and threw it into the counter. Then he flung a packet of 'Red-Lamp' cigarettes at Bakha, as a butcher might throw a bone to an insistent dog sniffing round the corner of his shop.[2]

However, Bakha is still supremely happy as he buys four *annas* worth of *jalebis*, and feels all is right with the world. The reversal is swift, as Bakha, unmindful of his 'alien' status in this space, accidentally touches a bystander. All hell breaks loose as all the people of *his* 'community' begin heaping abuse on his 'attempt' to touch a caste-Hindu. It is significant that the men abusing Bakha not only refuse to acknowledge him as one of their own but even refuse to acknowledge his very *humanity*, demeaning him repeatedly by using animal names:

> 'You swine, you dog, why didn't you shout and warn me of your approach!' … 'Don't you know, you brute, that you must not touch me!' … 'Dirty dog! Son of a bitch! The offspring of a pig!' … 'This dirty dog bumped right into me! So unmindfully do these sons of bitches walk in the streets! He was walking along without the slightest effort at announcing his approach, the swine![3]

It is equally significant that these men surround Bakha to threaten and abuse, but refuse to *touch* him, thereby heightening this sense of acute separateness:

> A few other men gathered round to see what the row was about … the pedestrians formed a circle around Bakha, keeping at a distance of several yards from him, but joining in to aid and encourage the aggrieved man in his denunciations. The poor lad ['s] … first impulse was to run, just to shoot across the throng, away, away, far away from the torment. But then he realised that he was surrounded by a barrier, not a physical barrier, because one push from his hefty shoulders would have been enough to unbalance the skeleton-like bodies of the Hindu merchants, but a moral one … And he could already hear in his ears the abuse that he would thus draw on himself.[4]

The only occasion Bakha is *touched* by the people of *his nation* is when the upper-caste crowd hit him to hurt and injure, all the while reminding him that, so far as caste-Hindus are concerned, even to punish a *bhangi* physically, necessitates a purificatory bath. The only person who establishes some connection (however fleeting or temporary) with Bakha, while this ritual act of deliberate humiliation and determined segregation is being played out, is the Muslim *tongawallah*, another 'alien' in a nation that has been predominantly imagined as upper-caste and Hindu.

It is this magic circle of hatred and derision that separates Bakha and his ilk, and creates the 'alien' within a so-called 'nation.' Anand repeatedly uses the image of *touch* to underline this sense of alienation and separateness. The shock that runs through Bakha's body when he discovers he is an *untouchable*, makes him look around desperately for some point of unity or solidarity. Bakha is forbidden even to come near the precincts of the temple, let alone touch it, or enter its portals, as his very presence will supposedly pollute the place of worship. All the while he feels alone, by the alien chants of the temple, the alien gods, and alien people who shun and berate him and loathe his touch.

However, just as caste-Hindus will *touch* Bakha only to hurt and injure, the Brahmin priest of the same temple (which segregates Bakha and Sohini on grounds of their ritual impurity) will *touch* Sohini (Bakha's sister) to sexually ravage and humiliate. Both these *touches* merely insult and alienate, rather than bring together. It is equally significant that these same people will *touch* the foul, onion-belching, dung-squirting bull because it is an act sanctioned by religion, but will shun human beings, creating walls of hatred and prejudice.

The ritual of humiliation and segregation is completed with the upper-caste Hindu housewife cursing him (again using animal epithets) for having polluted her doorsteps by sleeping near them, and throwing a piece of bread at him, just as one throws it at a dog.

This acute sense of separateness is partially alleviated when Bakha witnesses the Mahatma. This first sensation of equality, of oneness, a feeling of being more than an animal comes when Bakha hears Mahatma Gandhi speak at a public meeting. For the first time, Bakha feels human, and (and at least tentatively) a part of one people, one community, one nation. In *Untouchable*, Gandhi acts as much a real historical figure as an idea, a symbol of hope and change, which all sections of people—so long divided on lines of caste, class and religion—want desperately to cling on to, so that they may forge a new identity, and 'imagine' a united nation. The description of Bakha, witnessing all kinds of people running to meet Gandhi, is significant because for the first time, however accidentally or tentatively, Bakha is one with the people of his nation, and even when he has *touched* some, they don't seem to mind!

> At once the crowd, and Bakha among them, rushed towards the golbagh. He had not asked himself where he was going. He hadn't paused to think. The word 'Mahatma' was like a magical magnet to which he, like all the other people about him, rushed blindly … He was so much in a hurry that he didn't even remember the fact of his being an Untouchable, and actually touched a few people. But … no one noticed that a sweeper-boy had brushed past him. They hurried by.… It was as if they knew, by an instinct surer than that of conscious knowledge, that the things of the old civilisation must be destroyed in order to make room for those of the new. It seemed as if, in trampling on the blades of green grass, they were deliberately, brutally trampling on a part of themselves which they had begun to abhor, and from which they wanted to escape to Gandhi.[5]

Yet at the very moment when Bakha feels (for the first time) that he is part of one nation, and that people, divided on lines of caste, class and religion, are ready to bury their prejudices for this one instance and start afresh, he is also reminded of his liminal status as an alien within that 'imagined nation'. It is equally significant that Anand uses the image of *touch* once again, to convey this sense of 'inbetweenness', which plagues Bakha even at this moment of supreme happiness:

> But he became aware of the fact of being a sweeper by the contrast which his dirty khaki uniform presented to the white garments of most of the crowd. There was an insuperable barrier between himself and the crowd, the barrier of caste. He was part of a consciousness which he could share and yet not understand. He had been lifted from the gutter, through the barrier of space, to partake of a life which was his and yet not his. He was in the midst of a humanity which included him in its folds and yet debarred him from entering into a sentient, living, quivering contact with it.[6]

But Bakha knows instinctively that there is just one man who can break down these walls of prejudice, and enable him to become part of 'one nation'. 'Gandhi might unite them really. Bakha waited for Gandhi'.[7]

Obviously, Anand, at this stage is not just speaking of Gandhi the man, but Gandhi who is the idea of transformation and hope. Gandhi, with his unequivocal condemnation of the practice of untouchability, and his valorisation of the profession of scavenging as equal to any other 'respectable' profession, at least partially restores Bakha's sense of self-respect, and includes him (however tentatively) in this process of imagining a nation.

What the Mahatma also does is to free Bakha (at least temporarily) from compulsions to blindly ape British customs and dress habits and inscribe a viable self-image, thereby. Watching the frail, half-naked Mahatma, Bakha instinctively realizes the insubstantiality of European clothes as well as identities inscribed on their basis.[8]

For Bakha (and millions of marginalised people like him) what Gandhi does (along with the Marxist poet who explicates Gandhi's rather cryptic ideas) is to hold out promise (albeit tentative) of forging an indigenous identity, which is based on confidence, and a surer understanding of one's 'Indianness'.

Contextualizing *Untouchable*—Early and Later Dalit Writings

Mulk Raj Anand's *Untouchable* is an interesting example of early writing on Dalit problems by a writer who himself belonged to the 'upper castes' but whose broad humanistic sympathy was able to expose the inhuman structures of exploitation and deprivation in pre-colonial India, all in the name of 'religion' and 'tradition'. Some early examples of writings on such Dalit problems by non-Dalit writers is to be found in: A. Madhaviah's *Thillai Govindan* (1908), an English novel, embedded in Tamil cultural matrix; T. Suryanarayana's *Himavati* (1913), Venkata Parvatisvara Kavalu's *Matrimandiramu* (The Mother's Temple, 1919); Rabindranath Tagore's Bengali dance drama *Chandalika* (The Daughter of the Chandal or outcaste, 1938); Saratchandra Chattopadhyaya's Bengali novels such as *Abhagir Swarga* (The Paradise of the Hapless, 1926) and *Bamuner Meye* (The Brahmin's Daughter, 1920); Munshi

Premchand's *Sirf Ek Awaz* (Just One Cry), *Sadgati* (A Proper Post-death Ritual), and *Thakur Ka Kuan* (The Thakur's Well) in Hindi; Thagazhi Sivasankara Pillai's Malayalam novel *Oru Thotiyin Magan* (The Scavenger's Son, 1947); and Shivarama Karanth's Kannada novel *Chomana Dudi* (The Drums of Choma).

Untouchable can be better appreciated if the reader situates it within a tradition of protest literature addressing caste issues in India and considers it as a predecessor of Dalit writing, which engages specifically with this reality of marginalisation and deprivation of lower classes in modern India. A comparative reading of Anand's *Untouchable* and writings of later and professedly Dalit writers such as Daya Pawar, Lakshman Mane, Sharankumar Limbale, Om Prakash Valmiki or Bama, could help the reader to assess Anand's progressive ideology, and situate it within this tradition of activist and protest literature. It could also make the reader aware of the difference between these older 'fictions of sympathy' (written within the ambit of broadly Gandhian or progressive Marxist ideologies) which made an appeal to the upper caste reader's conscience, and Dalit fiction that emerged in the late 1950s and 1960s in Marathi (and later in Kannada, Tamil, Hindi, Bengali and other languages) to uphold the Ambedkarite dictum of 'educate, unite, organise', and use the experiences in the lives of the oppressed Dalit communities to provoke the reader's anger and violence and thereby mobilise them into action.

The character of Bakha too is an interesting example of portrayal of Dalit characters in the history of Indian writing. While Bakha has been socialised into believing in his essential inferiority, there lurks just beneath the surface of his apparent humility and deference, a volcanic substratum of anger and violence that is simply straining to erupt. He prefigures many of the dalit characters portrayed in later writings (often by writers belonging to these classes) where they are no longer satisfied with the solutions offered by the upper classes; solutions which offer sympathy but refuse to upset the apple-cart of age-old privileges. Bakha in his person prefigures this approaching storm of protest. *Untouchable* reminds us all over again of the necessity of addressing problems of systematic marginalisation and segregation of human beings in the name of religion/tradition, and redressing these issues before they erupt to tear apart the fabric of a so-called democratic and 'modern' Indian nation.

Notes

1. Hardiman. *Gandhi: In His Time and Ours*, New Delhi: Permanent Black, 2003, p.135.
2. *Untouchable* pp.33–34.
3. *Untouchable* pp.38–39.
4. *Untouchable*, p.39.
5. *Untouchable*, pp.126–27.
6. *Untouchable*, p.128.
7. *Untouchable*, p.128.
8. *Untouchable*, p.134.

Text and Context

Year	Anand's Life, Events and Publications	Social and Political Background	Other Important Literary Events
1905	Mulk Raj Anand is born in Peshawar in a well-to-do Kshatriya family. Father, head-clerk of the British Dogra Regiment. Mother Ishwar Kaur, unlettered but a great influence on the novelist.	Partition of Bengal by Lord Curzon. Nationwide protest and beginning of the high-tide of Indian nationalism.	Rabindranath Tagore writes 23 songs such as *Amar Sonar Bangla* (My golden Bengal), *Jodi Tor Dak Shune Keu na Ashe* (If your appeal falls upon deaf ears), and *Banglar mati, Banglar Jal* (The land and waters of Bengal), to protest against partition and inspire nationalistic feelings.
1908–1910	Father abandons Ismail faith and joins Arya Samaj. Anand becomes aware of multiplicity of faiths.	Rise of Hindu nationalism. Gandhi comes to the forefront of Indian anti-colonial resistance.	A. Madhaviah publishes *Thillai Govindan* (1908), the first English novel about evils of caste prejudice in Tamil society. M.K. Gandhi publishes his controversial *Hind Swaraj* (1910).

Year	Anand's Life, Events and Publications	Social And Political Background	Other Important Literary Events
1921–1922	Anand responds to Gandhi's call for nationwide Civil Disobedience Movement, and is consequently jailed. Flies to Bombay to escape from parental wrath and begins writing reviews in *Bombay Chronicle*.	Gandhi introduces removal of Untouchability as the central agenda of Congress movement for *Swaraj* or independent nation.	B.R. Ambedkar launches Marathi fortnightly journal *Muk Nayak* highlighting problems of 'untouchables' in India. James Joyce publishes *Ulysses*. T.S. Eliot publishes *The Wasteland*.
1925–1926	Mother pawns jewellery. Mentors like poet Iqbal raise funds to facilitate Anand's journey to England to complete his graduation. Anand joins the University College of London to research the thought of Locke, Hume and Berkeley. Begins reading *Communist Manifesto*.	B.R. Ambedkar launches *Bahishkrit Hitakarani Sabha* to fight for the rights of 'untouchables.' 'Self-Respect Movement' launched by the leader of Tamil Dalits, Periyar E.V. Ramaswami Naicker. Coal Miners' Strike and general labour unrest in Britain.	
1930–1932	Anand writes *History of Persian Painting* (published by Faber and Faber) and *Curries and other Indian Dishes* (1932).	Poona Pact between Gandhi and Ambedkar where the latter accedes to Gandhi's demand for a unified electorate, rather than a separate one for Dalits.	

YEAR	ANAND'S LIFE, EVENTS AND PUBLICATIONS	SOCIAL AND POLITICAL BACKGROUND	OTHER IMPORTANT LITERARY EVENTS
1935	*Untouchable* published.	Rise of aggressive nationalist parties such as Nazis and fascists in Europe.	R.K. Narayan's *Swami and Friends* published.
1936	*Coolie*		
1937	*Two Leaves and a Bud*		R. K. Narayan's *The Bachelor of Arts* published.
1939	*The Village*	World War II begins.	
1940	*Across the Black Waters*		
1942	*The Sword and the Sickle*		
1945	*The Big Heart*	World War II ends.	
1951	*Seven Summers*		
1953	*The Private Life of an Indian Prince*		
1960	*The Old Woman and the Cow*		
1963	*The Road*		
1964	*The Death of a Hero*		
1970	*Morning Face*	Anand selected for Sahitya Academy award.	
1976	*Confessions of a Lover*		
2005		Anand dies.	

UNTOUCHABLE

The outcastes' colony was a group of mud-walled houses that clustered together in two rows, under the shadow both of the town and the cantonment, but outside their boundaries and separate, from them. There lived the scavengers, the leather-workers, the washermen, the barbers, the water-carriers, the grass-cutters and other outcastes from Hindu society. A brook ran near the lane, once with crystal-clear water, now soiled by the dirt and filth of the public latrines situated about it, the odour of the hides and skins of dead carcases left to dry on its banks, the dung of donkeys, sheep, horses, cows and buffaloes heaped up to be made into fuel cakes, and the biting, choking, pungent fumes that oozed from its sides. The absence of a drainage system had, through the rains of various seasons, made of the quarter a marsh which gave out the most offensive stink. And altogether the ramparts of human and animal refuse that lay on the outskirts of this little colony, and the ugliness, the squalor and the misery which lay within it, made it an 'uncongenial' place to live in.

At least so thought Bakha, a young man of eighteen, strong and able-bodied, the son of Lakha, the Jemadar[1] of all the sweepers in the town and the cantonment, and officially in charge of the three rows of public latrines which lined the extremest end of the colony, by the brookside. But then he had been working in the barracks of a British regiment for some years on a sort of

[1]Head or Foreman.

probation with a remote uncle and had been caught by the glamour of the 'white man's' life. The Tommies had treated him as a human being and he had learnt to think of himself as superior to his fellow-outcastes. Otherwise, the rest of the outcastes, with the possible exception of Chota, the leather-worker's son, who oiled his hair profusely, and parted it like the Englishmen on one side, wore a pair of shorts at hockey and smoked cigarettes like them, and of Ram Charan, the washerman's son who aped Chota and Bakha in turn, were content with their lot.

Bakha thought of the uncongeniality of his home as he lay half awake in the morning of an autumn day, covered by a worn-out, greasy blanket, on a faded blue carpet which was spread on the floor in a corner of the twelve feet by five, dank, dingy, one-roomed mud-house. His sister slept on a cot next to him and his father and brother snored from under a patched, ochre-coloured quilt, on a broken string bed, further up.

The nights had been cold, as they always are in the town of Bulashah, as cold as the days are hot. And though, both during winter and summer, he slept with his day clothes on, the sharp, bitter wind that blew from the brook at dawn had penetrated to his skin, past the inadequate blanket, through the regulation overcoat, breeches, puttees and ammunition boots of the military uniform that clothed him.

He shivered as he turned on his side. But he didn't mind the cold very much, suffering it willingly because he could sacrifice a good many comforts for the sake of what he called 'fashun,' by which he understood the art of wearing trousers, breeches, coat, puttees, boots, etc., as worn by the British and Indian soldiers in India. 'You lover of your mother,' his father had once abusively said to him, 'take a quilt, spread a bedding on a string bed, and throw away that blanket of the *gora* white men; you will die of cold in that thin cloth.' But Bakha was a child of modern India. The clear-cut styles of European dress had impressed his naïve mind. This stark simplicity had furrowed his old Indian consciousness and cut deep new lines where all the considerations which made India evolve a skirty costume as best fitted for the human body, lay dormant. Bakha had looked at the Tommies, stared at them with wonder and amazement when he first went to live at the British regimental barracks with his uncle. He had had glimpses, during his sojourn there, of the life the Tommies lived, sleeping on strange, low canvas beds covered tightly with blankets, eating eggs, drinking tea and wine in tin mugs, going to parade and then walking down to the bazaar with cigarettes in their mouths and small silver-mounted canes in their hands. And he had soon become possessed with an overwhelming desire to live their life. He had been told they were sahibs, superior people. He had felt that to put on their clothes made one a sahib too. So he tried to copy them in everything, to copy them as well as he could in the exigencies of his peculiarly Indian circumstances. He had begged one Tommy for the gift of a pair of trousers. The man had given him a pair of breeches which he had to spare. A Hindu sepoy, for the good of his own soul, had been kind enough to make an endowment of a pair of boots and puttees. For the other items he had gone down to the rag-seller's shop in the town. He had looked longingly at that shop. Ever since he was a child he had walked past the wooden stall on which lay heaped the scarlet and khaki uniforms discarded or pawned by the Tommies, pith solar topees, peak caps, knives, forks, buttons, old books and other oddments of Anglo-Indian life. And he had hungered for the touch of them. But he had never mustered up courage enough to go up to the keeper of the shop and to ask him the price of anything, lest it should be a price he could not pay and lest the man should find out from his talk that he was a sweeper-boy. So he had stared and stared, stealthily noticing the variety of their queer, well-cut forms. 'I will look like a sahib,' he had secretly told himself. 'And I shall walk like them. Just as they do, in twos, with Chota as my companion. But I have no money to buy things.' And there his fantasy would break down and he would walk away from the shop rather crestfallen, with a heavy heart. Then he had had the good luck to come by some money at the British barracks. The pay which he received there had, of course, to be given to his father, but the bakshish which he had collected from the Tommies amounted to ten rupees, and although he couldn't buy all the things in the rag-seller's shop he wished to, he had been able to buy the jacket, the overcoat, the blanket he slept under, and have a few annas left over for the enjoyment of 'Red-Lamp' cigarettes. His father had been angry at his extravagance, and the boys of the outcastes' colony, even Chota and Ram Charan, cut jokes with him on account of his new rig-out, calling him 'Pilpali sahib' (imitation sahib). And he knew, of course, that except for his English clothes there was nothing English in his life. But he kept up his new form, rigidly adhering to his clothes day and night and guarding them from all base taint of Indianness, not even risking the formlessness of an Indian quilt, though he shivered with the cold at night.

A sharp tremor of cold ran through his hot, massive frame. The hair of his body almost stood on end. He turned on his side and waited in the half-dark for something he knew not what. These nights were awful. So cold and uncomfortable! He liked the days because during the day the sun shone and he could, after he had finished his work, brush his clothes with a rag and walk out into the street, the envy of all his friends and the most conspicuous man in the outcastes' colony. But the nights! 'I must get another blanket,' he said to himself. 'Then father won't ask me to put a quilt on. He always keeps abusing me. I do all his work for him. He appropriates the pay all right. He is afraid of the sepoys. They call him names. He abuses me. He is happy when they call him Jemadar. So proud of his izzat![1] He just goes about getting salaams from everybody. I don't take a moment's rest and yet he abuses me. And if I go to play with the boys he calls me in the middle of the game to come and attend to the latrines. He is old. He doesn't know anything of the sahibs. And now he will call me to get up, and it is *so* cold. He will keep

[1]Prestige.

lying in bed, and Rakha and Sohini will still be asleep, when I go to the latrines.' He wrinkled his dark, broad, round face with the feeling of pain that came up into his being and made his otherwise handsome features look knotted and ugly. And thus he lay, awaiting his father's call, hating to hear it, yet lying anxiously in expectation of—the rude bullying order to get up.

'Get up, ohe you Bakhya, you son of a pig,' came his father's voice, sure as a bullet to its target, from the midst of a, broken, jarring, interrupted snore. 'Get up and attend to the latrines or the sepoys will be angry.'

The old man seemed to awake instinctively, for a moment, just about that time every morning and then to relapse into his noisy sleep under the greasy, dense, thick, discoloured, patched quilt.

Bakha half opened his eyes and tried to lift his head from the earth as he heard his father's shout. He was angered at the abuse as he was already feeling rather depressed that morning. The high cheek-bones of his face became pallid with sullenness. His mind went back to the morning after his mother's death, when although he, Bakha, was awake, his father had thought he was asleep and presuming he was never going to get up, had shouted at him. That was the beginning of his father's subsequent early-morning calls, which he had begun at first to resist with a casual deafness, and which he now ignored irritatedly. It wasn't that he couldn't get up, because ordinarily he woke up from his slumber quite early, his mother having habituated him to getting up early. She used to give him a brass tankard full of a boiling hot mixture of water, tea-leaves and milk from the steaming earthen saucepan that always lay balanced on the two-bricks-with-a-space-in-between oven or fireplace in a corner of their one-roomed house. It was so delightful, the taste of that hot, sugary liquid, that Bakha's mouth always watered for it on the night before the morning on which he had to drink it. And after he had drunk it he used to put on his clothes and go to work at the latrines, happy and contented. When his mother died and the burden of looking after the family fell on him, there was no time left to look for such comforts and luxuries as an early morning tumblerful of tea. So he learnt to do without it, looking back, however, with fondness to the memory of those days when he lived in the enjoyment not only of the tasty, spicy delights of breakfast, but of all the splendrous details of life, the nice clothes which his mother bought him, the frequent visits to the town and the empty days, filled with play. He often thought of his mother, the small, dark figure, swathed simply in a tunic, a pair of baggy trousers and an apron, crouching as she went about cooking and cleaning the home, a bit too old-fashioned for his then already growing modern tastes, Indian to the core and sometimes uncomfortably so (as she did not like his affecting European clothes), but so loving, so good, and withal generous, giving, always giving, buying him things, kindness personified. He, didn't feel sad, however, to think that she was dead. He just couldn't summon sorrow to the world he lived in, the world of his English clothes and 'Red-Lamp' cigarettes, because it seemed she was not of that world, had no connection with it.

'Are you up? Get up, you illegally begotten came his father's shout again and stirred the boy to a feeling of despair.

'The bully!' Bakha exclaimed under his breath as he listened to the last accents of his father's voice die out in a clumsy, asthmatic cough. He just shook himself and turning his back to his father for sheer cussedness, averted the challenge of the dark, dingy, crowded, little room which seemed to have come with his father's abuse. He felt that his bones were stiff and his flesh numb with the cold. For a moment he felt feverish. A hot liquid trickled down from the corners of his eyes. One of his nostrils seemed to be blocked and he sniffed the air, trying to adjust his breathing to the congested climate of the corner where his face was turned. His throat too seemed to have been caught, for as he inhaled the air it seemed to irritate his trachea uncomfortably. He began to swallow air in order to relieve his nose and his throat. But when a breath of air pierced the cavity which was clogged the other became impenetrable. A cough shook the inner tissues of his throat and he spat furiously into the corner where he lay. He leaned on his elbow and blew his nose under the carpet on which he lay. Then he fell back, his legs gathered together and shrunken under the thin folds of his blanket, his head buried into his arms. He felt very cold. And he dozed off again.

'Oh, Bakhya! Oh, Bakhya! Oh, you scoundrel of a sweeper's son! Come and clear a latrine for me!' someone shouted from without.

Bakha flung the blanket off his body, stretched his legs and arms to shake off the half-sleep that still clung to him, and got up abruptly, yawning and rubbing his eyes. For a moment he bent, rolling the carpet and the blanket to make room for the activity of the day, then, thinking he heard the man outside shout again, he hurried to the door.

A small, thin man, naked except for a loin-cloth, stood outside with a small brass jug in his left hand, a round white cotton skull-cap on his head, a pair of wooden sandals on his feet, and the apron of his loin-cloth lifted to his nose.

It was Havildar Charat Singh, the famous hockey player of the 38th Dogras regiment, as celebrated for his humour as for the fact, which with characteristic Indian openness he acknowledged, that he suffered from chronic piles.

'Why aren't the latrines clean, you rogue of a Bakhe! There is not one fit to go near! I have walked all round! Do you know you are responsible for my piles? I caught the contagion sitting on one of those unclean latrines!'

'All right, Havildar ji, I will get one ready for you at once,' Bakha said cautiously as he proceeded to pick up his brush and basket from the place where these tools decorated the front wall of the house.

He worked away earnestly, quickly, without loss of effort. Brisk, yet steady, his capacity for active application to the task he had in hand seemed to flow like constant water from a natural spring. Each muscle of his body, hard as a rock when it came into play, seemed to shine forth like glass. He must have had immense pent-up resources lying deep, deep in his body, for as he rushed along with considerable skill and alacrity from one doorless latrine to another, cleaning, brushing, pouring phenoil, he seemed as easy as a wave sailing away on a deep-bedded, river. 'What a dexterous workman!' the onlooker would have said. And though his job was dirty he remained comparatively clean. He didn't even soil his sleeves, handling the commodes, sweeping and scrubbing them. 'A bit superior to his job,' they always said, 'not the kind of man who ought to be doing this.' For he looked intelligent, even sensitive, with a sort of dignity that does not belong to the ordinary scavenger, who is as a rule uncouth and unclean. It was perhaps his absorption in his task that gave him the look of distinction, or his exotic dress however loose and ill-fitting, that removed him above his odorous world. Havildar Charat Singh, who had the Hindu instinct for immaculate cleanliness, was puzzled when he emerged from his painful half an hour in the latrines and caught sight of Bakha. Here was a low-caste man who seemed clean! He became rather self-conscious, the prejudice of the 'twice-born[1]' high-caste Hindu against stink, even though he saw not the slightest suspicion of it in Bakha, rising into his mind. He smiled complacently. Then, however, he forgot his high caste and the ironic smile on his face became a childlike laugh.

'You are becoming a gentreman, ohe Bakhya! Where did you get that uniform?

Bakha was shy, knowing he had no right to indulge in such luxuries as apeing the high-caste people. He humbly mumbled:

'Huzoor it is all your blessing.'

Charat Singh was feeling kind, though he did not relax the grin which symbolised six thousand years of racial and class

[1]The Brahmins, the Kshatriyas, the two upper caste in Hindu society, justify their superiority by asserting that they have earned their position by the good deeds of multiple lives.

superiority. To express his good-will, however, he said:

'Come this afternoon, Bakhe. I shall give you a hockey stick.' He knew the boy played that game very well.

Bakha stretched himself up; he was astonished yet grateful at Charat Singh's offer. It was a godsend to him, this spontaneous gesture on the part of one of the best hockey players of the regiment. 'A hockey stick! I wonder if it will be a new one!' he thought to himself, and he stood smiling with a queer humility, overcome with gratitude. Charat Singh's generous promise had called forth that trait of servility in Bakha which he had inherited from his forefathers, the weakness, of the down-trodden, the helplessness of the poor and the indigent, suddenly receiving help, the passive contentment of the bottom dog suddenly illuminated by the prospect of fulfilment of a secret and long-cherished desire. He saluted his benefactor and bent down to his work again.

A soft smile lingered on his lips, the smile of a slave overjoyed at the condescension of his master, more akin to pride than to happiness. And he slowly slipped into a song. The steady heave of his body from one latrine to another made the whispered refrain a fairly audible note. And he went forward, with eager step, from job to job, a marvel of movement dancing through his work. Only, the sway of his body was so violent that once the folds of his turban came undone, and the buttons of his overcoat slipped from their worn-out holes. But this did not hinder his work. He clumsily gathered together his loose garments and proceeded with his business.

Men came one after another, towards the latrines. Most of them were Hindus, naked, except for the loin-cloth, brass jugs in hand and with the sacred thread twisted round their left ears. Occasionally came a Mohammedan, who wore a long white cotton tunic and baggy trousers, holding a big copper kettle in his hands.

Bakha broke the tempo of his measured activity to wipe the sweat off his brow with his sleeve. Its woollen texture felt nice and sharp against his skin, but left an irritating warmth behind. It was a pleasant irritation, however, and he went ahead with the renewed vigour that discomfort sometimes gives to the body. 'My work will soon be finished,' he said to himself, seeing that he was almost at the end of one part of his routine. But the end of one job meant to him no escape into the haven of luxury. Not that he shirked work or really liked doing nothing. For, although he didn't know it, to him work was a sort of intoxication which gave him a glowing health and plenty of easy sleep. So he worked on continuously, incessantly, without stopping for breath, even though the violent exertion of his limbs was making him gasp.

At last when he had got to the end of the third row of latrines for the second time during the morning, he felt a cramp in his back and stretched himself out from the bent posture he had maintained all the while. He looked in the direction of the town. There was a slight misty haze before him, a sort of screen which the smouldering fire in the chimney where he had burnt the refuse last night had sent up to mingle with the vaporous fleecy clouds that rose from the surface of the brook. Through the thin film he could see the half-naked brown bodies of the Hindus hurrying to the latrines. Some of those who had already visited the latrines could be seen scrubbing their little brass jugs with clay on the side of the brook. Others were bathing to the tune of 'Ram re Ram,' 'Hari Ram,'—crouching by the water, rubbing their hands, with a little soft earth; washing their feet, their faces; chewing little twigs bitten into the shape of brushes; rinsing their mouths, gargling and spitting noisily into the stream; douching their noses and blowing them furiously, ostentatiously. Ever since he had worked in the British barracks Bakha had been ashamed of the Indian way of performing ablutions, all that gargling and spitting, because he knew the Tommies disliked it. He remembered so well the Tommies' familiar abuse of the natives: '*Kala admi zamin par hagne wala*'(black man, you who relieve yourself on the ground). But he himself had been ashamed at the sight of Tommies running naked to their tub baths. 'Disgraceful,' he had said to himself. They were, however, sahibs. Whatever they did was 'fashun.' But his own countrymen—they were *natus* (natives). He felt amused as an Englishman might be amused, to see a Hindu loosen his dhoti to pour some water first over his navel and then down his back in a flurry of ecstatic hymn-singing. And he watched with contemptuous displeasure the indecent behaviour of a Mohammedan walking about with his hands buried deep in his trousers, purifying himself in the ritual manner, preparatory to his visit to the mosque. 'I wonder what they say in their prayers?' he asked himself. 'Why do they sit, stand, bend and kneel as if they were doing exercises?' Once, he remembered, he had asked Ali, the son of a regimental bandsman, why they did that, but Ali would not tell him and was angry, saying that Bakha was insulting his religion. And he recalled the familiar sight of all those naked Hindu men and women who could be seen squatting in the open, outside the city, every morning. 'So shameless,' he thought; 'they don't seem to care who looks at them, sitting there like that. It is on account of that that the goras white men call them *kala log zamin par hagne wala* (black man, you who relieve yourself on the ground). Why don't they come here?' But then he realised that if they came to the latrines his work would increase and he didn't relish the idea. He preferred to imagine himself sweeping the streets in the place of his father. '*That* is easy work,' he said to himself, 'I will only have to lift cow-dung and horse-dung with a shovel and sweep the dust of the road with a broom.'

'There is not a latrine clean. You must work for the pay you receive.'

Bakha turned abruptly and noticed Ramanand the peevish old black moneylender shouting at him in his sharp southern diction. He bowed with joined hands to Ramanand who was staring at him, a pair of gold rings studded with rubies in his ears, a transparent muslin loin-cloth and shirt on his portentous belly, and a funny string cap of a turban on his head. 'Maharaj,' he said and ran towards the latrines and busied himself with his job again.

He hardly realised that he had lapsed into activity, so vigorously did he attack his job. And he was completely oblivious during the quarter of an hour he took to finish a fourth round of the latrines, oblivious alike of the time and of the sweat trickling down his forehead, of the warmth in his body and of the sense of power that he felt as he ended up.

The spurts of smoke from the chimney near his house made him conscious of the next job he had to attend to. He went towards it half-heartedly, and after pausing for a while to pick up a trident-shaped shovel, began to stuff the aperture of the little brick pyramid with the straw in the baskets which he had collected from the latrines.

Little pieces of straw flew into the air as he shovelled the refuse into the chimney, the littlest pieces settling on his clothes, the slightly bigger ones settling on the ground where he had to collect them again with his broom. But he worked unconsciously. This forgetfulness or emptiness persisted in him over long periods. It was a sort of insensitivity created in him by the kind of work he had to do, a tough skin which must be a shield against all the most awful sensations. Stooping down over the baskets full of straw, he gathered shovelfuls and cast them into the grate till it seemed congested and it would take no more. Then he picked up a long poker and prodded the fire. Quickly it flared up, suddenly illuminating the furnace with its leaping red, gold and black flames, an angry consuming power, something apart, something detached from the heaps of straw it fed on.

The blood in Bakha's veins tingled with the heat as he stood before it. His dark face, round and solid and exquisitely well defined, lit with a queer sort of beauty. The toil of the body had built up for him a very fine physique. It seemed to suit him, to give a homogeneity, a wonderful wholeness to his body, so that you could turn round and say: 'Here is a man.' And it seemed to give him a nobility, strangely in contrast with his filthy profession and with the sub-human status to which he was condemned from birth.

This was a long task, lasting almost twenty minutes. Bakha, however, did not seem to feel the strain of it as he had felt the strain of his earlier occupation. The burning flame seemed to ally itself with him. It seemed to give him a sense of power, the power to destroy. It seemed to infuse into him a masterful instinct somewhat akin to sacrifice. It seemed as if burning or destruction was for him a form of physical culture.

When the chimney had consumed the last basket of straw and refuse Bakha closed its mouth and retreated. He felt thirsty. The edges of his lips were dry, He put back the shovel, the basket, the broom and the brushes in their place. Then he moved towards the door of his hut, sniffing the air full of smoke from the chimney, brushing his clothes and smoothing them out. His thirst became overpowering as he entered the room. Looking dazedly at the utensils lying about in a corner, he felt he wanted tea. But as he surveyed the room he heard his father still snoring under his patched quilt. His brother was not in the room. He knew at once where he would be—playing in the maidan by the street. As he stood staring round in order to get used to the comparative darkness, he saw that his sister was trying to light a fire between two bricks. She was blowing hard at it, lifting herself on her haunches as she crouched on the mud floor. Her head almost touched the ground, but each puff from her mouth succeeded only in raising a spurt of smoke and was beaten back by the wet wooden sticks that served as fuel. She sat back helpless when she heard her brother's footsteps. Her smoke-irritated eyes were full of water. She turned and saw her brother. Real tears began to flow down her cheeks.

'Will you get up and let me blow at it?' Bakha said. And without waiting for a reply he walked up to the corner of the room, sat down on his knees, shook the fuel and stooping, began to blow. His big, round mouth seemed like a real bellows as it sent the breath whirring into the fireplace and started first a few sparks, then a blazing fire through the damp sticks. He put the earthen pan over the little stove.

'There is no water in that,' his sister said.

'I will get some water from the pitcher,' he said, as he casually made towards the corner.

'There is no water in the pitcher either,' she answered.

'Oh!' he exclaimed under his breath, tired and exasperated. And for a moment he stood defeated where he had bent down to the pitcher.

'I shall go and get some water,' said Sohini meekly.

'All right,' agreed Bakha without any show of formality, and going out of doors sat down on the edge of a broken cane chair, the only article of furniture of European design which he had been able to acquire in pursuance of his ambition to live like an Englishman. Sohini picked up the pitcher, poised it easily on her head, and ran past her brother.

How a round base can be adjusted on a round top, how a sphere can rest on a sphere is a problem which may be of interest to those who think like Euclid or Archimedes. It never occurred to Sohini to ask herself anything like this as she balanced her pitcher on her head and went to and from her one-roomed home to the steps of the caste-well where she counted on the chance of some gentleman taking pity on her and giving her the water she needed. She had a sylph-like form, not thin but full-bodied within the limits of her graceful frame, well rounded on the hips, with an arched narrow waist from which descended the folds of her trousers and above which were her full, round, globular breasts, jerking slightly, for lack of a bodice, under her transparent muslin shirt. Bakha observed her as she walked along swaying. She was beautiful. He was proud of her with a pride not altogether that of a brother for a sister.

The outcastes were not allowed to mount the platform surrounding the well, because if they were ever to draw water from it, the Hindus of the three upper castes would consider the water polluted. Nor were they allowed access to the near-by brook as their use of it would contaminate the stream. They had no well of their own because it cost at least a thousand rupees to dig a well in such a hilly town as Bulashah. Perforce they had to collect at the foot of the caste Hindus' well and depend on the bounty of some of their superiors to pour water into their pitchers. More often than not there was no caste Hindu present. They were all rich enough to get the water-carriers to supply them with plenty of fresh water every morning for their baths and kitchens, and only those came to the well who were either fond of an open-air bath or too poor to pay for the water-carriers' services. So the outcastes had to wait for chance to bring some caste Hindu to the well, for luck to decide that he was kind, for Fate to ordain that he had time—to get their pitchers filled with water. They crowded round the well, congested the space below its high brick platform, morning, noon and night, joining their hands with servile humility to every passer-by, cursing their fate, and bemoaning their lot, if they were refused the help they wanted, praying, beseeching and blessing, if some generous soul condescended to listen to them, or to help them.

When Sohini reached the well there were already about ten other outcastes waiting. But there was no one to give them water. She had come as fast as she could to the well, full of fear and anxiety that she would have to wait her turn since she could see from a distance that there was already a crowd. She didn't feel disappointed so much as depressed to realise that she would be the tenth to receive water. She had sensed with her deep woman's instinct the feeling in her brother's soul. He was tired. He was thirsty. She had felt like a mother as she issued from her home to fetch water, a mother going out to fetch food or drink for her loved ones at home. Now as she sat in a row with her fellow-sufferers, her heart sank. There was no sign of any-one passing that way who could be a possible benefactor. But she was patient. She had in her an instinctive fortitude, obvious in her curious reserve, in her composed and peaceful bearing.

Gulabo, the washerwoman, the mother of Ram Charan, her brother's friend, had observed Sohini approach. She was a fair-complexioned, middle-aged woman, the regularity of whose supple body bore even in its decay the evidence of a form which must, in her youth, have been wonderful. But although her face was now covered with wrinkles she had pretensions to beauty and was notorious as an assertive old hussy who thought herself superior to every other outcaste, first because she claimed a high place in the hierarchy of the castes among the low castes, secondly, because a well-known Hindu gentleman in the town who had been her lover in her youth was still kind to her in her middle age.

Now Sohini being of the lowest caste among the outcastes would naturally be looked down upon by Gulabo. The delicate features of her rising beauty had added fuel to Gulabo's fire. The girl was a potential rival. Gulabo hated the very sight of her innocent, honest face, though she would not confess, even to herself, that she was jealous of the sweeper girl. But she unconsciously betrayed her feeling in the mockery and light-hearted abuse which she showered on Sohini. The consciousness of that prettiness which people's compliments stimulated in her, made the young woman vaguely surmise it all.

'Go back home,' said Gulabo mockingly. 'There is no one to give you water here! And, at any rate, there are so many of us ahead of you!'

Sohini smiled evasively, then recognising an elderly man in the company, she modestly drew her apron from her head a little over her eyes. And she sat still, crouching by her pitcher.

'Have you heard of such immodesty!' exclaimed Gulabo to Waziro, the weaver's wife who sat near her. 'This sweeper girl goes about without an apron over her head all day in town and in the cantonment.'

'Really!' exclaimed Waziro, pretending to be shocked though she knew Gulabo's evil tongue and had nothing against Sohini. 'You ought to be ashamed of yourself,' she said, winking an aside to the girl.

Sohini could not suppress her amusement at so comic an

assurance of friendliness as Waziro's and laughed.

'Think of it! Think of it! You bitch! You prostitute! wanton! And your mother hardly dead. Think of laughing in my face, laughing at me who am old enough to be your mother. Bitch!' the washerwoman exploded.

Sohini laughed still more hilariously at the ridiculous abruptness of Gulabo's abuse.

'Ari, you bitch! Do you take me for a buffoon? What are you laughing at, slut? Aren't you ashamed of showing your teeth to me in the presence of men, you prostitute?' shouted Gulabo, and she looked towards the old man and the little boys who were of the company.

Sohini now realised that the woman was angry. 'But I haven't done anything to annoy her,' she reflected. 'She herself began it all and is abusing me right and left. I didn't pick the quarrel. I have more cause to be angry than she has!'

'Bitch, why don't you speak! Prostitute, why don't you answer me?' Gulabo insisted.

'Please don't abuse me,' the girl said, 'I haven't said anything to you.'

'You annoy me with your silence, you illegally begotten! You eater of dung and drinker of urine! You bitch of a sweeper women! I will show you how to insult one old enough to be your mother.' And she rose with upraised arm and rushed at Sohini.

Waziro, the weaver's wife, ran after her and caught her just before she had time to hit the sweeper girl.

'Be calm, be calm; you must not do that,' she said as she dragged Gulabo back to her seat. 'No, you must not do that.'

A flutter of excitement travelled through the little group, exclamations, shouts and cries of 'Hai, Hai,' and strange looks of disgust, indignation and disapproval were exchanged. Sohini was a bit frightened at first and grew pale, but she kept intensely still and avoiding the shock, subsided into a listless apathy. As she looked away, however, and cast her eyes up to the blue heavens overhead, she felt a sort of dreariness, a pain, which, though she accepted it resignedly, brought a hurtfulness with it. Sad and wistful, she heaved a soft sigh and felt something in her heart asking for mercy. The sun overhead shot down bright arrows of heat, and inspired a feeling of the passing of time, a feeling that made her forget the unsolicited quarrel with Gulabo, but cast over her the miserable, soul-harrowing shadow of the vision of her brother waiting for her at home, thirsty after the morning's toil, dying for a cup of tea. And yet no caste Hindu seemed to be near.

Minutes passed in silence, only slightly disturbed by Gulabo's sobs and sighs. 'On the day of my little daughter's marriage too! This inauspicious sweeper woman has started my auspicious day so badly!' she was saying. But no one heeded her. And then at long last, a belated caste Hindu visitor to the latrines was passing. He was a sepoy from the neighbouring regiment.

'Oh, Maharaj! Maharaj! Won't you draw us some water, please? We beg you. We have been waiting here a long time, we will be grateful,' shouted the chorus of voices as they pressed towards him, some standing up, bending and joining their palms in beggary, others twisting their lips in various attitudes of servile appeal and abject humility as they remained seated.

Either the sepoy was a callous brute or in too much of a hurry. But he passed by without heeding the request of the group collected at the foot of the well.

Luckily for the crowd of outcastes, however, there was another man coming a little way behind, no less a person than Pundit Kali Nath, one of the priests in charge of the temple in the town. The crowd repeated their entreaties with more vehemence than before.

The Pundit hesitated, twitched his eyebrows and looked at the group frowning with the whole of his bony, hollow-cheeked, deeply-furrowed face. The appeal seemed, even to his dry-as-dust self, irresistible. But he was an ill-humoured old devil, and had it not been that, as he stood and reflected, he realised that the exercise at the well might do some good to the chronic constipation from which he suffered, he would not have consented to help the outcastes.

He moved slowly on to the brick platform of the well. His small, cautious steps and the peculiar contortions of his face showed that he was a prey to a morbid preoccupation with his inside. He took his own time to prepare for the task he had undertaken. He seemed to be immersed in thought, but was really engrossed in the rumblings in his belly. 'That rice,' he thought, 'the rice I ate yesterday, that must be responsible. My stomach seems jammed. Or was it the sweet jalebis I ate with my milk at the confectioner's? But the food at the home of Lalla Banarsi Das may have introduced complications.' He recalled the taste of the various delicacies to which he was so often treated by the pious. 'How nice and sweet is the milk-rice pudding, sticking to the white teeth and lingering in the mouth. And kara parshad, the semolina pudding; the hot, buttery masses of it melt almost as you put a morsel of it in the mouth. But the hubble-bubble usually keeps my stomach clean. What happened to this morning's smoke? I smoked for an hour to no effect. Strange!' During the time taken by these cogitations he had placed the brass jug in his hand to rest in a little hollow in the wooden frame of the well. The waiting crowd thought that it was the Brahmin's disgust at serving them, the outcastes, that brought such deep wrinkles on his face and made it look peeved and angry. They didn't realise that it was constipation and a want of vigour in his lanky little limbs. They soon realised this, for as, after a great many hesitant steps, he tied the iron can that lay near the frame to an edge of the hemp rope that skirted the pulley-wheel, and gently lowered it into the well, the handle slipped from his hand, because of the weight of the bucket, and revolved violently back, releasing all the coils of rope that were around it. He was a bit scared by the suddenness of the motion of the wheel. Then he pulled himself together and renewed his attack. But he was soon upset again. To draw out a can, full of water, required limbs which had been used to exercise more strenuous than the Pundit had ever performed, his whole life revolving round endless recitation of sacred verses and the writing of an occasional charm or horoscope with a reed pen. He exerted all his strength and strained to roll the handle on. His face was contorted, but not altogether unlit with pleasure, because already the exercise of his muscles made him feel much easier in the belly than he had done for days. The expectant outcastes were busy getting their pitchers ready, but as that only meant shifting themselves into position so to be nearest to this most bountiful, most generous of men, all their attention was fixed on him. And as that disclosed the apparent effort the athlete was making, they exerted all their energies, all their will-power to aid him in his task.

At length the can was on the brick platform. But the Brahmin becoming interested in the stirrings of his stomach, in the changing phases of his belly, looked, for a moment, absent-minded. A subtle wave of warmth seemed to have descended slowly down from his arms to the pit of his abdomen, and he felt a strange stirring above his navel such as he had not experienced for months, so pleasing was it in its intimations of the relief it would bring him. Then, unfortunately, a sharp pain shot through like a pin-prick on the right-hand side of his waist and his demeanour assumed the anxious, agitated look habitual to it.

'I am first, Pundit ji,' said Gulabo the washerwoman impetuously, and suddenly disturbed the Brahmin who was absorbed in himself.

He frowned at her and not noticing the vamping expression she had assumed, deprived her of the favourable attention that would have been her due if he had.

'No, I came first,' shouted an inconspicuous little boy.

'But you know that I was here before you,' shouted someone else.

And there was a general stampede towards the well that would, in ordinary circumstances, have flurried the priest into throwing water on all of them. But he had as good an eye for a pretty face as he had an ear for the sound of a request. Sohini had sat patiently away from the throng, the while it charged the well. The Pundit recognised her as the sweeper's daughter. He had seen her before, noticed her as she came to clean the latrines in the gullies in the town—the fresh young form whose full breasts with their dark beads of nipples stood out so conspicuously under her muslin shirt, whose innocent look of wonder seemed to stir the only soft chord in his person, hardened by the congenital weakness of his body, disillusioned by the congenital weakness of his mind, brazened by the authority he exercised over the faithful and the devout. And he was inclined to be kind to her.

'Oh, you Lakha's daughter, come here,' he said, 'you have been patient and the reward of patience, say the holy books, is supreme. Get away, you noisy curs, get out of the way!'

'But Pundit ji!' said Sohini, hesitating to receive the favour, not because she divined the Brahmin's admiration, but because she was afraid of all those who had come before her.

'Now come along,' urged the Pundit, irritated by the beginning in his belly of the urge for excretion, and exhilarated by the thought of doing the beautiful girl a favour. The girl advanced meekly and put her pitcher down under the platform. The priest lifted the can with a great effort. For a moment he successfully handled the water, being surcharged with the glow of that warmth which he felt being near Sohini, intoxicated by it. Then his normal weakness returned. So he splashed the water and the outcastes flew on all sides, half wet, half dry.

'Get out of the way!' he shouted as he poured the water into Sohini's pitcher. He was attempting to cover his weakness by bullying. At length the pitcher was three-quarters full.

'Have you got enough now?' asked the Pundit in triumph as he withdrew the empty can.

'Yes, Pundit ji,' Sohini whispered, her head bent in modesty, as she wiped the outside of the pitcher to lift it on to her head.

'Look, why don't you come and clean the courtyard of our house at the temple,' called the Brahmin as the girl withdrew.

'Tell your father to send you from to-day.' And he looked long at her, rather embarrassed, his rigid respectability fighting against the waves of amorousness that had begun to flow in his blood.

'You will come to-day,' he firmly said lest there should be any misunderstanding left in her mind about it.

Sohini was grateful for the favour he had shown her. She shyly nodded and went her way, her left hand on her waist, her right on the pitcher and a balance in her steps like the rhythm of a song. The washerwoman cast dark and angry glances at her as she herself sullenly drew nearer the well with the rest of the crowd which had now begun to appeal to a new-comer for help.

This was Lachman, a Hindu water-carrier, a Brahmin who in spite of his mean occupation was allowed to go and wash the utensils of the caste Hindus, to cook their food, to fetch their water, and to do other odd jobs about their houses. He was a young man, about twenty-six, with the intelligent though rather rugged features of the Brahmin who has come down in status. A bamboo pole to the extreme ends of which were adjusted four strings (supporting wooden brackets to carry pitchers) was on his shoulders. He rested it slowly on the ground and ascending the well, joined his hands in greeting to the Pundit, saying, 'Jay deva,' Long live the Gods, and respectfully relieved him of the job of drawing more water from the well. As he threw the can easily into the well, however, he looked sideways towards Sohini who was retreating home. He too had noticed her before and felt a stirring in his blood, the warm impulse of love, the strangely affecting desire of the soul to reach out to something beyond, at first in fear, then in hope and then with all the concentrated fury of a bodily and mental obsession. Sometimes he had playfully irritated her with mild jokes, when she came to the well and he happened to be there. She had responded with a modest smile and a subtle look of her shining, lustrous eyes. And he was, as he said, in the language characteristic of the Indian lover, 'dead over her.' The Pundit caught him in the act of looking back. Shame-faced. Lachman withdrew his gaze, and with that servility which he shared with the other menials, quietly turned to the job he had in hand. Soon the strength of his arm had brought the can full of water to the top of the well. He first filled the Pundit's little brass jug and Gulabo's pitcher, and then set about to help the others. The picture of Sohini disappeared from his mind.

She, however, figured conspicuously in the corner of the little mud-house which was her kitchen. Her father was abusing her, as he now sat on his bed, puff-puffing away at the cane tube of his hubble-bubble though he was still wrapped in his patched quilt.

'I thought you were dead or something, you daughter of a pig!' Lakha was shouting. 'No tea, no piece of bread, and I am dying of hunger! Put the tea on and call those sons of a pig, Bakha and Rakha, to me!' Then he frowned in the gruff manner of a man who was really good and kind at heart, but who knew he was weak and infirm and so bullied his children, to preserve his authority, lest he should be repudiated by them, refused and rejected as the difficult old rubbish he was.

Sohini obeyed him at once, shouting for her brothers as she put the earthen saucepan on the fire.

'Vay Bakhia, vay Rakhia, father is calling you!'

Bakha alone came into the room in answer to his sister's call, Rakha having slipped away to play, early in the morning.

The boy was wiping the sweat off his face and neck and breathing hard, for he had been to do another round at the latrines. His black eyes shed fire and his big, broad face was slightly contracted with fatigue. His throat was parched and dry.

I have a pain in my side,' said the old man to his son, as the boy came in and stood towering in the doorway, the whites of his eyes glaring. 'You go and sweep the temple courtyard and the main road for me, and call that swine of a Rakha, wherever he is, to come and attend to the latrines here.'

'Father, the Pundit of the temple wanted me to clean the family house at the temple,' said Sohini.

'Well then go and do so! *why do you eat my head?*' snapped Lakha peevishly.

'Is your pain very bad? asked Bakha ironically, to make his father conscious of his bad temper. 'I will rub your side with oil if you like.'

'No, no,' said the old man irritably, turning his face to hide the shame which his son's subtle protest aroused in him. He had no pain at all in his side, or anywhere, and was merely foxing, being in his old age, ineffectual, and excusing himself from work like a child. 'No, no,' he said, 'you go and attend to the work. I'll be all right.' And he smiled gently.

Meanwhile the mixture of tea-leaves, water, milk and sugar was ready. Sohini poured some of it into two earthen bowls, glazed on the inside. Bakha came, and lifting one, gave it to his father. Then he picked up the other and put it to his lips in hot haste. The sharp, warm taste of the liquid sent forth a queer delight spreading into his flesh. His tongue was slightly burnt with the small sips because he did not, as his father did, blow on the tea to cool it. This was another of the things he had learnt at the British barracks from the Tommies. His uncle had said that the goras didn't enjoy the full flavour of the tea because they did not blow on it. But Bakha considered that both his uncle's and his father's spattering sips were natu habits. He would have told his father that the sahibs didn't do that. But he was too respectful by habit to suggest such a thing, although, of course, for himself he accepted the custom of the English Tommies and followed it implicitly. After he had drunk his tea and eaten a piece of bread from the basket which Sohini put before her father, Bakha went out. He picked up the big broom of thin, very thin cane sticks with a stump of a wooden handle, and the basket with which his father used to go out sweeping the roads. Then he, walked away towards the town, realising, for the first time, the strange coincidence of his morning's wish with his father's sudden injunction.

The lane leading to the outcastes' street was soon left behind.

It seemed such a short lane to him to-day. Where the lane finished, the heat of the sun seemed to spread as from a bonfire out into the empty space of the grounds beyond the outcastes' colony. He sniffed at the clean, fresh air around the flat stretch of land before him and vaguely sensed a difference between the odorous, smoky world of refuse and the open, radiant world of the sun. He wanted to warm his flesh; he wanted the warmth to get behind the scales of the dry, powdery surface that had formed on his fingers; he wanted the blood in the blue veins that stood out on the back of his hand to melt. He turned his hands so as to show them to the sun. He lifted his face to the sun, open-eyed for a moment, then with the pupils of his eyes half closed, half open. And he lifted his chin upright. It was pleasing to him. It seemed to give him a thrill, a queer sensation which spread on the surface of his flesh where the tincture of warmth penetrated the numbed skin. He felt vigorous in this bracing atmosphere. Instinctively he rubbed his face in order to make it warm enough to take in the rays of the sun, to open out its pores. So he adjusted the broom and the basket under his arms and caressed his face with the palms of his hands. A couple of brisk rubs and he felt the blood in his cheeks rising to the high bones under the shadow of his eyes and into the ears which shone red-tipped and transparent at the sides of his head. He felt as he used to do when, on winter Sundays in his childhood, he used to strip himself naked, except for a loincloth, to stand in the sun, and rub mustard oil on his body. Recollecting this he looked up at the sun. He caught the full force of its glare, and was dazed. He stood lost for a moment, confused in the shimmering rays, feeling as though there were nothing but the sun, the sun, the sun, everywhere, in him, on him, before him and behind him. It was a pleasant sensation in spite of the disconcerting suddenness with which it had engulfed him. He felt suspended, as it were, in a region of buoyant tenseness.

As he emerged from the world of that rare, translucent lustre into which he had been lifted, he stumbled over a stone and muttered a curse. Looking ahead he saw that he was being observed by Ram Charan, the washerman's son, by Chota, the leather-worker's son, and his own brother, Rakha. He felt abashed at being seen absorbed in talking to himself. They always made a butt of him, ridiculing the weight of his body, the shape of his clothes, his gait, which was a bit like an elephant's, on account of his heavy, swaying buttocks, and a bit like a tiger's, lithe and supple. He thought they would mock at him if they saw him massaging his face or talking to himself, especially as he knew they knew that he was a devotee of 'fashun,' a weakness which they shared with him and yet for which they ridiculed him. Bakha would always retaliate by pointing at the washer-boy's lashless, browless eyes and saying: 'That comes of using too much soap to whiten your skin.' And there were other peculiarities about Ram Charan, the fact that he had Gulabo for a mother, and a rather pretty flirtatious sister, the fact that he was a very bony, thin little figure, and drove an ass, blind of one eye, to the waterside, which made the basis of a good joke. Chota he could not attack, for that regular-featured lad was the smartest fellow about the lane, with his neatly oiled hair, khaki shorts and white tennis shoes. Almost a model 'gentreman' Bakha thought him, the kind of person he admired and wanted to follow. With him, therefore, he had an intimate understanding which made the jokes they cut about each other always more tolerable.

'Come, o bey brother-in-law,' greeted Ram Charan, blinking his lashless eyes and looking up.

'I want to be your brother-in-law if you will let me', said Bakha, turning the washer-boy's light abuse into a mild joke based on the fact that he was known to everyone to be an admirer of Ram Charan's sister.

'Well, she is being married to-day, so you are too late,' replied Ram Charan, pleased to contemplate that Bakha would never be able to make the same joke again.

'Oh, is that why you are wearing such nice clothes to-day!' remarked Bakha. 'I see! What a fine waistcoat that! Only a bit frayed, that gold thread on the velvet. Why don't you iron it? And oh, I like that chain! By the way, is there a watch attached to it or is it merely for "fashun"?' Ram Charan flushed red and subsided. Chota sat quietly smiling at the interchange. Rakha was apparently feeling cold from the way he had made muffs for his hands of the long sleeves of the torn and battered overcoat he had inherited from Bakha and from the manner in which he was hugging his arms close to his chest. A few other outcastes were busy killing lice from the pleats of their shirts and trousers and too comfortable in the sun to bother to look up. As they sat or stood in the sun, showing their dark hands and feet, they had a curiously lackadaisical, lazy, lousy look about them. It seemed their insides were concentrated in the act of emergence, of a new birth, as it were, from the raw, bleak wintry feeling in their souls to the world of warmth. The taint of the dark, narrow, dingy little prison cells of their one-roomed homes lurked in them, however, even in the outdoor air. They were silent as if the act of liberation was too much for them to bear. The great life-giver had cut the inscrutable knots that tied them up in themselves. It had melted the innermost parts of their being. And their souls stared at the wonder of it all, the mystery of it, the miracle of it.

It was some time before they nodded a greeting to Bakha. But he understood them like that. For though he considered them his inferiors since he came back with sharpened wits from the British barracks, he still recognised them as his neighbours, the intimates with whose lives, whose thoughts, whose feelings he had to make a compromise. He didn't expect them to be formal. And as he stood for a while among them, he became a part of the strange, brooding, mysterious crowd that was seeking the warmth of the sun. One didn't need to employ a courtesy, a greeting to become part of this gathering as one does in the world where there is plenty of light and happiness. For in the lives of this riff-raff, this scum of the earth, these dregs of humanity, only silence, grim silence, the silence of death fighting for life, prevailed.

Once Bakha was with them, however, his own and their queer reactions to the beauty of the morning emerged.

'Why, O Bakhe,' said Chota, beaming with the happiness of the sun of which he seemed a favoured child as the light played on his dark, greasy face: 'Where are you off to-day?'

'My father is ill,' replied Bakha, 'so I am going to sweep the roads in the town and the temple courtyard in his stead.' Then he turned to his brother and said: 'Oh, Rakhia, why did you run away early in the morning? Father is ill and there is all the work at the latrines to do in my absence. Come, my brother, run back home. Sohini has kept some hot tea for you, too.'

Rakha, a short, long-faced, black, stumpy little man, seemed to resent his brother's reprimand. But he quickly got up and sullenly faced the path leading homewards.

'Don't you go! Don't go!' called Ram Charan naughtily after him. This, your brother, wants to be a 'gentreman' and to work on the roads while he wants you to do the dirty work at the latrines.'

'Don't buk buk, o bey brother-in-law,' said Bakha good-humouredly. 'Let him go and work for a bit.'

'Come and play khuti!' said Chota, turning to a packet of 'Red-Lamp' cigarettes he had fished out of a shirt pocket, to see how many it contained before offering one to Bakha. 'Come,' he said, 'we will go and join the others.' He referred to Clayton, a black-skinned bandsman, and Godu, the carpenter's son, who were playing marbles round a hole in the ground.

'Come,' urged Chota, 'we shall win some money.'

'No, I must go to my work,' Bakha said, sternly declining the suggestion. 'My father might see me and he will be angry.'

'Forget the old man, come for a while,' Chota insisted persuasively.

'Come, come,' seduced Ram Charan.

They were truants and expected the call of their parents any time. But they believed in dangerous living and had never missed a morning's sun, however much they were rebuked at home, or even beaten. Bakha had principles. With him duty came first, although he was a champion at all kinds of games and would have beaten them hollow at khuti. He seemed intent on his work and he was going to move on.

'All right, wait,' said Chota. 'There, I see the son of the burra babu coming. What about hockey to-day? The boys of the 31st Punjabis sent a "challenge" to play a match against us.'

'I shall come if my father allows me,' said Bakha. Then he looked aside and seeing two white-clad, delicate young boys, greeted them by raising his right hand to his forehead.

'Salaam, babu ji,' he said respectfully.

The elder of the two boys, a simple, innocent, rather plain child of ten, angular, bony, with a flat nose and prominent cheek-bones, smiled back kindly. There was a twinkle of recognition in the dark eyes of the little one, about eight years of age, with a mischievous egg-shaped face, alive in every feature from his big forehead to his pouting, thick lower lip and his determined little chin.

'Come, you boys!' greeted Ram Charan and Chota with an impudent swagger. 'What about hockey to-day? There is a match with the boys of the 31st Punjabis.'

'We shall play in the afternoon,' said the little one enthusiastically jumping where he stood, holding his brother's finger. He was hardly big enough to hold a stick and he ignored the fact that he hadn't been asked, because he knew the boys never allowed him to play, saying he was too small, and that they were afraid he would get hurt and would go and tell on them.

'All right, will you give us the sticks?' asked Ram Charan, cunningly taking advantage of the child's enthusiasm to exact a promise which, though it was more likely to be repudiated than kept, might serve as a precaution against the child's obstinacy if that mood came upon him that afternoon, as it often did when he was not asked to play.

The sons of the babu, being influential with the captain of the regimental hockey team, because of the exalted position of their father, had had a dozen or so discarded hockey sticks given to them. The boys of the neighbourhood who composed the 38th Dogras boys' eleven, were mostly the poor sons of the Untouchables, dependent on the bounty of the babus' sons for the loan of a stick every afternoon for a practice game. The elder of the two was always a very obliging boy. He willingly suffered his mother's abuse for playing with the outcastes. But the younger one had to be humoured before he would yield.

'Yes, I have brought a nice new stick from Havildar Charat Singh,' he said, 'and a new ball.' Then all of a sudden he turned peevishly to his brother, nudged him and exclaimed: 'Come, don't you want to go to school! We will be late!'

Bakha noticed the ardent, enthusiastic look that lighted up the little one's face. The anxiety of going to school! How beautiful it felt! How nice it must be to be able to read and write! One could read the papers after having been to school. One could talk to the sahibs. One wouldn't have to run to the scribe every time a letter came. And one wouldn't have to pay him to have one's letters written. He had often felt like reading Waris Shah's *Hir and Ranjah*.[1] And he had felt a burning desire, while he was in the British barracks, to speak the *tish-mish, tish-mish* which the Tommies spoke.

His uncle at the British barracks had told him when he first expressed the wish to be a sahib that he would have to go to school if he wanted to be one. And he had wept and cried to be allowed to go to school. But then his father had told him that schools were meant for the babus, not for the lowly sweepers. He hadn't quite understood the reason for that then. Later at the British barracks he realised why his father had not sent him to school.. He was a sweeper's son and could never be a babu. Later still he realised that there was no school which would admit him because the parents of the other children would not allow their sons to be contaminated by the touch of the low-caste man's

[1]An epic poem of the Punjab.

sons. How absurd, he thought, that was, since most of the Hindu children touched him willingly at hockey and wouldn't mind having him at school with them. But the masters woaldn't teach the outcastes, lest their fingers which guided the students across the text should touch the leaves of the outcastes' books and they be polluted. These old Hindus were cruel. He was a sweeper, he knew, but he could not consciously accept that fact. He had begun to work at the latrines at the age of six and resigned himself to the hereditary life of the craft, but he dreamed of becoming a sahib. Several times he had felt the impulse to study on his own. Life at the Tommies' barracks had fired his imagination. And he often sat in his spare time and tried to feel how it felt to read. Recently he had actually gone and bought a first primer of English. But his self-education hadn't proceeded beyond the alphabet. To-day as he stood in the sun looking at the eager little boy dragging his brother to school, a sudden impulse came on him to ask the babu's son to teach him.

'Babu ji,' he said, addressing the elder boy, 'in what class are you now?'

'In the fifth class,' the boy answered.

'Surely now you know enough to teach.'

'Yes,' the boy replied.

'Then, do you think it will be too much trouble for you to give me a lesson a day?' Seeing the boy hesitate, he added: 'I shall pay you for it.'

He spoke in a faint, faltering voice, and his humility increased in depth and sincerity with every syllable.

The babu's sons didn't get much pocket-money. Their parents were thrifty and considered, perhaps rightly, that a child should not eat irregularly, as the low-caste boys did, buying things in the bazaar. The elder boy had developed a strong materialistic instinct, hoarding the stray pice or two he received from anyone.

'Very well,' he said. 'I will. But the . . .' He wanted to change the topic, to make his suppressed desire for money less obvious. Bakha knew from his glance what he meant.

'I will pay you an anna per lesson.'

The babu's son smiled a hypocritical smile which seemed queer in so young a person. And he signified his assent, adding as an afterthought the conventional moneylover's phrase: 'Oh, the money doesn't matter.'

'Shall we begin this afternoon?' pleaded Bakha.

'Yes,' the boy agreed, and was inclined to stand to talk and cement the bond with pleasant words, but his brother was now very peevish and tugged at his sleeve, not only because he thought they were late for school, but also because he hated the idea of his brother becoming rich, was jealous of the money he would be earning.

'Come,' shouted the little one, 'the sun is almost overhead! We will be beaten for being late at school.'

Bakha divined the nature of the child's anger and tried to placate him by offering a bribe.

'You will also teach me, won't you, little brother? I will give you a pice a day.'

Bakha knew this would appease the boy's jealousy and obviate any chance of his telling upon his elder brother for spite. He knew if the little one told his mother that his elder brother was teaching a sweeper to read, she would fly into a rage and turn the poor boy out of the house. He knew her to be a pious Hindu lady.

The little one was too flurried to appreciate the value of the bribe. He looked towards school and was obsessed by the lateness of the hour. He pulled at the lower edge of his brother's tunic and dragged him away.

Bakha saw them depart. He felt elated at the prospect of the lesson he was to take in the afternoon and proceeded to go.

'Stop, O *Babu*! Now you are going to be a very big man,' shouted Ram Charan ironically. 'You won't even talk to us.'

'You are mad,' answered Bakha jovially. 'I must go, the sun is "coming on". And I have to clean the temple approach, and the courtyard.'

'All right, let me show you my madness at hockey to-day.'

'Very well,' Bakha said as he headed towards the gates of the town, his basket under one arm, his broom under the other, and in his heart a song as happy as the lark's.

Tan-nana-nan-tan, rang the bells of a bullock-cart behind him as, like other pedestrians, he was walking in the middle of the road. He jumped aside, dragging his boots in the dust, where, thanks to the inefficiency of the Municipal Committee, the pavement should have been but was not. The fine particles of dust that flew to his face as he walked and the creaking of the cart-wheels in the deep ruts seemed to give him an intense pleasure. Near the gates of the town were a number of stalls at which fuel was sold to those who came to burn their dead in the cremation ground a little way off. A funeral procession had stopped at one of these. They were carrying a corpse on an open stretcher. The body lay swathed in a red cloth painted with golden stars. Bakha stared at it and felt for a moment the grim fear of death, a fear akin to the terror of meeting a snake or a thief. Then he assured himself by thinking: 'Mother said, it is lucky to see a dead body when one is out in the streets.' And he walked on, past the little fruit-stalls where dirtily clad Muhammadans with clean-shaven heads and henna-dyed beards cut sugarcane into pieces, which lay in heaps before them, past the Hindu stall-keepers, who sold sweetmeats from round iron trays- balanced on little cane stools, till he came to the betel-leaf shop, where, surrounded by three large mirrors and lithographs of Hindu deities and beautiful European women, sat a dirty turbaned boy smearing the green, heartshaped betel leaves with red and white paint. A number of packets of 'Red-Lamp' and 'Scissors' cigarettes were arranged in boxes on his right and whole rows of biris native tobacco rolled in leaf on his left. From the reflection of his face in the looking-glass, which he shyly noticed, Bakha's eyes travelled to the cigarettes. He halted suddenly, and facing the shopkeeper with great humility, joined his hands and begged to know where he could put a coin to pay for a packet of 'Red-Lamp.' The shopkeeper pointed to a spot on the board near him. Bakha put his anna there. The betel-leaf-seller dashed some water over it from the jug with which he sprinkled the betel leaves now and again. Having thus purified it he picked up the nickel piece and threw it into the counter. Then he flung a packet of 'Red-Lamp' cigarettes at Bakha, as a butcher might throw a bone to an insistent dog sniffing round the corner of his shop.

Bakha picked up the packet and moved away. Then he opened it and took out a cigarette. He recalled that he had forgotten to buy a box of matches. He was too modest to go back, as though some deep instinct told him that as a sweeper-lad he should show himself in people's presences as little as possible. For a sweeper, a menial, to be seen smoking constituted an offence before the Lord. Bakha knew that it was considered a presumption on the part of the poor to smoke like the rich people. But he wanted to smoke all the same. Only he felt he should do so unobserved while he carried his broom and basket. He caught sight of a Muhammadan who was puffing at a big hubble-bubble sitting on a mattress spread on the dust at one of the many open-air barbers' stalls that gaudily flanked the way.

'Mian ji, will you oblige me with a piece of coal from your clay fire-pot?' he appealed.

'Bend down to it and light your cigarette, if that is what you want to do with the piece of coal,' replied the barber.

Bakha, not used to taking such liberties with anybody, even with the Muhammadans whom the Hindus considered outcastes and who were, therefore, much nearer him, felt somewhat embarrassed, but he bent down and lit his cigarette. He felt a happy, carefree man as he sauntered along, drawing the smoke and breathing it out through his nostrils. The coils of smoke rose slowly before his eyes and dissolved, but he was intent on the little white roll of tobacco which was becoming smaller every moment as its dark grey and red outer end smouldered away.

Passing through the huge brick-built gate of the town into the main street, he was engulfed in a sea of colour. Nearly a month had passed since he was last in the city, so little leisure did his job at the latrines allow him, and he couldn't help being swept away by the sensations that crowded in on him from every side. He followed the curves of the winding, irregular streets lined on each side with shops, covered with canvas or jute awnings and topped by projecting domed balconies. He became deeply engrossed in the things that were displayed for sale, and in the various people who thronged around them. His first sensation of the bazaar was of its smell, a pleasant aroma oozing from so many unpleasant things, drains, grains, fresh and decaying vegetables, spices, men and women and asafoetida. Then it was the kaleidoscope of colours, the red, the orange, the purple of the fruit in the tiers of baskets which were arranged around the Peshawari fruit-seller, dressed in a blue silk turban, a scarlet velvet waistcoat, embroidered with gold, a long white tunic and trousers; the gory red of the mutton hanging beside the butcher who was himself busy mincing meat on a log of wood, while his assistants roasted it on skewers over a charcoal fire, or fried it in the black iron pan; the pale-blond colour of the wheat shop; and the rainbow hues of the sweetmeat stall, not to speak of the various shades of turbans and skirts, from the deep black of the widows to the green, the pink, the mauve and the fawn of the newly-wedded brides, and all the tints of the shifting, changing crowd, from the Brahmin's white to the grass-cutter's coffee and the Pathan's swarthy brown.

Bakha felt confused, lost for a while. Then he looked steadily from the multi-coloured, jostling crowd to the beautifully arranged shops. There was the inquisitiveness of the child in his stare, absorbed here in the skill of a woodcutter and there in the manipulation of a sewing-machine by a tailor. 'Wonderful! Wonderful!' his instinct seemed to say, in response to the sights familiar to him and yet new. He caught the eye of Ganesh Nath, the bania, a sharp-tongued, mean little man, in view of whose pyramids of baskets full of flour, native sugar, dried chillies, peas and wheat he had sat begging for the gift of a tiny piece of salt and a smear of clarified butter. He withdrew his gaze immediately, because there had recently been a quarrel between the bania and his father on account of the compound interest Ganesh had demanded for the money Lakha had borrowed on the mortgage of his wife's trinkets to pay for her funeral. That was an unpleasant thing! He resisted the memory and drifted in his unconscious happiness towards the cloth shop where a big-bellied Lalla (Hindu gentleman), clad in an immaculately white loose muslin shirt, and loin-cloth was busy writing in curious hieroglyphics on a scroll book bound in ochre-coloured canvas, while his assistants unrolled bundles of Manchester cloth one after another, for inspection by an old couple from a village, talking incessantly the while of the 'tintint' and 'matchint,' just to impress the rustics into buying. Bakha was attracted by the woollen cloths that flanked the corners of the shop. That was the kind of cloth of which the sahibs' suits were made; the other cloth that he had seen lying before the yokels he could imagine turning soon into tunics and tehmets. All that was beneath his notice. But the woollen cloth, so glossy and nice! so expensive-looking! Not that he had any intention of buying, or any hope of wearing a kot-patloon suit; he felt for the money in his pocket to see if he had enough to pay an instalment on the purchase of cloth. There were only eight annas there. He remembered that he had promised to pay the babu's son for the English lesson. He crossed the street to where the Bengali sweetmeat-seller's shop was. His mouth began to water for the burfi, the sugar candy that lay covered with silver paper on a tray near the dirtily-clad, fat confectioner. 'Eight annas in my pocket,' he said to himself, 'dare I buy some sweets? If my father comes to know that I spend all my money on sweets,' he thought and hesitated, 'but come, I have only one life to live,' he said to himself, 'let me taste of the sweets; who knows, tomorrow I may be no more.' Standing in a corner, he stole a glance at the shop to see which was the cheapest thing he could buy. His eyes scanned the array of good things; rasgulas, gulabjamans and ludus. They were all so lushly, expensively smothered in syrup, that he knew they certainly could not be cheap, certainly not for him, because the shopkeepers always deceived the sweepers and the poor people, charging them much bigger prices, as if to compensate themselves for the pollution they courted by dealing with the outcastes. He caught sight of jalebis. He knew they were cheap. He had bought them before. He knew the rate at which they were sold, a rupee a seer (two pounds).

'Four annas' worth of jalebis,' Bakha said in a low voice as he courageously advanced from the corner where he had stood. His head was bent. He was vaguely ashamed and self-conscious at being seen buying sweets.

The confectioner smiled faintly at the crudeness of the sweeper's taste, for jalebis are rather coarse stuff and no one save a greedy low-caste man would ever buy four annas' worth of jalebis. But he was a shopkeeper. He affected a casual manner and picking up his scales abruptly, began to put the sweets in one pan against bits of stone and some black, round iron weights which he threw into the other. The alacrity with which he lifted the little string attached to the middle of the rod, balanced the scales for the shortest possible space of time and threw the sweets into a piece torn off an old *Daily Mail*, was as amazing as it was baffling to poor Bakha, who knew he had been cheated, but dared not complain. He caught the jalebis which the confectioner threw at him like a cricket ball, placed four nickel coins on the shoe-board for the confectioner's assistant who stood ready to splash some water on them, and he walked away embarrassed, yet happy.

His mouth was watering. He unfolded the paper in which the jalebis were wrapped and put a piece hastily into his mouth. The taste of the warm and sweet syrup was satisfying and delightful. He attacked the packet again. It was nice to fill one's mouth, he felt, because only then could you feel the full savour of the thing. It was wonderful to walk along like that, munching and looking at all the sights. The big signboards advertising the names of Indian merchants, lawyers and medical men, their degrees and professions, all in broad, huge blocks of letters, stared down at him from the upper stories of the shops. He wished he could read all the luridly painted boards. But he found consolation in recalling the arrangement he had made for beginning his lessons in English that afternoon. Then his gaze was drawn to a figure sitting in a window. He stared at her absorbed and un-self-conscious.

'Keep to the side of the road, you, low-caste vermin!' he suddenly heard someone shouting at him. 'Why don't you call, you swine, and announce your approach! Do you know you have touched me and defiled me, you cockeyed son of a bow-legged scorpion! Now I will have to go and take a bath to purify myself. And it was a new dhoti and shirt I put on this morning!'

Bakha stood amazed, embarrassed. He was deaf and dumb. His senses were paralysed. Only fear gripped his soul, fear and humility and servility. He was used to being spoken to roughly. But he had seldom been taken so unawares. The curious smile of humility which always hovered on his lips in the presence of high-caste men now became more pronounced. He lifted his face to the man opposite him, though his eyes were bent down. Then he stole a hurried glance at the man. The fellow's eyes were flaming and red-hot.

'You swine, you dog, why didn't you shout and warn me of your approach!' he shouted as he met Bakha's eyes. 'Don't you know, you brute, that you must not touch me!'

Bakha's mouth was open. But he couldn't utter a single word. He was about to apologise. He had already joined his hands instinctively. Now he bent his forehead over them, and he mumbled something. But the man didn't care what he said. Bakha was too confused in the tense atmosphere which surrounded him to repeat what he had said, or to speak coherently and audibly. The man was not satisfied with dumb humility.

'Dirty dog! Son of a bitch! The offspring of a pig!' he

shouted, his temper spluttering on his tongue and obstructing his speech, and the sense behind it, in its mad rush outwards. 'I . . . I'll have to go-o-o . . . and get washed—d—d . . . I . . . I was going to business and now . . . now, on account of *you*, I'll be late.'

A man had stopped alongside to see what was up, a white-clad man, wearing the distinctive dress of a rich Hindu merchant. The aggrieved one put his case before him, trying to suppress his rage all the while with his closed, trembling lips which hissed like a snake's:

'This dirty dog bumped right into me! So unmindfully do these sons of bitches walk in the streets! He was walking along without the slightest effort at announcing his approach, the swine!'

Bakha stood still, with his hands joined, though he dared to lift his forehead, perspiring and knotted with its hopeless and futile expression of meekness.

A few other men gathered round to see what the row was about, and as there are seldom any policemen about in Indian streets, the constabulary being highly corrupt, as it is drawn from amongst rogues and scoundrels, on the principle of 'set a thief to catch a thief,' the pedestrians formed a circle round Bakha, keeping at a distance of several yards from him, but joining in to aid and encourage the aggrieved man in his denunciations. The poor lad, confused still more by the conspicuous place he occupied in the middle of the crowd, felt like collapsing. His first impulse was to run, just to shoot across the throng, away, away, far away from the torment. But then he realised that he was surrounded by a barrier, not a physical barrier, because one push from his hefty shoulders would have been enough to unbalance the skeleton-like bodies of the Hindu merchants, but a moral one. He knew that contact with him, if he pushed through, would defile a great many more of these men. And he could already hear in his ears the abuse that he would thus draw on himself.

'Don't know what the world is coming to! These swine are

getting more and more uppish!' said a little old man. 'One of his brethren who cleans the lavatory of my house, announced the other day that he wanted two rupees a month instead of one rupee, and the food that he gets from us daily.'

'He walked like a Lat Sahib, like a Laften Gornor!' shouted the defiled one. 'Just think, folks, think of the enormity!'

'Yes, yes, I know,' chimed in a seedy old fellow, 'I don't know what the *kalijugs* of this age is coming to!'

'As if he owned the whole street!' exclaimed the touched man. 'The son of a dog!'

A street urchin, several of whom had pushed their way through people's legs to see the fun, took his cue from the vigorous complainant and shouted: 'Ohe, you son of a dog! Now tell us how you feel. You who used to beat us!'

'Now look, look,' urged the touched man, 'he has been beating innocent little children. He is a confirmed rogue!'

Bakha had stood mute so far. At this awkward concoction of the child's, his honest soul surged up in self-defence.

'When did I beat you?' he angrily asked the child.

'Now, now mark his insolence!' shouted the touched man. 'He adds insult to injury. He lies! look!'

'No, Lalla ji, it is not true that I beat this child, it is not true,' Bakha pleaded. 'I have erred now. I forgot to call. I beg your forgiveness. It won't happen again. I forgot. I beg your forgiveness. It won't happen again!'

But the crowd which pressed round him, staring, pulling grimaces, jeering and leering, was without a shadow of pity for his remorse. It stood unmoved, without heeding his apologies, and taking a sort of sadistic delight in watching him cower under the abuses and curses of its spokesman. Those who were silent seemed to sense in the indignation of the more vociferous members of the crowd, an expression of their own awakening lust for power.

To Bakha, every second seemed an endless age of woe and suffering. His whole demeanour was concentrated in humility, and in his heart there was a queer stirring. His legs trembled and shook under him. He felt they would fail him. He was really sorry and tried hard to convey his repentance to his tormentors. But the barrier of space that the crowd had placed between themselves and him seemed to prevent his feeling from getting across. And he stood still while they raged and fumed and sneered in fury; 'Careless, irresponsible swine!' 'They don't want to work.' 'They laze about!' 'They ought to be wiped off the surface of the earth!'

Luckily for Bakha, a tonga-wallah came up, goading a rickety old mare which struggled in its shafts to carry a jolting, bolting box-like structure and shouted a warning (for lack of a bell or a horn) for the crowd to disperse as he reined in his horse in time to prevent an accident. The crowd scattered to safety, blurting out vain abuse, exclamations of amusement and disgust, according to age and taste. The touched man was apparently not yet satisfied. He stood where he was, though aware that he would be forced to move by the oncoming vehicle, as for the first time for many years he had had an occasion to display his strength. He felt his four-foot-ten frame assume the towering stature of a giant with the false sense of power that the exertion of his will, unopposed against the docile sweeper-boy, had called forth.

'Look out, eh, Lalla ji,' shouted the tonga-wallah with an impudence characteristic of his profession. The touched man gave him an indignant, impatient look and signed to him, with a flourish of his hand, to wait.

'Don't you thrust your eyeballs at me,' the tonga-wallah answered back, and was going to move on, when, all of a sudden, he gripped his reins fast.

'You've touched me,' he had heard the Lalla say to Bakha. 'I will have to bathe now and purify myself anyhow. Well, take this for your damned irresponsibility, you son of a swine!' And the tonga-wallah heard a sharp, clear slap through the air.

Bakha's turban fell off and the jalebis in the paper bag in his hand were scattered in the dust. He stood aghast. Then his whole countenance lit with fire and his hands were no more joined. Tears welled up in his eyes and rolled down his cheeks. The strength, the power of his giant body glistened with the desire for revenge in his eyes, while horror, rage, indignation swept over his frame. In a moment he had lost all his humility, and he would have lost his temper too, but the man who had struck him the blow had slipped beyond reach into the street.

'Leave him, never mind, let him go, come along, tie your turban,' consoled the tonga-wallah, who being a Muhammadan and thus also an Untouchable from the orthodox Hindu point of view, shared the outcaste's resentment to a certain degree.

Bakha hurried aside and putting his basket and broom down, wrapped the folds of his turban anyhow. Then wiping the tears off his face with his hands he picked up his tools and started walking.

'You be sure to shout now, you illegally begotten!' said a shopkeeper from a side, 'if you have learnt your lesson!' Bakha hurried away. He felt that everyone was looking at him. He bore the shopkeeper's abuse silently and went on. A little later he slowed down, and quite automatically he began to shout: '*Posh* keep away, *posh*, sweeper coming, *posh*, *posh*, sweeper coming, *posh*, *posh*, sweeper coming!'

But there was a smouldering rage in his soul. His feelings would rise like spurts of smoke from a half-smothered fire, in fitful, unbalanced jerks when the recollection of some abuse or rebuke he had suffered kindled a spark in the ashes of remorse inside him. And in the smoky atmosphere of his mind arose dim ghosts of forms peopling the scene he had been through. The picture of the touched man stood in the forefront, among several indistinct faces, his bloodshot eyes, his little body with the sunken cheeks, his dry, thin lips, his ridiculously agitated manner, his abuse; and there was the circle of the crowd, jeering, scoffing, abusing, while he himself stood with joined hands in the centre. 'Why was all this?' he asked himself in the soundless speech of cells receiving and transmitting emotions, which was his usual way of communicating with himself. 'Why was all this fuss? Why was I so humble? I could have struck him! And to think that I was so eager to come to the town this morning. Why didn't I shout to warn the people of my approach? That comes of not looking after one's work. I should have begun to sweep the thoroughfare. I should have seen the high-caste people in the street. That man! That he should have hit me! My poor jalebis! I should have eaten them. But why couldn't I say something? Couldn't I have joined my hands to him and then gone away? The slap on my face! The coward! How he ran away, like a dog with his tail between his legs. That child! The liar! Let me come across him one day. He knew I was being abused. Not one of them spoke for me. The cruel crowd! All of them abused, abused, abused. Why are we always abused? The santry inspictor and the Sahib that day abused my father. They always abuse us. Because we are sweepers. Because we touch dung. They hate dung. I hate it too. That's why I came here. I was tired of working on the latrines every day. That's why they don't touch us, the high-castes. The tonga-wallah was kind. He made me weep telling me, in that way, to take my things and walk along. But he is a Muhammadan. They don't mind touching us, the Muhammadans and the sahibs. It is only the Hindus, and the outcastes who are not sweepers. For them I am a sweeper, sweeper—untouchable! Untouchable! Untouchable! That's the word! Untouchable! I am an Untouchable!'

Like a ray of light shooting through the darkness, the recognition of his position, the significance of his lot dawned upon him. It illuminated the inner chambers of his mind. Everything that had happened to him traced its course up to this light and got the answer. The contempt of those who came to the latrines daily and complained that there weren't any latrines clean, the sneers of the people in the outcastes' colony, the abuse of the crowd which had gathered round him this morning. It was all explicable now. A shock of which this was the name had passed through his perceptions, previously numb and torpid, and had sent a quiver into his being, stirred his nerves of sight, hearing, smell, touch and taste, all into a quickening. 'I am an Untouchable!' he said to himself, 'an Untouchable!' He repeated the words in his mind, for it was still a bit hazy and he felt afraid it might be immersed in the darkness again. Then, aware of his position, he began to shout aloud the warning word with which he used to announce his approach: '*Posh*, *posh*, sweeper coming.' The undertone, 'Untouchable, Untouchable,' was in his heart; the warning shout, '*Posh*, *posh*, sweeper coming!' was in his mouth. His pace quickened and it formed itself into a regular army stop into which his ammunition boots always fell so easily. He noticed that the thumping of his heavy feet on the ground excited too much attention. So he slowed down a little.

He became conscious that people were looking at him. He looked about himself to see why he was arousing all that attention. He felt the folds of his turban coming loose over his forehead. He wanted to retreat to a corner and tie it up properly. But he couldn't stop right in the middle,of the street. So he walked to a corner. Feeling that he might be observed, he assumed a look of abstraction, as if he was harassed by the thought of some important work he had in hand. And he stared round. He felt a fool knowing that he was acting. He unrolled his turban and began to wrap it hard round his head.

A bright, busy scene surrounded him where he lingered. The burning inside had emptied his mind of its content and he stood firm, struggling to express each shock as it impinged on his tight-stretched senses. A huge, big-humped, small-horned, spotted old brahminee bull was ruminating with half-closed eyes near him. The stink from its mouth as it belched, strangely unlike any odour which had assaulted Bakha's nostrils that day, was nauseating. And the liquid dung which the bull had excreted and which Bakha knew it was his duty to sweep off, sickened him. But presently he saw a well-dressed wrinkled old Hindu, wearing, like a rich man, a muslin scarf over his left shoulder, advance to the place where the bull was enjoying its siesta and touch the animal with his forefingers. That was a Hindu custom, Bakha knew. What the meaning of it was, he didn't know. His truant memory ran back to a scene which he had seen occur so many times in the town. The figure of a bull roaming aimlessly about, then walking leisurely up to a vegetable stall, sniffing at the row of baskets and getting away with a mouthful of cabbage, spinach or carrots. The keeper only abused it mildly, threatened it with his hand, without striking it. The bull moved a yard or two away munching the mouthful of vegetables it had purloined, and then it renewed its attack on the shop as soon as the keeper had turned his head away. 'How queer, the Hindus don't feed their cows although they call the cow "mother"!' Bakha thought. 'Their cattle which go to graze at the brookside are so skinny and feeble. Their cows can't yield more than two seers of milk a day.' He recalled with great self-righteousness, how when his father had a buffalo given him in charity (or rather out of superstition) by a rich Hindu merchant who desired sons and was advised by the Brahmins to bestow some cattle on the sweepers, they used to feed it daily with grain and tended it so well that it yielded twelve seers of milk a day. And these people feed their cows on mere remainders of food and even on the grain, sifted, as he well knew (for he had to do the sifting), from the cowdung. 'But they are kind to the cows. This bull must enjoy making its daily haul on those onions. That is why it smells.'

So far he had succeeded in isolating himself from his surroundings, but a cart came loaded with turnips and carrots and was emptied on to the ground. He stepped forward a few yards hurriedly. But a heap of decaying, rotten vegetables were littered over the baskets here. The putrid stink of this decomposing waste made him hurry away. He stared blankly for a while as he went along, without stirring his eyelids. The hot and crowded bazaar blazed with light. He was perspiring. His broad, frank face ordinarily so human, so variable, so changing, with its glistening high cheek-bones, its broad nose, the nostrils of which dilated like those of an Arab horse, his fine full quivering underlip so alive always, was set and impassive, silent, a bit grim and deathly.

'*Posh*, *posh*, sweeper coming,' he whispered as he resumed his steps and advanced into what was neither a broad, busy street nor a narrow alley, but something of both, with a few odd shops occupied by companies of native bandsmen who play European instruments of music under the leadership of some retired army bandmaster, and are greatly in demand at the marriage and birth parties held in the gulleys of crowded cities. A stray grocer's shop or the betel-leaf-seller's punctuated the 'four-faced street' as it was called, and there was a modern flour mill to which went those fastidious old Indian women who loved coarse flour and could not digest the fine which was sold in the shops, or who loved economy and bought wheat wholesale and had it ground. An ancient oil-mill stood in a corner, in a large, dark room, in which the bullock went round and round revolving a wooden pestle into a wooden mortar fixed in the centre from the ceiling. Bakha had known this street ever since his childhood, was used to the deep pits and admired its straight barrack-like look. The English musical instruments and the gold-embroidered uniforms that hung from the band shops, especially in the shop of Jehangir, the celebrated owner of the finest band in the city, were very congenial to his English-apeing mind. He felt sobered by the comparative quiet of this street. The few shops in it made no claims on his attention and he felt less confused in its atmosphere. The sight of the brass instruments and uniforms in the band shop took his mind back to the military band of the 38th Dogras which he saw almost every day practising in the cantonment, and he partly forgot the insult and the injury which he had suffered; he felt soothed; his grief was assuaged.

Out of the silent street, he turned the corner under a house which bridged the thoroughfare and he went along a row of stalls where cheap nickel jewellery was being electroplated. As a child, Bakha had often expressed a desire to wear rings on his fingers, and liked to look at his mother adorned with silver ornaments. Now that he had been to the British barracks and known that the English didn't like jewellery, he was full of disgust for the florid, minutely studded designs of the native ornaments. So he walked along without noticing the big ear-rings and nose-rings and hair-flowers and other gold-plated ornaments which shone out from the background of green paper against which the smiths had ingeniously set them. A seller of cloth remnants loaded on a three-wheeled box-like carriage was haggling with some white-aproned Hindu women right in the middle of the street. Bakha waited for a minute to see if they would clear the road to enable him to pass. He was too tired to shout and stood awhile contemplating the cheap German lithographs of Hindu deities which a Sikh craftsman was fixing into expensive-looking frames. The picture of an Englishwoman, very scantily dressed and reclining with a flower in her hand, seduced Bakha's eyes away from the Hindu deities. The shopkeeper, noticing the basket and broom in Bakha's hand, gave him a stern look of disapproval and asked him to move on. The sweeper-boy lifted his face and pushing ahead called '*Posh*, *posh*, sweeper coming' to the throng of buyers at the remnant-seller's stall. Dragging at the pieces of cloth and loudly bargaining, it was with difficulty that the irritable Mohammedan keeper of the stall could wrest his wares from the grasp of his customers or apprise them of the coming of the Untouchable. When, at last, he managed to do so, they dispersed, talking, whispering, furious, happy, melancholy, ahead of Bakha, and thronged round the bangle-sellers, who were shaking their glass wares to dazzle and attract the young brides in the crowd, who timidly walked behind their mothers and mothers-in-law, adorned in their gold-embroidered silk aprons and Benarsi skirts towards the temple where Bakha was going. He shouted his call again, a little wearily, '*Posh*, *posh*, sweeper coming.' But the eager ardent women had forgotten the instigation of their last move and talking vociferously from their heaving, opera-star chests, did not listen till he reiterated his shout more vigorously.

At length he was allowed right of way and sighted the temple, a colossal, huge turreted structure of massive stone and carved masonry, the florid exuberance of whose detailed and intricate decoration struck a strange kind of awe into his being. Bakha had never quite got over his sense of fear born of the respect for these twelve-headed and ten-armed gods and goddesses which was inculcated in him in his childhood. And as he looked up from the shadow of the high wall falling on the courtyard through which he was walking, he was impressed by some unknown force that seemed to lurk there and to make the place too heavy to breathe in. A few slate-coloured pigeons flew and rested in the little empty niches among the profuse carvings. The sight of them, so cool in their fawn-blue, and the sound of their cooing seemed to calm him. He surveyed the courtyard with the pertinacity of his sweeper's instinct, surveyed the droppings and the flowers, the heap of leaves and dust which he had come to clear.

He threw the basket and the broom he had in his hand on the ground and girt up his loins to attack his job as he, stood in the shadow of a banyan-tree that spread its dense foliage over the temple courtyard. A brass cage of a miniature temple with the beautifully polished image of a snake enclosed in it, lay on a small stone structure which surrounded the giant trunk of the banyan-tree. It arrested his attention. 'What is that snake image?' he asked himself casually. 'What does it mean? Perhaps a snake lives at the root of the tree,' his naïve mind answered. And he was slightly afraid, stepping away from the place instinctively. Then as he saw a regular stream of people pass through the courtyard after touching the foot of the altar of the miniature temple under the banyan-tree, his nerves were steadied. He drew near to the place where he had dropped his basket and his broom, shouting his call the while, lest the disaster of the morning be repeated through his negligence. This crowd was much more orthodox, this crowd which passed up and down the big broad stairs, in and out of the open doorway, this dense crowd, jostling in its blue, white, red and green trappings of cotton and silk. Bakha stared beyond the throng with his inner eye, not daring to look beyond the gate with the overt, lifted eye of the ordinary man curious to know, to solve a mystery, but like the slave stealing an enquiry into the affairs of his master. 'What have these people come here to worship?' he asked himself.

'*Ram*, Ram, *Sri*, *Sri*, *Hari*, *Narayan*, *Sri Krishna*,'[1] a devotee sang as he almost brushed past the Untouchable. '*Hey Hanuman jodah*,[2] *Kali Mai*.'[3]

Bakha had got his answer. The word 'Ram' he had heard very often, also 'Sri, Sri,' and he had seen a red shrine with a monkey carved on a wall, caged from without with brass bars—that he knew was called the shrine of Hanuman. The black shrine showing a jet-black woman with a flaming-red tongue, ten-armed and with a garland of skulls round her neck—that was called the shrine of Kali. Krishna was the blue god who played the flute in the coloured pictures of the betel-leaf-seller's shop in the street. But who was Hari, Narayan? And he was more completely baffled when a man passed by repeating: '*Om*, *Om*, *Shanti Deva*.'[4] Who was Shanti Deva? Was he in the temple?

'There is no chance of seeing anything if I stand here,' he mused. 'I shall go and look.' But he hadn't the courage to go. He felt weak. He realised that an Untouchable going into a temple polluted it past purification. His father would be angry if he knew that he hadn't done any work this morning. Somebody might come and see him roaming about and think he was a thief.

But the edge of his curiosity became more and more acute as he stood there. He suddenly dismissed his thoughts and with

[1]Names of various incarnations of the supreme god.

[2]The monkey god who helped Rama, the hero of the Ramayana, to fight against his enemy Ravana.

[3]The supreme god in its female form as the divine mother.

[4]An invocation to the gods.

a determined, hurried step went towards the stairs, looking to this side and that, with a tense, heavy head, but unafraid. A murderer might have advanced 'like that, one confident in his consummate mastery of the art of killing. But he soon lost his grace in the low stoop which the dead weight of years of habitual bending cast on him. He became the humble, oppressed under-dog that he was by birth, afraid of everything, creeping slowly up,, in a curiously hesitant, cringing movement. After he had mounted the first two steps, he stood completely demoralised with fear and retreated to the place from which he had started. He picked up his broom by its short wooden handle and began to sweep the ground. The particles of dust flew in a small, very small cloud before him, pale white and radiating bright gleams of gold where the sun-rays touched them. But Bakha didn't notice that. To him the litter of banyan leaves, flower petals, the droppings of pigeons, stray sticks and the dust, which his broom soon collected in its sweep, was more immediate, though even of this he was fairly unmindful till the dust flew to his nostrils and he tied the edge of his turban across his nose. And he jogged along, slowly and slowly, step by step, with an apathy peculiar to him. This was a slow business as compared to the work at the latrines, but though slow and wearying, not so unpleasant.

He collected the litter in small heaps, because he knew he could not push any more of it with his small broom, right round the courtyard. He had purposed to collect these small heaps, one by one, in his basket later on. When the heaps were ready, he waited for a moment to wipe the sweat off his brow. The temple stood challengingly before him. He bent down and began to collect the heaps which his broom had piled up. The unfailing sense of direction of his inner impulse landed him near the steps of the temple again. But now he was afraid. The temple seemed to advance towards him like a monster, and to envelop him. He hesitated for a while. Then his will strengthened. With a sudden onslaught he had captured five steps of the fifteen that led to the door of the temple. There he stopped, his heart drumming fiercely in his chest, which bent forward like that of an athletic runner on the starting-line, his head thrown back. The force of another impulse pushed him a step or two further up. Here he was almost thrown out of equilibrium by an accidental knock on his knee and stood tottering, threatened with a fall. But he gripped the steps hard, and recovering his balance, rushed headlong to the top step. From here, as he lay, he could peer through with his head raised above the marble threshold, lowered (luckily for him) by the rubbings of the heads of the devout, and affording a glimpse, just a glimpse, of the sanctuary which had so far been a secret, a hidden mystery to him. In the innermost recesses of the tall, dark sanctum, beyond the brass gates, past what seemed. a maze of corridors, Bakha's eyes probed the depths of a raised platform. There, from a background of gold-embroidered silk and velvet draperies, stood out various brass images dimly shrouded in the soft tremors of incense that rose from a dish at their feet. A priest sat half naked, with a tuft of hair on the top of his shaven head, unduly prominent as it tied itself in an inscrutable knot. An open book lay on a bookstand before him, amidst the paraphernalia of brass utensils, conch-shells and other ritualistic objects. A tall man, evidently also a priest, naked, save for a loin-cloth, darkhaired and supple, with a sacred thread throwing into relief the beautiful curves of his graceful body, got up and blew a conch-shell. Bakha saw, peered, stared hard, and realised that the morning service had begun. After the loud soprano of '*Om, Shanti Deva*'[1] the seated priest lifted his hard voice, jarring on the bell which tinkled in his left hand, into unison with the brass notes of the conch. The quiet little shrine of a moment ago had become a living, feeling reality. Worshippers flocked from the inner corridors of the temple towards the platform of the gods, and stood beneath the dome, singing '*Arti, Arti . . .*'[2] in a chorus. The loud flourish of the first

[1]An invocation to the gods.

[2]Idem.

conch note floated into a sweet, lingering melody, soft and clear, yet potent with a strength of the most mysteriously affecting kind, a strength sustained enough to raise one's hair, as it proceeded to a finish in the last hoarse shout of triumphant worship: '*Sri Ram Chandar ki Jai*' (Long live the Great God Ram).

Bakha was profoundly moved. He was affected by the rhythm of the song. His blood had coursed along the balanced melodic line to the final note of strength with such sheer vigour that his hands joined unconsciously, and his head hung in the worship of the unknown god.

But a cry disturbed him: 'Polluted, polluted, polluted.' A shout rang through the air. He was completely unnerved. His eyes were covered with darkness. He couldn't see anything. His tongue and throat were parched. He wanted to utter a cry, a cry of fear, but his voice failed him. He opened his mouth wide to speak. It was no use. Beads of sweat covered his forehead. He tried to raise himself ftom the awkward attitude of prostration, but his limbs had no strength left in them. For a second he was as if dead.

Then as suddenly as he had been overpowered he asserted himself. He lifted his head and looked round. The scales fell from his eyes. He could see the little man with a drooping moustache whom he knew to be a priest of the temple, racing up the courtyard, trembling, stumbling, tottering, falling, with his arms lifted in the air, and in his mouth the hushed cry 'polluted, polluted, polluted.'

'I have been seen, undone,' the sentence quickly flashed across Bakha's mind. But he espied the figure of a woman behind the shouting priest. He stood amazed, though, still afraid, still feeling that he was doomed. He was unaware, however, of the form the doom would take.

But he soon knew. A thumping crowd of worshippers rushed out of the temple, and stood arrayed as in the grand finale of an opera show. The lanky little priest stood with upraised hands, a few steps below him. His sister, Sohini (for that was the woman he had seen behind the priest), lingered modestly in the courtyard.

'Polluted, polluted, polluted!' shouted the Brahmin below. The crowd above him took the cue and shouted after him, waving their hands, some in fear, others in anger, but all in a terrible orgy of excitement. One of the crowd struck out an individual note.

'Get off the steps, you scavenger! Off with you! You have defiled our whole service You have defiled our temple! Now we will have to pay for the purificatory ceremony. Get down, get away, you dog!'

Bakha ran down the steps, past the priest below him, to his sister. He had two impulses, that of fear for himself, for the crime he knew he had committed, another of fear for his sister, for the crime she might have committed, since she stood there speechless.

'You people have only been polluted from a distance,' Bakha heard the little priest shriek. 'I have been defiled by contact.'

The distance, the distance!' the worshippers from the top of the steps were shouting. 'A temple can be polluted according to the Holy Books by a low-caste man coming within sixty-nine yards of it, and here he was actually on the steps, at the door. We are ruined. We will need to have a sacrificial fire in order to purify ourselves and our shrine.'

'But I .... I . . .' shouted the lanky priest histrionically, and never finished his sentence.

The crowd on the temple steps believed that he had suffered most terribly, and sympathised, for it had seen the sweeper-boy rush past him. They didn't ask about the way he had been polluted. They didn't know the story that Sohini told Bakha at the door of the courtyard with sobs and tears.

'That man, that man,' she said, 'that man made suggestions to me, when I was cleaning the lavatory of his house there. And when I screamed, he came out shouting that he had been defiled.'

Bakha rushed back to the middle of the courtyard, dragging his sister behind him, and he searched for the figure of the priest in the crowd. The man was no longer to be seen, and even the surging crowd seemed to show its heels as it saw the giant stride of the sweeper advance frighteningly towards the temple. Bakha stopped still in his determined advance when he saw the crowd fly back. His fist was clenched. His eyes flared wild and red, and his teeth ground between them the challenge: 'I could show you what that Brahmin dog has done!'

He felt he could kill them all. He looked ruthless, a deadly pale and livid with anger and rage. A similar incident he had heard about, rose to his mind in a flash. A young rustic had teased a friend's sister as she was coming home through the fields after collecting fuel. Her brother had gone straight to the fields with an axe in his hand and murdered the fellow. 'Such an insult!' he thought. 'That he should attack a young and innocent girl. And then the hypocrisy of it! This man, a Brahmin, he lies and accuses me of polluting him, after—father of fathers, I hope he didn't violate my sister.' A suspicion stole into his mind that he might have. He was stung to the quick, and turning to Sohini asked her loudly:

'Tell me, tell me, that he didn't do anything to you!'

Sohini was weeping. She shook her head in negation. She couldn't speak.

Bakha was reassured a bit. 'But no, the attempt!' he thought; 'the man must have made indecent suggestions to her. I wonder what he did. Father of fathers! I could kill that man. I could kill that man!' He was being tormented with the anxiety to know what had really happened, and yet he hesitated to question his sister again lest she should begin to cry. But his doubts and misgivings about her were too much for him.

'Tell me, Sohini,' he said, turning fiercely to his sister, how far did he go?'

She sobbed and didn't reply.

'Tell me! Tell me! I will kill him if . . .' he shouted.

'He-e-e just teased me,' she at last yielded. 'And then when I was bending down to work, he came and held me by my breasts.'

'The son of a pig!' Bakha exclaimed. 'I will go and kill him!' And he rushed blindly towards the courtyard.

'No, no. Come back. Let's go away,' called Sohini after him, arresting his progress by dragging hard at a lapel of his overcoat.

He stood staring at the temple for a moment. There was not a soul to be seen out of doors. All was still. He felt the cells of his body lapse back chilled. His eyes caught sight of the magnificent sculptures over the doors extending right up to the pinnacle. They seemed vast and fearful and oppressive. He was cowed back. The sense of fear came creeping into him. He felt as if the gods were staring at him. They looked so real although they were not like anything he had ever seen on earth. They seemed hard, their eyes fixed as they ogled out of their niches, with ten arms and five heads. He bent his head low. His eyes were dimmed. His clenched fists relaxed and fell loosely by his side. He felt weak and he wanted support. It was with difficulty that he steadied his gait and retraced his steps, with Sohini, to the outer gate.

The sight of her walking along with him, however, sent a wave of anguish into his soul. So frail she, looked and so beautiful. Bakha was conscious of the charm of his sister. Her slim, pale-brown figure, soft and warm and glowing, shot through with a lustre that set off her ornaments, the rings in her ears, the bangles on her arms, to a ravishing effect, was so silent and subtly modest and full of a strange tenderness and light. He could not think of her brutalised by anyone, even by a husband married to her according to the rites of religion. He looked at her and somehow a picture of her future life seemed to come before him. She had a husband—a man who had her, possessed her. He loathed the ghost of her would-be husband that he conjured up. He could see the stranger holding her full breasts and she responding with a modest acquiescence. He hated the thought of that man touching her. He felt he would be losing something. He dared not think what he would be losing. He dared not think that he himself—'I am her brother,' he said to himself, to rectify his thoughts which seemed to be going wrong. But there seemed no difference to his naked mind between his own feeling for her and what might be a husband's love. He dismissed the whole picture. Facing his mind was the figure of the little priest. That made his blood boil. He felt a wild desire to retaliate, retaliation meaning to him just doing anything to the man, from belabouring him with blows to killing him if need be. For though the serfdom of thousands of years had humbled him, the tropical emotions that welled up in him under an open sky had lessened his respect for life. He came of peasant stock, his ancestors having come down in the social scale by their change of profession. The blood of his peasant ancestors, free to live their own life even though they may have been slaves, raced in him now.

'I could have given him a bit of my mind,' he exclaimed to himself.

A superb specimen of humanity he seemed whenever he made the high resolve to say something, to go and do something, his fine form rising like a tiger at bay. And yet there was a futility written on his face. He could not overstep the barriers which the conventions of his superiors had built up to protect their weakness against him. He could not invade the magic circle which protects a priest from attack by anybody, especially by a low-caste man. So in the highest moment of his strength, the slave in him asserted itself, and he lapsed back, wild with torture, biting his lips, ruminating his grievances.

A busy street lay before the brother and sister when they emerged from the temple. Bakha looked out to it vaguely. He could not concentrate on the riot of variety that was displayed in it. He had no patience to see anything or to hear anything, and he didn't want to speak. 'Why didn't I go and kill that hypocrite!' he cried out silently. 'I could have sacrificed myself for Sohini. Everyone will know about her. My poor sister! How can she show her face to the world after this? But why didn't she let me go and kill that man? Why was she born a girl in our house to bring disgrace upon us? So beautiful! So beautiful and so accursed! I wish she had been the ugliest woman in the world! Then no one would have teased her!' But he couldn't bear the thought of her being ugly. His pride in her beauty seemed to be hurt. And he just wished: 'Oh, God, why was she born, why was she born.' Then, however, he saw her bending and wiping her eyes with her apron. With a sudden burst of tenderness and humility he gripped her arm close and dragged her along, writhing with the conflicts in his soul, trembling with despair.

A few steps and he felt more easy. His breath came and went more evenly. His big, raw-boned body, strung into a lithe, active frame by his overpowering passion, became rather heavy. His instinctive fear of the people in the street, all so quick to notice the vagaries of individuals, rude and ill-mannered if they saw something ridiculous or sublime, made him recollect himself. He contemplated his experience now in the spirit of resignation which he had inherited through the long centuries down through his countless outcaste ancestors, fixed, yet flowing like a wave, confirmed at the beginning of each generation by the discipline of the caste ideal.

'Do you go home, Sohini,' he said to his sister, who walked behind him, ashamed and crestfallen, with the stain upon her honour she thought it was to have been the object of a scene. 'Yes, do you go home,' he said, 'and I'll go and get the food. Take this basket and broom with you.'

She moved her head in assent without looking up at him. Then she took the basket and broom from his hand and drawing her apron to cover her face, she walked away towards the city gates.

A glance in the direction of his sister, and Bakha walked slowly away from the house of God. '*Posh*, *posh*, sweeper coming,' he suddenly remembered his warning call, as he just avoided touching a barefooted shopkeeper who was running like a holy bull from shop to shop. When he had thus unconsciously passed through the congested iron-monger's bazaar, past a humanity whose panting rush in its varied, rather hybrid clothes, neither English nor Indian, he took for granted, he found himself standing outside an alley which spread like a yawn between a fruit shop and an old perfumer's. Beneath the emptiness in his inside lay suppressed a confusion arising from the overpowering contradictions of his feelings. But outwardly he was calm and unperturbed. He stood still for a moment, to exercise his sense of direction, as he had been walking almost in a coma. 'To the houses in this alley for food,' he said to himself and turned into the lane.

A stray dog, thin, flea-bitten and diseased, was relieving itself. Another which was all bones, was licking at some decayed food on a refuse-heap that lay blocking the drain. Right across the passage further up lay a cow. Bakha observed the dirt and filth that lay about, casually. But the animals seemed to infuriate him. He approached the dogs, and jumping sharply surprised them into making off with a squeak and a squeal. The bovine insensibility of the cow that lay stretched before him was, however, hard to break through. Lest he should be accused of disturbing the holy mother by the rich owners at whose doors she lay stretched, he held it by the horns to protect his legs against its well-known ferocity, and picked his way across. More heaps of rubbish littered all over the small, old brick pavement meant to him only more reminders of his sister's careless performance of her duties that morning. He excused her, however, by thinking of her suffering. Nobody who had been insulted as she had, could be expected to do her work properly. He didn't want to confess that his defence of her was unreasonable, in that she was supposed to have been here before she went to clean the house in the temple. A huge din of coppersmiths hammering and rehammering copper in their irregular little dark shops engulfed him and he walked more comfortably for a while, for the noise was pleasant, even cheering from a distance, and helped to drown his conscience with regard to his sister's negligence. Deeper in the square, however, the 'thak, thak, thak' that issued from the collection of shops became unbearable. He would have rushed into the little sub-alley where he had to go and call for food but that the ablutions of a devout Hindu on the platform of the street well in the middle of the lane offered the prospect of Bakha getting well sprinkled with the holy water that rained off from the well-oiled body, naked save for a loin-cloth. Bakha waited until his holiness had emptied a canful of water on his head and slung the empty vessel back into the well. Then he sauntered into the dark, damp gulley, where two fat men could hardly pass each other. He felt calmer because it was cool here and the noise of the copper-beaters was fainter. But the test of his nerves was yet to come. For being an outcaste he could not insult the sanctity of the houses by climbing the stairs to the top floors where the kitchens were, but had to shout and announce his arrival from below.

'Bread for the sweeper, mother. Bread for the sweeper,' he called, standing at the door of the first house. His voice died down to the echo of 'thak, thak, thak,' which stole into the alley.

'The sweeper has come for bread, mother! The sweeper has come for the bread,' he shouted a little louder.

But it was of no avail.

He penetrated further into the alley, and standing near a point where the doors of four houses were near each other, he shouted his call: 'Bread for the sweeper, mother; bread for the sweeper.'

Yet no one seemed to-hear him on the tops of the houses. He wished it had been the afternoon, because he knew that at that time the housewives were always downstairs sitting in the halls of their houses, or on the drains in the gulley, gossiping or plying the spinning-wheel. But the vision of a number of them squatting in the gulley and wailing with each other's aprons over their heads, or beating their breasts in mourning for the dead, came before his eyes and he felt shy.

'Bread for the sweeper, mother,' he shouted again.

There was no response. His legs were aching. There was a

lethargy in his bones, a curious numbness. His mind refused to work. Feeling defeated, he sat down on the wooden platform of a house in the lane. He was tired and disgusted, more tired than disgusted, for he had almost forgotten the cause of his disgust, his experiences of the morning. A sort of sleepiness seemed to steal into his bones. He struggled hard against it by keeping his eyes open. Then he tightly leaned against the hard wood of the huge hall door as a concession to his fatigued limbs. He knew that his place was on the damp brick pavement on the side of the drain which carried water from the filth-pipes of all the houses. But for a while he simply didn't care. Bringing his legs together he crouched into a corner and gave himself up to the soft urgings of the darkness that seemed to envelop him. Before long he had succumbed to sleep.

Unfortunately for his tired body, it was an uneasy half sleep that he enjoyed, the hindrances in the labyrinthine depths of his unconscious weaving strange, weird fantasies and dreams. He saw himself driven in a bullock-cart through the thronging streets of a most marvellous city, encountering a wedding procession of gaily-dressed, laughing people, preceded by a litter, covered with ochre-coloured draperies, carried by four men, who were themselves preceded by a Sikh band, dressed in the uniform of the English Army, carrying clarinets, bugles, flutes,.super-saxophones and drums, walking in loose formation, and playing not the harmonies which he had heard in the cantonment, but tuneless wails, weird and disturbing. Then he was on the platform of a railway station. Before him stood a train of forty closed iron freight wagons with an engine at each end. Somewhere in a long row he could espy open trucks, two laden with boulders of stone and bulks of timber. He saw himself getting onto the top of one of these loads and sitting there, a bundle by his side, an umbrella with a carved silver handle in his hand, a solar topee on his head and the tube of his father's hookah in his mouth. Suddenly he could see the closed iron freight wagons move. Almost simultaneously he could hear squeaks, creaks, execrations, lamentations and general excitement, as if someone had been murdered on a near but invisible siding. Full of fear and pity he imagined himself bending over the end of the wagon. He discovered that they were only some blue-uniformed railway coolies pushing a coach into a shed. He was next transplanted to a small village with very narrow streets, muddy and heavily cambered with rills of water running on either side. He could see cows wandering about and two big carts, heavy laden, get stuck in the slush as they came from opposite directions. A number of sparrows alighted on the heaps of grain in the open shops and helped themselves to food. A carrion crow soared down to the bruised neck of a bullock and began to peck at it. Then he watched a little girl who stood outside a sweet-shop. The child advanced smiling, holding aloft the food she had bought. The crow swooped down and snatched at her hand and threw her food onto the heap of litter lying near the gutter. She began to cry. A silversmith, handsome, immense, who had sat before a charcoal fire fashioning ornaments, looked up, smiled understandingly, and with his tongs placed a burning ember on her uplifted hand. The child toddled off happily through a narrow entry, pleased that she was carrying the nucleus of warmth for her mother's hearth . . . Then Bakha saw himself in the compound of a school where boys in yellow turbans were reading aloud as their master sat, cane in hand, exercising a vigilant scrutiny over his wards. The monitor of the class passed successively to each of his fellows on the benches a verse which they declaimed after him. Behind a network of streets in the wonder city ran a stream by which stood a palace, whose domed inner roof was supported by stone trusses and whose wealth of stone carving compelled attention. Bakha looked at it with wonder and admiration and gasped. He entered and saw how it had been hewed out of a rock. Its roof was painted in red and gold and black and green. By colonnades of immense and richly ornamented columns forming a nave and an aisle at the far end, stood men crowding round an emaciated man. Out of the dome some soldiers emerged and chattering, talking, smiling, happy, they carried him to a vast plain, a burning-ground, where the embers of the incinerations of the previous evening still smouldered, sending delicate spirals of smoke from the mounds of human bodies. A number of holy men stood beside the dead bodies, pouring the ashes of the dead into their hair, drinking hemp and dancing in an orgy of destruction. A gora sahib was looking on from a corner. He smiled at the scene. Bakha saw one of the holy men, an ascetic whose years were said to exceed ten thousand and who sat naked and with shaven head in silent contemplation, perform a magic trick by which the sahib was turned into a little black dog. Bakha thought of offering him a gift but the holy man's followers told him he shouldn't. Bakha stood wondering how the man lived. Then a swarm of monkeys jumped down from a tree and—

'*Alakh*, *alakh*'[1] came a call and awoke him. The dream completely faded out in the glare that the sunshine cast leaning over the tall houses. Bakha knew it was noon and that just at that time every holy man and beggar seeks the doors of the devout for alms which he has earned by the dedication of his person to God. Almost at once he collected himself together, rubbed his eyes and felt: 'I shall soon get bread.' He knew that the housewives sat waiting for the ash-smeared sadhus (ascetics) and did not eat their food before dispensing hospitality to the holy men. 'I shall soon get food,' he thought, and he looked up at the sadhu without getting up. The man was staring down at him. Bakha fell back into the drowsy listlessness of a moment ago.

'*Bham*, *bham*, *bhole Nath*,'[2] cried the sadhu in the peculiar lingo of Sadhuhood, shaking the bangles on his arms, which brought two women rushing to the terraces of their house-tops.

'I am bringing the food, sadhu ji,' shouted the lady at whose doorstep Bakha was at rest. But she stopped short when she saw the sweeper's body knotted up on the wooden platform outside her house.

---

[1]An invocation of the ascetics.

[2]Idem.

'You eater of your masters,' she shouted, 'may the vessel of your life never float in the sea of existence! May you perish and die! You have defiled my house! Go! Get up, get up! You eater of your masters! Why didn't you shout if you wanted food? Is this your father's house that you come and rest here?'

Bakha got up as abruptly as the woman's tone had changed from kindness to the holy man to cruelty to him. And rubbing his eyes and trying to shake off the lethargy that lay thick like hot air about him, he apologised.

'Forgive me, mother. I shouted for bread, but you were perhaps busy and didn't hear me. I was tired and sat down.'

'But, you eater of your masters! why did you sit down on my doorstep, if you had to sit down at all? You have defiled my religion! You should have sat there in the gulley! Now I will have to sprinkle holy water all over the house! You spoiler of my salt! Oh, how terrible! You sweepers have lifted your heads to the sky, nowadays! This bad luck on a Tuesday morning too! And after I had been to the temple! . . .' She saw the sadhu waiting and checked her copious flow of remonstrance and abuse. Bakha didn't look up to her but he knew she was dark with anger.

'Be patient, sadhu ji,' her voice came again. 'I shall just go and get you your food. This eater of his masters has even burnt the bread I was baking by detaining me here.' She retreated from her vantage point on the terrace.

Meanwhile the other woman, as quiet as she was heavy, came down the stairs with a handful of rice in one hand and a chapati in the other. The first she put into the holy man's bag, the second she handed over to Bakha, adding kindly: 'My child, you shouldn't sit on people's doorstops like this.'

'May you live long and all your family prosper!' said the sadhu as he received the alms. 'Isn't there a little lentil of which you could make the holy man a gift?'

'Yes, sadhu ji,' she said, 'to-morrow, from to-morrow, you shall have lentil! I am busy cooking.' And she rushed upstairs saying she was busy cooking.

The owner of the defiled house came down now, as voluble as she was short of volume. She stared eagle-eyed at Bakha and remonstrated: 'Wah! You have wrought strange work this morning, defiling my home!' Then she turned to the holy man and heaped a steaming hot vegetable curry and a potful of cooked rice onto the sadhu's black skull of a begging-bowl. 'Please accept this,' she said, 'the house is all right; he didn't really pollute it. I wonder if you have a cure for my son's fever which you could bring me.'

'May the gods bless you and your children,' said the holy man. 'I will bring you some herbs in the morning.' And he turned his back after having exacted his dues for looking after the souls of his disciples.

'May you die,' the woman cursed Bakha, thinking she had acquired enough merit by being good to the holy man and wouldn't lose much of it by being unkind to the sweeper. 'What have you done to earn your food to-day, you or your sister? She never cleaned the lane this morning, and you have defiled my home. Come, clean the drain a bit and then you can have this bread. Come, do a bit of work now that you have defiled my home.'

Bakha looked at the lady for a while. Then cowed down by her abuse, he set to work to sweep the gutter with a small broom which, he knew, his sister always hid under the wooden platform where he, sat.

'Mother,' shouted a little child from the top of the house, 'I want to go to the lavatory.'

'No, you can't go,' replied the mother, who stood superintending the sweeper's work. 'You can't go upstairs, it will lie there all day,' she said. 'Come here, come downstairs, quick, and go here in the drain. The sweeper will clear it away.'

'No,' insisted the obstinate boy, who felt shy to sit in a public place.

His mother rushed up to fetch him. She had forgotten to give Bakha the bread she had brought for him. On reaching the top of her house she sent her son without the bread, and since she didn't want to undertake another journey down. she called to Bakha while he was in the middle of his job.

'*Vay* Bakhya, take this. Here's your bread coming down.' And she flung it at him.

Bakha laid aside the broom and tried hard to be the good cricketer he usually was, but the thin, paper-like pancake floated in the air and fell like a kite on to the brick pavement of the gully. He picked it up quietly and wrapped it in a duster with the other bread he had received. He was too disgusted to clean the drain after this, especially as the little boy sat relieving himself before him. He threw the little broom aside and made off without saying a thank-you.

'Aren't they a superior lot these days!' exclaimed the lady, disappointed at not receiving a courtesy. 'They are getting more and more uppish.'

'I have finished, mother,' her son shouted.

'Rub yourself on the ground, my child, if there is no one to give you water at the pickle-maker's next door,' she said, and she went back to her kitchen.

All the accumulated fury of the morning was in Bakha's soul and the rage of this fresh insult. He felt that he had got up from his sleep almost cured of the unpleasant memories of the morning, but now there was an ache in the back of his head. A subtle heat was mounting from his spine, drying the blood in his body and shrinking his face. 'I wish that hadn't happened at the temple,' he said to himself. 'Then Sohini would have come for the bread. Why did I come to the lane?' He moved in a sort of trance. Black and filthy, yet orderly with that dignity and decorum which his exotic dress gave him, he was possessed by a curious fire. 'I shouldn't have picked up that bread from the pavement,' he said, and he sighed. That seemed to relax him.

Meanwhile he began to feel hungry as if rats were running about in his belly searching for food. He began to spit a white flocculent spittle on the dust as he hurried out of the town, homewards. His limbs sagged. He felt the sweat trickling down his face from under his turban as soon as he got into the open. He looked up to the sun. It stood right above him. Bakha's face quickened with the awareness of the sun 'coming on.' His body had a wonderful time sense, as it really had a sense of other things. 'How can I go home with only two chapatis under my arm?' the feeling came to him. 'Father will be sure to ask if I have brought any delicacies. It isn't my fault that I have only two cakes. He is sure to ask why Sohini didn't go down to get the food. I shall have to tell him the whole story. He will be angry!' He remembered how, when he was a child, his father had abused him because he came and reported that a sepoy had frightened him. 'Father always takes sides with the others. Never with his own family. How can I tell him about the priest? He won't believe it. And he will burst out if I say anything about the incident in the street: "The only day that I send you down to the town to work, you go and pick a quarrel." That is what he will say: "When will you learn to do your job properly?" ' Bakha felt that rather than bear this he would go and tell a lie. 'But then he is sure to know because Sohini didn't go to fetch the food. He must have asked her why she came home so early. Perhaps it will be best not to say anything. But he is sure to ask. Oh, never mind, let come what may.' And he closed his mind to the conflict, and became absorbed in a stray eagle and a few specks of cloud.

With a mind occupied by things, Bakha didn't find the way home very long. He could see his family basking in the sunshine outside the house. There was no provision for lights in the sweepers' street, so most of the inhabitants compensated themselves for the nights spent in utter darkness amid the smoke of smouldering hearth fires in their small congested houses, by spending most of their time in the open air. In the summer, of course, this was difficult, even though they made awnings of the string beds on which they slept at night, by covering them with coarse, unwanted rags of jute cloth, and sat under them all day.

During the winter, however, they came out of their homes as soon as the sun was up and lived out in it till the evening fell and it was too cold.

Sohini had kept up the outdoor kitchen which her mother had made adjoining the door of her house. It was not strictly a kitchen in the Hindu manner, for there were no four lines defining its limits, according to those laws of hygiene which are the basis of Hindu piety. A couple of brooms stood out next to the fireplace, an empty refuse-basket, a can, two earthen pitchers and a chipped enamelled jug lay scattered about. Most of the utensils were of clay, darkened by the soot of many fires, and never washed since Bakha's mother had died, for Sohini was young and inexperienced, and had a great deal too much work to do outside the house to devote herself assiduously to housework. Besides, there was a scarcity of water. And since, on account of their profession and the filthy surroundings in which they were forced to live, they needed more than a pitcherful of water, but could not get it, they just did without; till sanitation, cleanliness and hygiene had lost its meaning for them.

'Where is Rakha?' Bakha asked his sister, as he gave her the duster containing the bread.

She kept quiet, but Lakha, his father, answered:

'The rascal has gone to get food at the *langar* (the kitchen) in the barracks.'

The old man was sitting on his bedstead, now stretched out near the kitchen, puffing away at his hookah, each puff a short asthmatic cough. He looked well groomed. He had evidently been plucking superfluous hair from his face with a pair of tweezers which he always kept under his pillow near a painted native looking-glass, because his bristling white beard looked trimmed up into clean edges and sides. There was a kindly look in his eyes due probably to the easy and comfortable morning he had had. But his lips were tightly set and his brow was wrinkled under his cleanly tied blue turban. Grumpiness was not too far away from him to summon if need be.

'Have you brought anything nice to eat?' he asked Bakha. 'I am just hungering for some pickles, spinach and maize-flour bread.'

'I have brought only two chapatis,' replied Bakha. The feeling came to him which had possessed him throughout his journey, of the struggle between making a clean breast of it all and lying.

'You are a good-for-nothing scoundrel,' muttered Lakha. 'I hope that the rascal brings something nice from the barracks.'

As he said so the Jemadar's mouth watered and his mind travelled to the great big piles of cooked food which he had received on the occasion of marriages in the alleys of the city. There were fried bread and chingri puffs, vegetables, curries and semolina pudding, sweets and tasty pickles—remainders from the trays of high-caste men, and sometimes portions direct from the kitchens. Those were unforgettable days, so pleasing to Lakha that he had always watched the development of each and every girl in the alleys where he worked and asked their parents when the auspicious occasion of their marriage would be celebrated. It may be that Lakha is to blame for most of the child marriages in Bulashah. The parents of the potential brides always remembered Lakha, giving him a suit of clothes and generous portions of food. Another occasion he remembered was when the regiment, to which he was attached, came back from the war, for during the rejoicings on its return there were grand feasts, and he, as the Jemadar of all the sweepers, was in charge of the distribution of the remainders of food. He recalled how the wooden box where his wife kept sweets was never empty that year.

'I don't know the people in the town very well, and I didn't call at all the houses for food,' said Bakha to excuse himself to his father. The remark disturbed Lakha's gastronomic fantasy.

'You should try and get to know them. You have got to work for them all your life, my son, after I die.'

Bakha felt the keen edge of his sense of anticipation draw before his eyes the horrible prospect of all the future days of service in the town and the insults that would come with them. He could see himself being shouted at by a crowd; he could see a little priest fling his arms in the air and cry, 'defiled, defiled.' He could see the lady who had thrown the bread down at him reprimanding him for not cleaning the gutter. 'No, no,' his mind seemed to say, 'never,' and there appeared before him the vague form of a Bakha clad in a superior military uniform, cleaning the commodes of the sahibs in the British barracks. 'Yes, much rather,' he said to himself to confirm the picture.

It was a queer mixture of awe and romance, the alternation of his hatred for his own town and the love for the world to which he looked out. Men get used to a place, become familiar with it, and then comes a stage when the fascination of the unknown, the exotic, dominates them. It is the impulse which tries to create a new harmony, frowning upon the familiar which has grown stale and dreary with too much use. The mind which has once peeped into the wonderland of the new, contemplated various aspects of it with longing and desire, is shocked and disappointed when living reality pulls in the reins of the wild horse of fancy. But how pleasant men find it to look at the world with the open, hopeful, astonished eyes of the child! The vagaries of Bakha's naïve tastes can be both explained and excused. He didn't like his home, his street, his town, because he had been to work at the Tommies' barracks, and obtained glimpses of another world, strange and beautiful; he had grown out of his native shoes into the ammunition boots that he had secured as a gift. And with this and other strange and exotic items of dress he had built up a new world, which was commendable, if for nothing else, because it represented a change from the old ossified order and the stagnating conventions of the life to which he was born. He was a pioneer in his own way, although he had never heard of that word, and was completely unconscious that it could be applied to him.

'What is the matter with you to-day?' asked Bakha's father, noticing the wild light in the boy's eyes and his listless manner. 'Are you tired?'

This started a panic in Bakha's soul. Should he tell or should he not? The sympathetic tone of the enquiry stirred the chords of his soul deeply. He could have wept at the apprehension implicit in his father's manner. He hesitated for a moment. Then, in a struggle to maintain the secret, he answered:

'Nothing,' he said, 'there is nothing.'

'Nothing! There is nothing!' echoed his father. 'Surely something is the matter. Come, tell the truth.'

Bakha felt he would break down and fall to pieces with his obstinate desire to suppress the secret. He was touched by the strange sympathy evinced by his father. He felt suffocated. He felt he couldn't sustain that mood for long. So he burst out with an explosion more sudden than the manner with which he was normally wont to utter a speech:

'They insulted me this morning, they abused me because as I was walking along a man happened to touch me. He gave me a blow. And a crowd gathered round me, abusing and—' He couldn't continue. He was possessed by an overpowering feeling of self-pity.

'My son,' said Lakha, with a forced mixture of anger and kindliness, 'didn't you give a warning of your approach?'

This burnt Bakha's soul. He sat tormented to think that he had told his father about his experience. 'I knew he would say that if I told him the truth,' he thought.

'Why weren't you more careful, my boy?' Lakha strained himself to be more kind than angry on noticing that his son was very agitated.

'But, father, what is the use?' Bakha shouted. 'They would ill-treat us even if we shouted. They think we are mere dirt because we clean their dirt. That pundit in the temple tried to molest Sohini and then came shouting: 'Polluted, polluted.' The woman of the big house in the silversmith's gulley threw the bread at me from the fourth story. I won't go down to the town again. I have done with this job.'

Lakha was touched. A queer self-conscious smile hovered on

the edges of his moustache, a smile of impotent rage.

'You didn't abuse or hit back, did you?' he asked. His sense of fear for his son for the consequences of such a crime, should he have been provoked to commit it, was mixed with that servile humility of his which could never entertain the prospect of retaliation against the high-caste men.

'No, but I was sorry afterwards that I didn't,' replied Bakha. 'I could have given them a bit of my mind.'

'No, no, my son, no,' said Lakha, 'we can't do that. They are our superiors. One word of theirs is sufficient to overbalance all that we might say before the police. They are our masters. We must respect them and do as they tell us. Some of them are kind.'

He looked at his son's face. It had relaxed a bit from the deliberate, tense expression it had assumed, to a sort of resigned cynicism, as if he didn't care. But the old man sensed that the boy was grieved and hurt, and he sensed also that he hated the high-caste people. He sought to assuage his son's grief, to placate his wrath.

'You know,' he began in the impersonal manner with which he always lifted himself from the lousy old man he was to the superior dignity of an aged father, 'You know, when you were a little child, I had a nasty experience too. You were ill with fever, and I went to the house of Hakim Bhagawan Das, in this very town. I shouted and shouted, but no one heard me. A babu was passing through the *Dawai Khana* (dispensary) of the Doctor and I said to him:

' "Babu ji, Babu ji, God will make you prosperous. Please make my message reach the ears of the Hakim ji. I have been shouting, shouting, and have even asked some people to tell the Hakim Sahib that I have a prayer to make to him. My child is suffering from fever. He has been unconscious since last night and I want the Hakim ji to give him some medicine."

' "Keep away, keep away," said the babu, "don't come riding on at me. Do you want me to have another bath this morning? The Hakim Sahib has to attend to us people who go to offices first, and there are so many of us waiting. You have nothing to do all day. Come another time or wait."

'And with this he walked into the dispensary.

'I remained standing. Whenever anyone passed by I would place my head at their feet and ask them to tell the Hakim. But who would listen to a sweeper? Everyone was concerned about himself.

'For an hour I stood like that in a corner, near the heap of litter which I had collected, and I was feeling as if a scorpion was stinging me. That I couldn't buy medicine for my son when I was willing to pay my hard-earned money for it, troubled me. I had seen many bottles full of medicine in the house of the Hakim ji and I knew that one of those bottles contained the medicine for you, and yet I couldn't get it. My heart was with you and my body was outside the house of the Hakim. I had torn my heart away from the room where you lay with your mother, and prayed to God to make my difficulty easy. But nothing happened. I began to think I was seeing you die. It seemed as if someone was giving me a blow in my side and saying "come and see the face of your son for the last time." I ran back home.

' "Have you brought the medicine?" asked your mother, rushing out to me.

'You, of course, only half opened your eyes and you were too delirious to recognise me. They told me they would soon bring you down on the floor.[1] So I ran back to the Hakim's house. Your mother shouted and said: "What is the good of medicine now?" But I ran and ran. When I got to the Hakim's house I just lifted the curtain and went straight in. I caught the Hakim's feet and said: 'Still there is a little breath left in my child's body, Hakim ji, I shall be your slave all my life. *The meaning of my life is my child*. Hakim ji, take pity. God will be kind to you."

[1]The Hindus do not allow a person to die in bed, but bring the dying to rest as near the earth as possible; the idea being that from the earth we come, to earth we return.

' "Bhangi! (Sweeper) Bhangi!" There was an uproar in the medicine house. People began to disperse hither and thither as the Hakim's feet had become defiled. He was red and pale in turn, and shouted at the highest pitch of his voice: 'Chandal! (low-caste) by whose orders have you come here? And then you join hands and hold my feet and say you will become my slave for ever. You have polluted hundreds of rupees worth of medicine. Will you pay for it?"

'I began to shed tears,' Lakha continued, 'and said: "Maharaj, Great One, I forgot. *Your shoe on my head.* I am not in my senses. Maharaj, you are my father and mother. I can't compensate for the medicines. I can only serve you. Will you come and give some medicine to my child? He is on his death-bed!"

'Hakim ji just shook his head and exclaimed: "Serve me! Serve me! How can you serve me? Have you ever received medicine here that you come rushing in?"

'I said: "Sarkar (Sir), I went away after standing outside for some time. I tried to fall at the feet of every passer-by and prayed them to tell to the Sarkar, your honour, that my child was suffering. But Sarkar, this is the time of kindness, be compassionate at this time, another time you can take even my life. Only save my child. All night I have been rocking him in my arms, thinking that if he survives the night, I shall come and fetch medicine from you with the rising of the sun. Who could have heard my call in the middle of the night if I had come here then?"

'With this the Hakim ji's heart melted to some extent and he began to write a prescription. Just at that time your uncle came running and shouted from without: "Ohe, Lakha! Ohe, Lakha! The boy is passing away!"

'I ran out. Hakim ji had dropped his pen. When I came home I found that you were very bad and they had put you on the floor for the fourth time, and your mother was crying.

'In a little while there was a knock at the door. And what do you think? Your uncle goes out and finds the Hakim ji himself, come to grace our house. He was a good man. He felt your pulse and saved your life.'

'He might have killed me,' Bakha commented.

'No, no,' said Lakha. 'They are really kind. We must realise that it is religion which prevents them from touching us.' He had never throughout his narrative renounced his deep-rooted sense of inferiority and the docile acceptance of the laws of fate.

Bakha had felt stirred in the deepest cells of his body as his father narrated the story. Every time his father mentioned his name, every time he referred to his dangerous illness, Bakha felt a strain of self-pity run through him which made him hot and cold at the same time, raised his hair on end and brought tears gushing to his eyes. It was by sheer exertion of his will power that he kept his weakness from actually letting the tears drop from his eyes. In a few moments, however, he was his own-strong self again.

'This rascal of a Rakha must have strayed away to play somewhere,' grumbled the old man. 'Whether you want to eat or not, I must. Sohini, give me some bread.'

'There is no salad,' said Sohini. 'Would you like to take it with some of the tea left over from the morning?'

'*What is taste to the palate of holy men, let it come with cream*,' the old man sang the familiar Indian proverb in reply. Sohini proceeded to put the smoke-bottomed handi full of tea-leaves, water and milk to boil.

Bakha crouched down to a tin jug and gingerly sprinkled a few drops of water on his hands and his face. He had heard his father ask for the food and he slightly resented it. 'I feel hungry too,' he thought. 'Perhaps much hungrier than he does. He has been sitting here all day.' The boy was, of course, too kind and self-sacrificing to believe that he grudged his old father the food that he was going to eat, but a feeling of disgust ran through him, the objection to the force of that biological expedient in him which, in its race across the stream of life, was sweeping everything out of its course. To the young and healthy animal in him, with the strength of his close-knit sinews, his old father was as good as dead. a putrefying corpse like that of a stray dog or cat on the rubbish-heap.

Rakha was at length in sight, a basket of food on his bare clean-shaven head, a pan slung by a string handle in his hand, and his feet dragging a pair of Bakha's old ammunition boots, laceless and noisy and too big for him. His tattered flannel shirt, grimy with the blowings of his ever-running nose, obstructed his walk slightly. The discomfort resulting from this, the fatigue, assumed or genuine, due to the work he had put in that morning, gave a rather drawn, long-jawed look to his dirty face on which the flies congregated in abundance to taste-of the sweet delights of the saliva on the corners of his lips. The quizzical, not-there look defined by his small eyes and his narrow, very narrow forehead, was positively ugly. And yet his ears, long and transparent in the sunlight, had something intelligent about them, something impish. He seemed a true child of the outcaste colony, where there are no drains, no light, no water; of the marshland where people live among the latrines of the townsmen, and in the stink of their own dung scattered about here, there and everywhere; of the world where the day is dark as the night and the night pitch-dark. He had wallowed in its mire, bathed in its marshes, played among its rubbish-heaps; his listless, lazy, lousy manner was a result of his surroundings. He was the vehicle of a life-force, the culminating point in the destiny of which would never come, because malaria lingered in his bones, and that disease does not kill but merely dissipates the energy. He was a friend of the flies and the mosquitoes, their boon companion since his childhood.

'So you have got back after all,' Bakha exclaimed when Rakha was within hearing distance.

His younger brother did not reply, but came sulkily up to where Sohini sat in the kitchen and, depositing his loads of food before her, sat down in the dust, exploring the heap of crumbs in his basket. He ate big morsels. His mouth filled on one side. It looked grotesque.

'At least wash your hands, you wild animal!' said Bakha, irritated by the sight of his brother's running nose.

'You mind your own business,' retorted the young boy as if

he based his defence on the solid foundation of his superior moral force, which indeed he did, because he knew his father sat on the bed, the person who loved him more than he loved Bakha.

'Look at yourself in the mirror! What a picture you look!' exclaimed Bakha.

'Don't keep on finding fault with him,' put in Lakha. 'Stop quarrelling, occasionally, at least.'

'Come and eat a piece of bread,' said Sohini to her elder brother sympathetically.

Bakha got up from his chair unwillingly and, crouching by the kitchen, casually dipped his hand in the basket. There was a heap of food there, broken pieces of chapatis, some whole ones and lentil curry in a bowl.

They all ate from the same basket and the same bowl, not apportioning the food in different plates as the Hindus do, for the original Hindu instinct for cleanliness had disappeared long ago. Only Bakha felt a thrill of loathing go through him for his brother after he had eaten his first few morsels of the day. He changed his position slightly, so that he had his back turned towards his brother. But his hand touched a piece of sticky, wet bread. He shrank back from the basket. The picture of a sepoy washing his hands in his round brass tray, over the leavings of bread and salad, and then throwing them in Rakha's basket appeared before him. He had himself gone so often to beg for food and the only thing he hated about it was the sight of those bits of bread softened by the water poured upon them. He had a queer warm feeling of water running under his tongue from across the sides of his mouth. He felt sick. He tried to drop the soft crumb he had got hold of, but some of it stuck to his fingers still. It was nauseating. He rose from the floor.

'You were saying you were hungry!' said Lakha, when he saw his son get up so suddenly from the meal.

Bakha bent over the tin vessel from the mouth of which he was sprinkling drops of water on his hand. He didn't know what to say in reply. 'He won't understand if I tell him that I feel sick,' he said to himself. 'I will make an excuse. But what—' Suddenly a pretence occurred to him.

'I have to go to Ram Charan's house to see his sister's marriage—and to receive my share of the sweets,' he said. The last he added tactfully, to fortify himself against any objection his father might have to his going, by appealing to the old man's greed.

The true reason for the sudden impulse that had come so usefully in the invention of his lie was inexplicable to anyone, even to himself. For even he did not realise why he was going to see the wedding of Ram Charan's sister. He hadn't been invited to go by Gulabo (of course he could not have been invited by her, quarrelsome as she was, abusing even such a docile person as Bakha for one thing or another, especially for his encouraging her son to truancy) or by Ram Charan. And he couldn't have been asked by Ram Charan's sister, because she had never talked to him since she was ten. Why then was he going? What had made him decide so suddenly on such an extraordinary adventure?

He only knew that he wanted to get away from home, his father, his brother, his sister, everyone. But he wouldn't confess even to himself that he was going to see Ram Charan's sister for the last time. A picture of her appeared from the past before his mind's eye. She was a tiny girl with shaven head, wearing a miniature skirt of gaudy red cotton with a white pattern, that the washerwomen wear. She looked like a juggler's little monkey. He himself was then a boy of eight, in a gold-embroidered cap which his father had begged from a moneylender who had three small sons whose discarded clothes fitted Lakha's three children exactly. Bakha remembered how, while he had been playing with her brother and Chota in the barracks, they had come home and started to play at marriage. Ram Charan's little sister was made to act the wife because she wore a skirt. Bakha was chosen to play the husband because he was wearing the gold-embroidered cap. The rest of the boys took the part of members of the marriage party. Bakha recalled how he had been ragged by Chota for acting as the husband of a shaven-headed, ridiculous little girl, and how he (Bakha) had been angry with him, although he himself thought she looked funny. There was something wistful about her, a soft light in her eyes, for which she had become endeared to him and for which, he, remembered, he had actually quarrelled with his friend. Since then, of course, she had grown up to be a tall girl with a face as brown as ripe wheat and hair as black as the rain clouds. And Bakha always felt proud of having once acted as her husband. Being very reticent and shy, however, he seldom dared even to look at her. But in the depths of his being he had felt waves of confusion at the thought of her. Now at the age of fourteen she was being married off to a young washerman attached as a follower to the 31st Punjabis regiment. He had heard of this arrangement a year ago. It was common knowledge in the sweepers' street that Gulabo had taken two hundred rupees for the hand of her daughter. Chota had told him that. He remembered the evening on which he had heard it, for it had been somewhat of a shock to him, and he had felt a regret in his soul, as if a spring of water had burst like a doleful lyric melody in the hard rock of his body. During the dreary hours of his routine work at the latrines, subsequently, he had often heard the delicate strain of that sad, elfin music. But he had never quite comprehended the source from which it came. In the darkness of his home at night, when he lay half asleep, something in him secretly led him towards the vague sylph-like form which he could have squeezed in the embrace of his arms, and still he could not connect the feelings he had at such moments with the ripples that surged up in him whenever he caught sight of Ram Charan's sister.

As he walked towards her home to-day, however, he recalled occasions on which his vague flowings towards her had become more defined. His large eyes had rested with adoration on her face as she met him once going to the shops to buy some kerosene oil in an old wine-bottle. Then from the dark undeclared places of his soul arose another picture of her in his memory—as she came through the darkness before the dawn from the banks of the brook where, he knew, she and the other women of the outcastes' colony went every day, taking advantage of the privacy which the half-light afforded, to perform their toilets unseen by men. He remembered that he had been about the latrines and had at first felt a thrill of delight, then a sensation more vital. He had pictured her quite naked as he had seen his mother quite often when he was a child, and his sister, and other little children. An impulse had arisen like a sudden gust of wind to his brain, and darkened his thoughts. He had felt as if he could forcibly gather the girl in his embrace and ravish her. Then he had put his hand across his eyes and shuddered in horror at the thought. He had cursed himself for such a vision. His reputation as a docile, good, respectable boy seemed at stake. He had wondered at himself: 'How could I, who am known to, everyone as Bakha the good, have such an unholy design?' Nevertheless, the picture had persisted. The more he tried to blot it out, the more definite it had become, until, when he had ceased to bother about his sensual feelings, his phantasy had vanished.

As he recalled these things, he seemed to feel ashamed. He had felt that shame also on the occasion when those things first happened. In a frantic effort to escape from himself, to escape from the secret, buried desire he had for the girl, he casually took a turning off the track which led to the washermen's houses, and wandered aimlessly into a lane which ended in the washermen's ghats by the waterside.

Shioh! Shioh! Shi! A few washermen were shouting as they tore the garments of their customers and broke their buttons on slabs of stone by the edges of the brook. Their dark legs were immersed in the water up to the knee and their bodies from the rumps upwards were swathed in the thick folds of loin-cloths up to the waists, where their shirts were tucked in. They doubled over the stones with supple movements and struck the garments with a loud swinging sweep which was graceful in itself even if it did not do any good to the cloth. Bakha had often stood watching this operation. In his childhood, of course, he had been fascinated by it, so that he wished to become a washerman. It was Ram Charan, true son of his mother, Gulabo, if he, wasn't his father's son, but of the rich man, his mother's lover, who had knocked the bottom out of that ambition by telling Bakha that though he (Ram Charan) touched him and played with him, he was a Hindu, while Bakha was a mere sweeper. Bakha was too young then to understand the distinction implied in the washer-boy's arrogant claim, or else he would have slapped Ram Charan's face. But now he knew that there were degrees of castes among the low-caste, and that he was of the lowest.

He looked hard among the few washermen who beat clothes upon the slabs of stone. He anxiously explored among the stray washermen's donkeys which grazed on the side of the brook, wildly thinking that Ram Charan might be there. He looked across the yards of space on which the washed, wet clothes lay drying in the hot afternoon sun. But he was looking in vain. For how could Ram Charan have absented himself from so auspicious an occasion as his sister's marriage and be working here! 'Only, did Ram Charan not absent himself at the time of his father's death and go fishing with us?' Bakha thought. 'He might be here to-day.' Then he thought: 'Perhaps his father wasn't his father, but he is his sister's brother. I will have to go to his place after all.'

He began to walk back. He felt shy. He didn't know how he could approach the house where festivities were going on. 'All the members of the washermen's brotherhood will be there, dressed in their best clothes, singing strange southern music. How shall I be able to stand there and look?' He felt ashamed to picture the scene. He was highly strung to-day. A strange leprosy seemed to have struck his tissues, his vertebrae seemed to be eaten up from within. 'How shall I be able to call Ram Charan when I get there?' he said.

Between the intervals of wiping the sweat off his brow, his ordinary self came back. The nervousness descended into the crowded world of his entrails, leaving the surface of his mind clean like a slate. He got to the kerb of the outcastes' street and stopped still, suddenly, within ten yards of Ram Charan's house. He had the pleasantest surprise. Chota stood, leaning by a wooden pillar, staring with wonder at the crowd of men and women gathered in the one-roomed mud-house and outside on the veranda.

Bakha advanced gingerly towards the wooden pillar and came and stood by Chota. His friend turned with surprise at him and cordially pressed him by the hand. Then they both fell to staring at the dazed, happy crowd before them. Bakha noticed how white the starched linen, which the washermen wore, seemed against their black skins. At first, however, he could not concentrate his gaze on the individuals. He felt afraid to lift his eyes beyond the veranda to the cavernous room scarcely illuminated by the glowing sun outside. A wave of warmth descended down the back of his head. Through the haze he could see a man from within looking at him. He felt quivers of self-consciousness pass through him. The thought of Ram Charan's sister came into collision with the sight of her. His heart sank within him. He was sweating. Luckily for him, the double beat of a drum tore the air and lifted all the confusion in Bakha's soul on the flapping, hovering wings of the song that accompanied it. It was a queer refrain, sudden as thunder, as it ranged over three notes of the minor scale, sung in unison by the whole assembly. In the very beginning it was a shrill wail, which went through the tympanum of the ear to the head, and seemed to make the listener mad with its ever-sharpening frenzy, as lightning which pokes its sharp spears of power through the head and leaves it athrob. Before they proceeded very far, the song had mounted above the drum and established the reign of an exhilarating rhythm. Bakha floated on the strain as he might have done on a swing. Then as the melody arose steeply to its full height of enthusiasm in the swaying, rolling, rocking, yelling frames of the washermen and washerwomen, Bakha again felt cold and impassive with self-consciousness. He touched Chota's arm nervously, hiding his movement in the blaze of riotous excess to which the washermen had carried their song. Chota greeted him with a broad grin as cordial as the contagious spirit of happiness in the atmosphere could make it.

'I shall call Ram Charan,' said Chota, and quite unafraid and unashamed to face the crowd of singing washermen he called Ram Charan, who sat dressed in a rather contradictory style of Eastern and Western habiliments—a large khaki topee on his small head, a muslin shirt, clean and white, but torn near the collar, and a pair of shorts on his thin, bare black legs.

At first Ram Charan was too absorbed, eating the *ludus* (sugar-plums) which his mother was distributing with the tankards of native wine, for Chota's message to pass from the washerman near him to whom he had entrusted it, through the forest of heads, to Ram Charan. Then luckily for his friends, as Ram Charan stood up to sprinkle the red colour over the white clothes of the crowd through a crude spray made out of a tin can, the ceremonial little mischief-maker was lifted amid the happy cries and shouts of hilarious laughter of the white-clad men, now spotted profusely with scarlet, and thrown out.

'Come,' he greeted Chota and Bakha, blinking his lashless eyes, and ran ahead.

'Give, o bey brother-in-law, give us some of the sweets,' said Chota.

Ram Charan had not forgotten to fill the pockets of his shorts, and his large silk handkerchief, stolen from the laundry bag of some rich merchant, with sugar-plums.

'Keep quiet for a while,' said Ram Charan, suddenly turning back to see if his mother was aware of the direction he was going to take.

She was.

'Oh, you illegally begotten!' came her voice shrilly, audible above all the other noises. 'Are you running away to play with that dirty sweeper and leather-worker on the very day of your sister's marriage? You ought to be ashamed of yourself, you little dog!'

'Shut up, you bitch!' replied Ram Charan, as was his wont, for he had been hardened into an impudent, obstinate young rascal by the persistency of his mother's abuse. And with Chota at his heels and Bakha following clumsily behind, he led the way towards the heath which sloped gently towards the north of the outcastes' colony.

'Give us some of those sugar-plums, brother-in-law!' insisted Chota, greedy and gay. 'I have waited for an hour for you outside your noisy house.'

'You shall have some as soon as we get to the hill,' assured Ram Charan. 'I have brought them for you and Bakha, not for anyone else. Now let us run, for my mother might come after me.' And he carried himself with the assurance of one who has suddenly come into power. Chota at least, if not Bakha, paid him the homage which he expected as his due because he had a dozen sugar-plums in his possession.

'Come, O elephant,' he rebuked Bakha for his coldness, 'show your teeth and lift your legs. You shall have some sweets soon.'

Bakha dismissed the impudence of his joke with a grunt and followed quietly. He was feeling quite detached from the human world, swathed in a sort of unadulterated melancholy.

The hand of nature was stretching itself out towards him, for the tall grass on the slopes of Bulashah Hills was in sight, and he had opened his heart to it, lifted by the cool breeze that wafted him away from the crowds, the ugliness and the noise of the outcastes' street. He looked across at the swaying loveliness before him and the little hillocks over which it spread under a sunny sky, so transcendingly blue and beautiful that he felt like standing dumb and motionless before it. He listened to the incoherent whistling of the shrubs. They were the voices he knew so well. He was glad that his friends were ahead of him and that the thrum was not broken, for the curve of his soul seemed to bend over the heights, straining to woo nature in solitude and silence. It seemed to him he would be unhappy if he heard even one human voice. His inside seemed to know that it wouldn't be soothed if there were the slightest obstruction between him and the outer world. It didn't even occur to him to ask why he had come here. He was just swamped by the merest fringe of the magnificent fields that spread before him. He. had been startled into an awareness of the mystery of vegetable moods.

As he rambled along, however, he felt he wanted an adventure in friendship to humanise the solitary excursion of the stoic in him. But he didn't want to call Ram Charan, or Chota, to come and share his joy with him. He fell back to a memory of the adventures he had had here in his childhood. He remembered the time in his early days when he used to come to the heath with all the other boys, to fight battles for the imaginary fort they had built by fixing a flag on the top of the hill. The bamboo bows with which they flung arrows at each other came before him and the imitation toy pistols with their sparks. How enthusiastic all the boys used to feel about him then! They had made him their *Jernel* (general). He recalled with pride the pitched battle they had fought against the boys of the 28th Sikhs and won. They were helter-skelter battles, not quite like the organised manoeuvres of the regiments, fought with guns. 'But then,' he said to himself, 'they were the games played in childhood. I wouldn't play those games now. I can hardly spare time to play hockey, with my father shouting at me all the time.' He felt a bit lonely thinking such thoughts. He switched his mind on to the landscape in that vague groping manner in which his mind always felt its way across things. On the slopes, carpeted with grass, there flourished a wilderness of flowers, of which the shades changed at various intervals. There were the yellow buttercups, which had seemed to Bakha always like the mustard-seed flower of his village near

Sialkot; then there were the long-stalked, single-headed daisies, alternating with grades of purple and white anemones—to Bakha all flowers, mere flowers, for he didn't know their names. A pool of water in long grass and ferns looked like a large basin round which the silver birches bent down and, smitten by the wind, seemed to be drinking. Here every passer-by quenched his thirst from the water that sprang from a natural spring.

Descending down to it, with his nostrils full of fresh air, and his heart as light as the spirits of the sparrows which chirped, Bakha seemed nevertheless unaroused and unresponsive as a child turning aside from every wayside flower, for though he had the receptivity of the man who is willing to lend his senses to experience, he had an unenlightened will. Necessity had forced him to the contemplation of the charms of nature, merely superficially. Heredity had furrowed no deep grooves in his soul where flowers could grow or grass abound. The cumulative influence of careful selection had imprisoned, his free will in the shackles of slavery to the dreary routine of one occupational environment. He could not reach out from the narrow and limited personality he had inherited to his larger yearning. It was a discord between person and circumstance by which a lion like him lay enmeshed in a net while many a common criminal wore a rajah's crown. His wealth of unconscious experience, however, was extraordinary. It was a kind of crude sense of the world, in the round, such as the peasant who can do the job has, while the laboratory agriculturalist is scratching his head, or like the Arab seaman who sails the seas in a small boat and casually determines his direction by the position of the sun, or like the beggar singer who recites an epic from door to door. But it wanted the force and vivacity of thought to transmute his vague sense into the superior instinct of the *really* civilised man.

As he sauntered along a spark of some intuition suddenly set him ablaze. He was fired with a desire to burst out from the shadow of silence and obscurity in which he lay enshrouded.

He rushed down to the slope, towards the trees that stood by the pool below him. The soft breeze came whispering up to him and made his blood tingle with its soft, fresh coolness. The sun on the curve of the sky before him was being reflected from the sheen of the rippling water with a restlessness like the pain in Bakha's soul. He descended through the meadows, rank with herbage, before he had breathed more than a breath. He lay down on the bank of the pool and immediately lent himself to the stillness about him, making not the slightest stir, even though the position in which he leaned back exposed his eyes uncomfortably to the sun. In a moment or two his frame seemed to have sunk into insignificance, drowned as it were in a pit of silence, while the things on the sunny bank began to take life, each little stem of plant becoming a big leaf, distinct and important. The whole valley seemed to him aglow with life.

But the rich and exuberant spaces about him seemed to have sucked all his energy away. He lay as if dead. His empty belly had provoked the subtle urgings of sleep into play. He was dozing.

He had hardly dozed off before Chota came and began to tickle his nose with a straw. With one wild sneeze the sweeper-lad got up and sat with his trunk upright in the face of his friends' double-barrelled laughter. Bakha was no killjoy to be annoyed by so ordinary a practical joke and willingly let himself be made a fool of. But the incidents of the morning had cast a shadow over him and there was something forced in his smile as against the spontaneous heartiness of his companions. Chota noticed this. He saw that there, was something tense about it, something accusing, as if Bakha really disapproved of the joke which had been played on him.

'What is the matter with you, brother-in-law?' he asked.

'Nothing,' replied Bakha. 'You were running. I came slowly.'

'You didn't look for us?'

'I was tired. I wanted to sleep. I couldn't sleep very well last night.'

'Because you will be a gentreman and won't put a quilt over you as your father says,' joked Chota. He learnt from Rakha all that happened to Bakha at home, all the abuse that their father inflicted upon him, and he used to tease him about it.

'Shut up,' retorted Bakha playfully, 'you are more of a gentreman than I am, and look at this brother-in-law to-day; he is wearing a sahib's topee and shorts.'

Although they all aspired to copy English customs, they were not altogether unconscious of the falseness of their instinct, and could see the edge of their elders' sarcastic reproach: '*Look at this gentreman!*' and repeated it amongst each other.

'What about those sugar-plums?' Bakha continued, referring to Ram Charan. He wasn't particularly keen to have them although he would have liked to eat one.

'Here is your portion,' said Ram Charan, unfolding the handkerchief which he carried.

There were three sugar-plums in it, all slightly broken.

'Throw me one,' said Bakha.

'Take it,' said Ram Charan.

But Bakha hesitated and didn't hold his hands out.

'Take it, why don't you take it?' Ram Charan grumbled.

'No, give it to me, throw it,' Bakha said.

Both Ram Charan and Chota were surprised. Never before had they seen Bakha behave like that. Ram Charan was admitted to be of the higher caste among them, because he was a washerman. Chota, the leather-worker's son, came next in the hierarchy, and Bakha was of the third and lowest category. But among the trio they had banished all thought of distinction, except when the snobbery of caste feeling supplied the basis for putting on airs for a joke. They had eaten together, if not of things in the preparation of which water had been used, at least dry things, this being in imitation of the line drawn by the Hindus between themselves and the Mohammedans and Christians. Sweets they had often shared together, and they had handled soda-water bottles anyhow, at all those formal hockey matches they played once a year, with the boys' teams of the various regiments in the Bulashah Brigade.

'What has happened to you?' queried Chota in a voice full of deep concern, and then he added caressingly: 'Come, friend, tell us.'

'Nothing, it's nothing,' said Bakha.

'Come, come, we are your friends,' implored Chota.

Bakha told them how when he left them that morning he was walking through the town, a man happened to brush past him, and how he began to abuse him, and summoned a large crowd; and how before he could get away, he had slapped him.

'Why didn't you strike back?' Chota asked, enraged.

'That wasn't the only thing,' continued Bakha. And he narrated how the priest tried to molest his sister and then came shouting at them both: 'Polluted, polluted.'

'You wait till the illegally begotten comes to our street side. We will skin the fellow,' shouted Chota indignantly.

'There was another insult waiting for me further up,' Bakha added, and he narrated the story of how the woman in the silversmith's alley had flung the bread down at him from the top of her house.

'Comrade, we're sorry,' assured Chota. 'Come, be brave, forget all this. What can we do? We are outcastes.' He patted Bakha comfortingly. 'Come,' he consoled again, 'forget all about it. We will go and play hockey. Let that *brother-in-law* of a priest come down our street, and we will teach him the lesson of his life.'

'Come, let's go,' put in Ram Charan, who was slightly embarrassed by Bakha's narrative, and growingly afraid that his mother would curse him if he absented himself from home too long. 'I'll have to put in an appearance at home before I can come and play hockey,' he said, looking from Chota to Bakha.

'Come,' urged Chota soothingly, with a deep strain of melancholy in his voice.

Bakha got to his feet and the three of them began to walk quietly homewards.

Ram Charan was beginning to feel very embarrassed by the silence, so embarrassed that he thought it no fit occasion to remain adorned with such a symbol of greatness as his solar hat. So he lifted his strange, large headgear off its small, uneasy seat and followed sheepishly.

Bakha's soul seemed to lie bare before his friends, bruised and tender. Chota felt with him. He allied himself with Bakha's mood.

The sympathy that the repetition of his narrative evoked from his friends accentuated Bakha's self-pity. He began, as he walked along, to feel the heart-burnings of the morning. He felt furious, his fury heightening with the invisible strength that the presence of his two friends gave him. 'Chota and I could teach that immoral wretch of a Brahmin a lesson,' he reflected.

'What do you say to our catching hold of the swine one day?' put in Chota.

This is strange, Bakha felt, that Chota should think of the same thing at the same time as I. But he felt unequal to the suggestion as he felt unequal to his own desire.

'What is the use?' he replied, sighing. He didn't want to refuse to wreak his vengeance too openly. And then he felt sad and pensive, because he couldn't rise to the realisation of his own urges. He resolved to tighten himself. He gnashed his teeth. A warmth rose to his ears. He felt a quickening in his blood. Then came the sweep of his ever-recurring emotions. He boiled with rage. 'Horrible, horrible,' his soul seemed to cry out within him. He felt the most excruciating mental pain he had ever felt in his body. He shivered. His broad, impassive face was pale with hostility. But he couldn't do anything. He hung his head and walked with a drooping chest. His frame seemed to be burdened with the weight of an inexpressible, unrelieved power. He was deliberately trying to hide his stature in his stoop, as if he were afraid of being seen at all.

'Where is that brother-in-law, Ram Charan?' said Chota to relieve the tension.

'Looking for mushrooms,' Bakha joked. With this his knitted brows relaxed and his furrowed forehead became uncreased. The cowed defiance of his manner gave place to an easy, natural air. He was absorbed in the spectacle of the town of Bulashah sleeping snugly in the afternoon hush at the foot of the hill. From the clump of trees, visible beyond the distant north gate, to the cantonment in the south, from the mango groves in the east to the little group of houses of the outcastes' colony, the white-blue lower sky was defined into a lovely pattern by the golden domes of the temples, the flat roofs of the houses and the carved terraces with big blue clay flower-pots fixed to their sides. And then the thatched hut of his home in the swamps and shallows presented itself to his gaze. The contrast of the tremulous line of foliage which lay near him and beyond, the green, green mango orchards and the marshland which surrounded his home, was a stark one.

'I think I shall also go and show my face at home before I come to play hockey,' said Chota suddenly. 'There is too much sunshine yet.'

'All right, Havildar Charat Singh said he would give me a hockey stick if I called this afternoon,' Bakha said, 'I shall go and get it.'

'All right, you go and get the stick,' agreed Chota. 'Charan and I will join you before the match begins. Meanwhile we shall take this footpath.'

They had reached a small lane which led to the outcastes' colony through cactus hedges. They branched off.

Bakha strode along in the open through the stones in the old river-bed that stretched itself between the hills and the barracks of the 38th Dogras. He felt that he had just invented this business with Charat Singh because he didn't want to go home, because he didn't want to see his father, his brother, his sister, because he didn't want to go and work at the latrines—at least, not to-day. For a moment he felt a compunction that he was trying to escape. But he had grown out of his surroundings and he just hated the thought of being in the neighbourhood of his mud-house.

Somewhere in him he felt he could never get away from it, but to the greater part of him the place didn't exist. It had been effaced clean off the map of his being.

There was not a soul to be seen about in the compound of the barracks. Even the quarter-guard seemed empty and forlorn, except for the two dummy-like sentries who walked up and down the veranda outside the magazine which Bakha knew to be behind the locked doors. Only a solar topee seemed to Bakha alive, instinct'with life, there, as it hung on the wall. There were many legends current about this hat. Some said it was a symbol of authority of the *sahib logs* (white men) who ruled over the regiment. Others said that the hat had been forgotten in the regimental office by a sahib (officer) once, and since, being a sahib (rich man), he didn't care to reclaim his lost property, it had been kept on at the quarter-guard. Again, it was rumoured that a sahib had once been court-martialled for shooting a sepoy, and since he was a white man and could never be put behind the bars in the lock-up at the quarterguard, his hat and belt and sword had been imprisoned instead. The sahib had suddenly disappeared. Some people said he had been helped by the officer commanding the regiment to escape overnight in order to evade the sentence of imprisonment pronounced by the judges, and only the hat had remained at the quarter-guard. If, on the other hand, you asked one of the sentries whose hat it was, they always told you it belonged to a sahib (an officer) who had just gone into the grounds and would be soon returning to take it. But nobody ever asked questions about this hat except the children of the 38th Dogras. The younger among these children believed what the sentries said and ran away, for great was the fear attaching to the persons of the sahibs, like the dread of pale-white ghosts, ghouls and hobgoblins, because they were rumoured to be very irritable, liable to strike you with their canes if you looked at them. The elder boys knew it was a lie invented by the sentries to drive the curious little boys away, as they remembered having seen that hat for years in the same place, and realised it couldn't have been just left there by a sahib every time they saw it.

But even they didn't really know why the sentries invented the lie. They didn't realise that the sepoys too wanted the hat, not because they could wear it, either with their uniform or their mufti, but because they thought of the wonder it would arouse in the hills at home, the interest it would arouse among the villagers. People would come to see it for miles, as they came to see their *vardi* (uniform) and their white clothes, with ogling eyes and admiring glances. How proud, they thought, they would feel carrying this symbol of Sahibhood in their luggage, going home to Kangra or Hoshiarpur.

But why had all these stories about the solar hat got round? Because there wasn't a child about the 38th Dogras who hadn't cast lingering eyes at this hat. The spirit of modernity had worked havoc among the youth of the regiment. The consciousness of every child was full of a desire to wear Western dress, and since most of the boys about the place were the sons of babus, bandsmen, sepoys, sweepers, washermen and shopkeepers, all too poor to afrord the luxury of a complete European outfit, they eagerly stretched their hands to seize any particular article they could see anywhere, feeling that the possession of something European was better than the possession of nothing European. A hat with its curious distinction of shape and form, with the peculiar quality of honour that it presents to the Indian eye because it adorns the noblest part of the body, had a fascination such as no other item of European dress possessed.

Bakha had for years looked with longing at the solar topee that hung on the peg in the veranda of the 38th Dogras' quarter-guard. Ever since he was a little child he had contemplated it with the wonder-struck gaze of the lover and the devotee. Whenever he was given the chance of going out sweeping in the compounds of the 38th Dogras' barracks, he invariably chose the quarter-guard side, for there he could steal glances at the object he coveted, and plan various devices to win it. Those were nice thoughts, those connected with the schemes he concocted in order to possess that hat.

One of the ways in which it could be acquired, he had thought, was to make friends with one of the non-commissioned officers in charge of the quarter-guard. But it was impracticable. There was never the same non-commissioned officer in charge of the quarter-guard for two days and nights together. The guard changed every twelve hours, and considering it was one N.C.O. from one of the many platoons of one of the twelve companies in the regiment, you could never hope to see the same non-commissioned oflicer at the quarter-guard twice in your life.

That scheme failing, Bakha had thought of asking one of the sentries. When he was a child he had once dared to do that, but then the sentry had sent him away with the yarn about the sahib who had left it for a moment while he was in the grounds, and who would soon come back to get it. Now, however, he dared not ask. Some of the sepoys gave themselves such airs. 'They might abuse me,' he said to himself. 'Better any time to ask a Havildar. Every Havildar is an experienced person with long service and surely knows my father, the Jemadar of the sweepers. He will be kind even if he doesn't actually give me the hat.' But he could not bring himself to ask, he just couldn't. 'Why is it,' he had often asked himself, 'that I can't go and ask now but dared to do so when I was a child?' He couldn't find the answer to this. He didn't know that with the growth of years he had lost the freedom, the wild, careless, dauntless freedom of the child, that he had lost his courage, that he was afraid.

Then he deceived himself by believing that he didn't really want the hat, because he could get any number of them at the rag shop or from some Tommy in the British barracks. But he still longed for the hat. For years he had pined for it. And now he stood contemplating it with the same interest, the same curiosity, the same desire to possess it, with which he had looked at it during these years. It was not too clean a topee. The dust of years had settled on it. The khaki cloth-cover, with the quilt-like pattern, had faded to a dirty white, and, of course, no one knew what it was like inside.

Bakha stared at it hard, as he stood in a corner of the quarter-guard off the track where the sentries paraded to and fro. It didn't seem to move any nearer towards him. 'What can I do?' he asked himself. 'Go and ask that sentry,' his mind told him. 'But no, he might not understand,' the doubt arose, 'he might not understand what I am talking about if I, a sweeper, suddenly put it to him that I want the hat. He looks rather stern. There is no chance of getting near him.'

He looked round to see if there were anyone else about. There wasn't a soul. He guessed that everyone was having a siesta. He felt an irresistible desire to go and steal the hat. If only that sentry was not there. 'One could do it,' he thought, 'when the sentry turns his face away and walks to the other end of his beat. But someone might come and surprise me. It is too big a thing, this hat, to conceal. Besides if I stole it, I could never wear it. Everyone in the regiment knows about it. No, it is impossible. No, there is no way of getting it.' Once more he cast a loving glance at it and walked away towards the barracks at the nearer end of which, he knew lived Havildar Charat Singh.

It wasn't far. A hundred yards or so. The time involved in covering this space Bakha occupied with a picture of himself playing hockey with the solar topee on. He saw himself running about in it. How important he looked, the idol of all the boys. Then it occurred to him that solar topees are not worn at hockey. 'How foolish my thoughts are,' he said. He was slightly ashamed of his predilection in favour of English dress, but he derived consolation from the fact that he had never made such a fool of himself as Ram Charan did by wearing a hat and shorts at his sister's marriage.

He crossed through a ditch and was in sight of the long rows of barracks. The particular one he wanted was only ten yards ahead of him. It had a long veranda. He reached the room at the near end of it. That was Havildar Charat Singh's place. He walked past it, because he was embarrassed. He was always ashamed of being seen. He felt like a thief. Luckily for his self-consciousness, the door of the room was shut. There was no way for him to know whether the Havildar was at home. An ordinary person could go and shout for the Havildar, or could go and strike the latch. He was a sweeper and dared not go within defiling distance of the veranda. Bakha wished that the system which the Emperor Jehangir had invented, if the story of the babu's son was right, now prevailed, of a bell in the Emperor's house which was attached to a string at the outer gates and by the pulling of which the King could be informed of the applicants waiting for admission. He had to shout for his food in the town. He had no way of getting into touch with Ram Charan or Chota when he went to their houses except by shouting, and that meant Ram Charan's mother and Chota's father recognising his voice, and shouting back abusively at him for trying to seduce their sons to play truant. And now, of course, he couldn't shout or do anything. The Havildar might be asleep. The sepoys might be having their siesta too. And they would be disturbed.

He walked to and fro outside the veranda. Then he lay down under a tree. His thoughts began to drift. 'I don't know what I can do. I hope he remembers the promise he made this morning. Otherwise all this time will be wasted for nothing. My father must be cursing me. I haven't worked all the afternoon. But never mind. Let Rakha do it for a change. I have been doing it all this while. What if I take an afternoon off?' His eyes drifted to the kitchen where the food for Charat Singh's company was cooked. He remembered he had been there quite often to get food when he was a child, when his father was attached to 'B' company as an ordinary sweeper. The figures of the hockey-playing members of this company passed through his mind. There was Hoshiar Singh, who played centre-half, the pivot of the team. There was Lekh Ram, who played centre-forward. There was Shiv Singh, who played right full-back. And, of course, there was the redoubtable Charat Singh, who kept goal. He recalled the story current about Charat Singh, that the days he didn't spend playing hockey he spent in hospital, suffering from the wounds and bruises he received playing hockey. He could picture the man keeping goal in the matches against the British regiment. He always stood leaning by the goalpost till the ball came his way and he just fell upon it. The number of scars he had on his body equalled in number, said the babu's son, the marks of sword and lance on the body of the Rajput warrior Rana Sanga, the conqueror of Akbar, the great Moghul. And the most delightful of the injuries which he had ever sustained was to have had his teeth knocked out, for he had had them replaced with a row of false ones, mounted with gold, which had led to many a joke, when someone ingeniously suggested that the proverb 'A straw in the beard of a thief' should be changed to 'Gold teeth in the mouth of the thief.'

Bakha had not fully given himself up to his reverie when he saw Charat Singh come out of his door, brass jug in hand. The Havildar sat down on the veranda profusely splashing water into his eyes and on his face. Too absorbed in his toilet and still half asleep, he didn't notice Bakha sitting under the *Kikir* tree. The sweeper-boy got up with a half-embarrassed, half-daring look, and lifting his hand to his brow, said: 'Salaam, Havildar ji.'

'Come, ohe Bakhia, how are you?' said Charat Singh enthusiastically. 'I have not seen you about at the regimental hockey matches lately. Where do you keep yourself hidden?'

'I have to work, Havildar ji,' Bakha replied.

'Oh, work, work, blow work!' exclaimed Charat Singh, forgetful in the manifestation of his present goodwill that he had himself shouted at Bakha for neglecting his work that morning.

Bakha was conscious of this anomaly. But he was altogether too favourably inclined towards Charat Singh to let anything stand in the way of his admiration for the hockey hero. There was a comfortable, homely glow radiating from the smile that the Havildar wore. Bakha felt happy in his presence. 'For this man,' he said to himself, 'I wouldn't mind being a sweeper all my life. I would do anything for him.'

Charat Singh got up and wiped his face with the edge of his coarse homespun loin-cloth. Then he picked up a little hookah with a coco-nut shell for a water-basin, and a delicately-carved marionette-like stem crowned by a red clay basin for charcoal and tobacco. He separated the earthen pot from the neck of the hubble-bubble and said to Bakha:

'Go and get me two pieces of coal from the kitchen.'

The boy stood wonder-struck. That a Hindu should entrust him with the job of fetching glowing charcoal in the chilm which he was going to put on his hookah and smoke! For a moment he looked as if an electric shock had passed through him. Then the strange suggestion produced a pleasant thrill in his being; it exhilarated him. He took the chilm from Charat Singh and, wrapped in an atmosphere of delight, walked towards the kitchen fifty yards away.

'Call the cook also to me,' shouted Charat Singh after him, 'and tell him to bring my tea.'

'Very good, Havildar ji,' said Bakha, and walked away without looking back, lest he should prove unequal to the unique honour that the Hindu had done him by entrusting him with so intimate a job as fetching coal in his clay basin. 'What? Is it wet or dry?' he asked himself. 'Could it be defiled, I wonder?' The answer came back to him: 'Oh, yes, the tobacco is wet. Of course it could be defiled.' For a moment he doubted whether Charat Singh was conscious and in his senses when he entrusted him with the job. 'He might be forgetful and suddenly realise what he had done. Did he forget that I am a sweeper? He couldn't have done, I was just talking to him about my work. And he saw me this morning. How could he have forgotten?' Thus reassured he was grateful to God that such men as Charat Singh existed. He walked with a steady step, with a happy step, deliberately controlled, lest he should excite anyone's attention about the barracks, and be seen carrying the Havildar's clay basin. It was with difficulty, however, that he prevented himself from stumbling, for his soul was full of love and adoration and worship for the man who had thought it fit to entrust him, an unclean menial, with the job and his eyes were turned inwards.

He went and stood in sight of a kitchen cubicle where a cook sat by the earthen fireplace peeling potatoes, while a big brass saucepan sent coils of steam shooting out from under its lid.

'Will you give me some pieces of coal for Havildar Charat Singh, please?'

The cook looked at Bakha for a moment, as much as to ask: 'Who are you?' He thought he had seen the face somewhere but he couldn't place him. 'He might be one of the sappers,' he concluded charitably, seeing that the man held Havildar Charat Singh's clay basin in his hand. As the sappers, in spite of their dark colour and dirty clothes, are of the grass-cutter caste, no one would object to sending one of them on an errand to fetch fire. Besides, the cook was indebted to Havildar Charat Singh. The Havildar had given him a clean new shirt and a white turban before he went on leave. He lifted two sticks of wood fuel from the fire and stuck them on the ground before Bakha. The sweeper picked up the live, burning pieces of coal in his hand one by one, and put them in the firepot. He suddenly recalled the figure of the little girl in his dream of the morning on whose hands the silversmith had placed a burning ember.

'*Mehrbani*' (thank you), he said, when he had half filled the firepot with coal. 'The Havildar says he wants his tea.' He tried to put a great deal of humility into an unfortunately abrupt sentence.

Then he walked back to where Charat Singh sat in an easy-chair he had drawn out from somewhere, and he handed him the firepot. The Havildar casually stretched his hand and, accepting the pot, put it on his coco-nut shell hookah and gurgled away for all he was worth.

Bakha was feeling impatient now, and he sat near the veranda on a brick. He didn't know why he felt impatient. It was because of the hookah. It always made him impatient. And then he was eager for the hockey stick. The Havildar hadn't said a word about it. 'Had he forgotten?' Bakha wondered. So as he sat waiting, he itched a bit with the empty awkwardness that yawned between him and Charat Singh. The cook came bearing a long brass tumbler and a jug of tea and the Havildar relieved his friend of his nervousness in an easy unconscious manner.

'Get that pan from which the sparrows drink water,' he said to Bakha, pointing to the foot of a wooden pillar. 'Pour out the water from it.'

Bakha did as he was directed, and the vessel was clean in his hand. To his great surprise Charat Singh got up and began to pour tea out of his tumbler into the pan.

'No, no, sir,' Bakha protested in the familiar Indian guests' manner.

Charat Singh poured out the tea.

'Drink it, drink it, my son.'

'I am very grateful, Havildar ji,' said Bakha. 'It is very kind of you.'

'Drink it, drink the tea, you work hard; it will relieve your fatigue,' said Charat Singh.

When Bakha had gulped down the liquid, he rose and replaced the vessel. Meanwhile Charat Singh had poured the contents of his jug into the tumbler and sipped it quietly.

'Now what about a hockey stick for you!' he said, licking his lips and his thin moustache with the tip of his tongue.

Bakha looked up and tried to assume a grateful expression. He didn't have to try very hard, for in, a second he seemed to have dwarfed himself to the littlest little being on earth, and followed the Havildar noiselessly. His face was hot with the tea, his teeth shone even in their slavish smile, his whole body and mind were tense with admiration and gratitude to his benefactor. 'What has happened to change my *kismet* (fate) all of a sudden?' he asked himself. 'Such kindness from the Havildar, who is a Hindu, and one of the most important men about the regiment!' He followed Charat Singh with his gaze, curiously amazed.

The Havildar opened a door by the side of his room and

disappeared for a moment. Then he came out with an almost brand-new hockey stick, which must have been used only once. He handed it to Bakha as casually as he had given him the firepot to go and fill with charcoal.

'But it is new, Havildar ji,' Bakha said as he took it.

'Now run along, new or not new, it doesn't matter,' said Charat Singh. 'Conceal it under your coat and don't tell anyone. Go, my lad.'

Bakha bent his head and evaded the Havildar's eyes. He couldn't look at so generous a person. He was overcome by the man's kindness. He was grateful, grateful, haltingly grateful, falteringly grateful, stumblingly grateful, so grateful that he didn't know how he could walk the ten yards to the corner to be out of the sight of his benevolent and generous host. The whole atmosphere was charged with embarrassment. He felt uncomfortable as he walked away. 'Strange! strange! wonderful! kind man! I didn't know he was so kind. I should have known. He always has such a humorous way about him! Kind, good man! He gave me a new stick, a brand-new stick!' He impatiently drew the stick from the folds of his overcoat where he had hidden it. It was a beautiful broad-bladed stick, marked with English stamps, and therefore, to Bakha, the best stick that had been manufactured in the world. It had a leather handle. 'Beautiful! Beautiful!' his heart seemed to be shouting in its thumping, mad rush of exhilaration. He turned the corner and went across the ditch, so that he was out of sight of his benefactor. Assured now that nobody would see the foolish pride and pleasure that he was taking in his prize, he rested it on the ground in the position in which it is usual to place a stick before hitting the ball. He bent it. It was elastic and bent finely. *That* Bakha knew was the test of a good stick. He hurriedly rubbed off the dust that had touched the lower part of the stick and holding it fast in his hands, as if he were afraid someone would come and snatch it from him, he tried to assure himself and make himself believe that he possessed it, so incredulous was he of the fact that he owned it. In spite of the fact that he held it tight, he couldn't shake off the feeling that he was dreaming, until he got to the edge of the playing-fields outside the gymnasium, behind the Indian officers' quarters, and began to hit a little round stone about. Then he suddenly realised that the stick might break, or get scarred, that way. He clutched it hard, and pressed it to his body, and tried to recollect his thoughts: 'So my normal good luck has returned. If only that thing hadn't happened this morning!'

Bakha tried to recall Charat Singh's face.

It had a slight suspicion of forgetfulness about it. 'I hope he knew what he was doing,' Bakha thought. 'I hope he wasn't absent-minded. He may have been. Dare I play with the stick? It might be spoiled, and in case he suddenly realises he has given away something he didn't want to give, it will be terrible because I can't return his stick battered or broken or even used. And, of course, I can't buy a new stick like this. But there is no question of that. Didn't he say: 'New or not new, take it and run away, and don't tell anyone.' Of course he knew what he was doing. I am mad to think that he was forgetful. So kind a person, and I think *this* about him. I am a pig to do that.' He didn't want to think at all, since he felt his thoughts becoming ungenerous. 'How beautiful the afternoon is,' he said, and he tilted his face up from the curve of, his thought to sniff the bite in the air which came from the hills in the north. He was aware of the transparent autumn sunshine, just warm enough to fill a heart wrapped in warm clothes with pleasure. The cup of Bakha's life was filled to overflowing with the happiness of the lucid, shining afternoon, as the bowl of the sky was filled with a clear and warm sunshine. He could have jumped for joy.

He was just going to, then he felt someone might see him. Someone was sure to be about. A passing sepoy or someone from among the boys. So there was no way of extending happiness into space except by walking about.

He began to walk. Each step he took was a strut, his chest thrown out, his head lifted high and his legs stiff, as if they were made of wood. The awkward sway of his rump had, for a moment, become the haughty gait of a proud soldier

Then he caught a glimpse of himself foolishly strutting about and he grew self-conscious. He stopped suddenly, uncomfortably. His newly-assumed confidence had been shattered.

He was impatient now. He wished someone would come and relieve his loneliness. If only a sepoy were passing, he would look at him. And if one of the boys came, he would show him the stick he had acquired. He wished that Chota would come. He would like to have shown him the stick. Or Ram Charan. 'But no, I must not show it to Ram Charan. Else he will go to Charat Singh and worry him by demanding a similar stick. The Havildar said I wasn't to tell anyone. He will be angry with me if Ram Charan takes it into his head to go and beg for a stick.' He wished the babu's sons would come. They had the ball. The elder boy had promised to give him a lesson in English. Perhaps he could give it to him before the game started. He wished someone would come, someone to fill his mind, which had dried up, become suddenly empty.

He walked about aimlessly now. His limbs were loose. His face turned now to this side, now to that, with a halfconscious look. At last he espied the babu's son, the little boy, rushing out of the hall of his house, a big stick in his little hand, food in his mouth and sweets tied up in the lap of his tunic. Bakha knew how eager the little one was to play hockey. He began to advance towards the child with an easy step, made awkward by a consciousness of his low position, and with a smile of humility on his face. He liked the babu's sons, respected them, not only because they were high-caste Hindus whom he, as a sweeper's son, had to respect, but also because their father held a position of extraordinary importance in the regiment, almost second to the Colonel Sahib himself.

The little one came up to him with a wild gesture of enthusiasm and said:

'Look, here is the new stick I told you about this morning. Charat Singh gave it to me.'

'Oh, it is very beautiful!' Bakha commented. 'But,' he continued jocularly, 'look at mine, it is better than yours. Ha, ha, mine is more beautiful than yours.'

'Let me see,' said the little one.

Bakha handed him the stick.

'Oh, it is the same kind exactly!' shouted the child.

Bakha felt that Charat Singh had apparently not done him an exceptional favour. But it was a favour all right. 'The babu's sons were the babu's sons. He would, of course, give them sticks. That he had given one to him, a sweeper, was an extraordinary favour.'

'Are you prepared for the match? Ohe, Bakhe,' said the child, as if he were a full-grown skipper.

'Yes, I am ready,' said Bakha smilingly, and without betraying the slightest sign of that sympathy which he felt for the child, seeing him so enthusiastic and knowing he wouldn't be allowed to play. He liked the little one, so brimful of energy and enthusiasm.

'Where is your elder brother?' Bakha asked the child.

'He is finishing his meal. He is coming. I shall go and fetch the hockey sticks and the ball. The boys will soon be here.' And he ran home abruptly, leaving Bakha curiously affected.

'Poor little boy, and they won't let him play. He is so eager. He will be an extraordinary man when he grows up. A big babu perhaps. Or a sahib. His eyes twinkle so!—'

'Ohe, Bakhe,' someone disturbed his thoughts.

He turned round and saw Chota and Ram Charan followed by various boys, the armourer's sons, Naimat and Asmat; the tailor-master's son Ibrahim; the bandmaster's sons, Ali, Abdulla, Hassan and Hussein, and hosts of strangers, presumably the boys of the 31st Punjabis. Bakha advanced towards them. Chota ran up to him and whispered: 'I have told them that you are the sahib's bearer: they don't know that you are a sweeper.'

'All right,' Bakha agreed. He knew that it had been done to convince some of the orthodox boys of the 31st Punjabis team that they wouldn't be polluted.

'Look, I have got a wonderful new stick,' said Bakha. He showed it to his friend. Then he said: 'Don't tell Ram Charan about it. Charat Singh gave it to me. I shall score no end of goals with it.'

'Wonderful! Wonderful! Marvellous! Beautiful!' exclaimed Chota. 'Brother-in-law, you are lucky!' He slapped Bakha's back and raised a small cloud of dust from his thick overcoat.

'Boys, get ready,' he shouted as he turned.

When the time for the election of the team came, the babu's little son brought and dumped the sticks before Chota and expected his reward. But Chota had already chosen his eleven.

'Let the child play,' Bakha put in on the little one's behalf.

'No, he will be troublesome,' Chota whispered. 'We can't let him play. It is a match with the big boys. He will get hurt and then there will be trouble.'

Bakha didn't want to insist too much. He knew that Chota and the little one didn't get on very well, and he was helpless seeing he liked them both equally, hurt to see the child ignored by everyone except his elder brother, who was trying to console him by saying that even he might not be asked to play, so important was the match, and between such big boys.

The child bore the disappointment more easily when it came, after the consolation his brother had offered and the friendliness reflected in Bakha's smiles. Ignored and helpless, he sought to interest himself in the match by volunteering to be the referee. But Chota wouldn't have him even as a referee. The little one now looked sorry for himself. The match had begun. He stood by the heaps of the boys' clothes which lay on the side of the hockey ground. He wished he were as big as Chota. Then he would be asked to play. Also then he could wear shorts like him. And he would look like a real sahib because he was not so dark as Chota.

Bakha came, for a second, to throw off his overcoat near the little one. He had started playing without having discarded it.

'Keep a watch over it, little brother, won't you?' he said to the child, as if by entrusting him with the job he was trying to console him for his non-inclusion in the team. Then he ran back to his place.

The little one could have cried at that moment. But the game, the play—Bakha was going to score a goal.

It was an extraordinary spectacle. The crowd of boys in the field hopped to and fro like grasshoppers. There was no organisation in the game they played. Bakha had rolled the ball, dribbling, dodging to the goal of the 31st Punjabis boys. But then he had been caught, enmeshed, by a throng of defenders of the goal, struggling, shouting,shoving to hit the ball out. Bakha managed, however, to scoop past the legs of all the boys and drove the ball into the space between the posts.

Defeated by superior tactics, the goalkeeper spitefully struck Bakha a blow on the legs. Upon this Chota, Ram Charan, Ali, Abdulla and all the rest of the 38th Dogra boys fell upon the goalkeeper of the 31st Punjabis.

Soon there was a free fight.

'Foul! Foul!' shouted the captain of the 31st Punjabis team.

'No foul! No foul!' responded Chota, drawing himself up to his full height angrily.

The captain of the 31st Punjabis advanced hotly, tearing the hordes asunder, and gripped Chota by the collar. And, once more, the boys were fighting, scratching, hitting, kicking, yelling. One, two, three, four, five, the little hands worked their sticks, rudely, heavily, vigorously, and the blusterings of the horde reached such a pitch of excitement that you could see the ruthlessness of the savage hunters in them. Chota had gripped his antagonist by the shoulder and for a time these two wrestled furiously, wildly, tearing each other's clothes and punching each other. Then Chota's enemy, unable to endure his transgressions, called to his followers and ran back a few yards.

'Throw stones at them, stones,' shouted Chota.

At this the boys of the 38th Dogras seemed to separate from their enemies, to run on one side and to begin hurling small stones at them.

In their intense excitement they didn't notice the little boy who stood near the clothes between them and their enemies, receiving the full weight of the stone bombardment. Most of the stones, however. passed high over the child's head and, though frightened, he was safe. But a bad throw from Ram Charan's hand caught him a rap on the skull. He gave a sharp, piercing shriek and fell unconscious. All the boys rushed to him. Streams of blood were pouring from the back of his head. Bakha picked him up in his arms and took him to the hall of his house. Unfortunately for him, the child's mother had heard the row they had been making and casually came to see if her children were safe. She met Bakha face to face.

'You eater of your masters, you dirty sweeper!' she shouted. 'What have you done to my son?'

Bakha was going to open his mouth and tell her what had happened. But even while she asked, she knew from the trickling of the blood from her son's skull, from his deathly, pale, senseless face.

'Oh, you eater of your masters! What have you done? You have killed my son!' she wailed, flinging her hands across her breasts and turning blue and red with fear. 'Give him to me! Give me my child! You have defiled my house, besides wounding my son!'

'Mother, mother, what are you saying?' interposed her elder son. 'It was not he. He didn't wound him. It was the washerwoman's son Ram Charan.'

'Get away, get away, you eater of your masters!' she shoutec at him. 'May you die! Why didn't you look after your brother?'

Bakha handed over the child, and afraid, humble, silent as a ghost, withdrew. He felt dejected, utterly miserable. Was the pleasure of Charat Singh's generosity only to be enjoyed for half an hour? What had he done to deserve such treatment? He loved the child. He had been very sorry when Chota refused to let him join the game. Then why should the boy's mother abuse him when he had tried to be kind? She hadn't even let him tell her how it all happened. 'Of course, I polluted the child. I couldn't help doing so. I knew my touch would pollute. But it was impossible not to pick him up. He was dazed, the poor little thing. And she abused me. I only get abuse and derision wherever I go. Pollution, pollution, I do nothing else but pollute people. They all say that: "Polluted, polluted!" She was perhaps justified though. Her son was injured. She could have said anything. It was my fault and of the other boys too. Why did we start that quarrel? It started on account of the goal I scored. Cursed me! The poor child! I hope he is not badly hurt. If only Chota had let him join the game, the little one would not have been standing where he was, and then he might have escaped getting hurt. Now where have all the boys gone?'

For the first time he became conscious that he had been walking alone. He looked around. Only the sparrows on the waste land of the sweepers' lane twittered accusingly at him in the pale afternoon light. With a sudden shudder of unutterable weariness he clutched the stick which he carried under his arm, and turned into a by-path leading to his home across decayed walnut leaves.

Before he came within sight of his home, he stopped and looked for a convenient spot where he might hide his hockey stick. He couldn't take it home. His father would at once fly into a rage about his wasting valuable time playing when there was all the work to do at the latrines. There was a long hedge of cactus away from the path. He turned towards it. There was a convenient hollow in the middle of the bush. He stepped over with a high stride into the hollow and laid the stick there. Then he bent down a few oar-shaped cactus leaves on to it and covered it against bad weather. After that he hurried, lest he should be seen hiding the stick by someone who might come later and filch it.

When Bakha returned his father sat smoking his hubble-bubble in the English wicker-chair. For a moment Lakha was unaware of his son's presence. Then suddenly he seemed to rise from his seat and wave his close-fisted hand menacingly at Bakha and to shout:

'You son of a pig! You son of a dog! You ran away! You have been away all the afternoon and now you come back! You illegally begotten! Have you become a nabob that you go wandering about when you know that there is work here for you to do? The sepoys have been shouting!'

Bakha was cool in the face of this warm reception. He was too wearied by the succession of revived memories to cope with anything now. He stood obstinately still while his father's invective continued.

'Son of a pig! You have no care for your old father. You go out in the morning and you come back at night. Who is going to do the work at the latrines? I brought you up. Won't you give me some rest in my old age? There you go trying to be a sahib when you are a sweeper's son. You illegally begotten! Dog! Pig!'

Bakha moved slowly under the rain of abuse towards the latrines. He was going to pick up a broom but he saw that his brother Rakha held it. He stopped short and looked up at his brother.

'So you have come back,' shouted Rakha self-righteously. He stared hard at his elder brother. There was the pride of the favourite in his glance.

Bakha knew that the boy was preening himself because he had put in an afternoon's work and had won his father's partiality. He didn't hate him for his overbearing manner, however. He thought of him as a child, as he really loved him. And he would have borne his impudence and his father's abuse as his due, but the boy refused to give him the broom and his father persisted in his denunciation.

'Son of a pig! illegally begotten! He has no sense of shame! *Play, play, play and wander all day*. As if he has nothing else to do!'

Bakha felt he couldn't bear the constant iteration of the same sentiments. He knew the way in which his father nagged him, persistently, stubbornly, without waiting for breath. He made for the latrines.

'Get away, you swine, run away from my presence,' shouted his father. 'Don't touch that broom or I shall kill you. Go away! Get out of my house. And don't come back! Don't let us see your face again!'

Before now, Bakha had often borne the brunt of his misery with a resigned air of fatalism. He had quietly suffered his father's abuse and satire, and even occasional beatings with a calm that betokened his intense docility and gentleness. He would never lift his head, or his hand, to defend himself against anyone. To-day, however, he had had more than enough. The spirit of fire which lay buried in the mass of his flesh had ignited this morning and lay smouldering. A little more fuel and it flared up, like a wild flame.

He tore across the plain without even looking back. It was as though a demon had taken possession of him. He was not conscious of the shattering moment which had suddenly determined his flight. Nor was he aware of the feeling of revulsion that had filled the moment. It seemed as if the demon in him held a cruel sword with which it hacked everything in its way and, by the force of the hacking, acquired a more sinister power, frightening in its intensity and weirdly fascinating in its transmutation of Bakha's body into a wild yet marvellously controlled medium.

He advanced eagerly. The old river lay on his right like a stormy sea of discontent whose mountainous waves the wind had swept, till the boulders and rocks reared up in knife-edges against the sky or rolled quietly over the earth. So different from what was on his left, the monotone of dusty plain, with short patterns of mauve and silver and grey where the sun's rays played upon the crest, and deep purple shadows in its fissures and its folds.

As he moved over the fringe of flat earth facing the plain, the rim of the upturned sky was taking on the gold and silver hues of the afternoon sun, and the world lay encircled in a ribbon of crimson. Here he slackened his pace, for it was here that he had felt the first glow of the early morning sun creeping into his bones. It was through this plain that he had gone out to the world, full of the spirit of adventure.

The wide expanse was empty except for the interminable thread of men entering the mud-houses which clustered in the north like mushrooms, surrounded by rubbish-heaps filled with broken bottles, old tins, dead cats and deep in mud. So lofty did he feel in his mood of righteous indignation that he had the strange sensation of being a giant, of commanding a full view of everything in the hollows and the hills.

'Unlucky, unlucky day! What have I done to deserve all this?' he cried in exasperation.

A sepoy on his way to the latrines was approaching. He jumped aside into a ditch so as not to be seen. He didn't want to meet anybody. He wanted to be alone and quiet, to compose himself. When the man had passed, he crept out of the ditch and made for a *pipal*-tree which stood in the plain surrounded by a clay platform. He sat down under it, facing the sun.

Now he felt desolate and the fact dawned on him that he was homeless. He had often been turned out like that. As a matter of fact when his father was angry he always threatened him and his brother with eviction. He remembered that once after his mother's death his father had locked him out all night, for not looking after the house properly. It was a winter night. The east wind blew and he was sleepy. He was tired from the day's work and yawned as he curled himself up in his overcoat behind two refuse-baskets. How he had smarted under the pain of that callousness and cruelty. Could he be the same father who, according to his own version, had gone praying to the doctor for medicine? Bakha recalled he had not spoken to his father for days after that incident. Then his grief about his unhappy position had become less violent, less rebellious. He had begun to work very hard. It had seemed to him that the punishment was good for him. For he felt he had learnt through it to put his heart into his work. He had matured. He had learnt to scrub floors, cook, fetch water besides doing his job cleaning the latrines and carting manure for sale to the fields. And in spite of the poor nourishment he got, he had developed into a big strong man, broad-shouldered, heavy-hipped, supple-armed, as near the Indian ideal of the wrestler as he wished to be.

But this present disgrace! This could do no good, he thought. It was undeserved. Why should his father object to his taking a half-holiday once in his life, especially as he knew he had been insulted in the town this morning and didn't feel like working? Then he had not spent the afternoon uselessly. He had got a new stick. But that, it occurred to him, was something which his father could not appreciate. He didn't like him to play hockey. That was what all the trouble was about, 'Rakha must have told about me,' he muttered, 'because he could not go to play. What a day I have had! Unlucky, inauspicious day! I wish I could die!' And he sat nursing his head in his hands, utterly given up to despair.

He had sat for a long while like that, his head in his hands. He felt sick and stifled with the knowledge that he was homeless and unwanted even by his own father. He had unconsciously chosen to sit down in a place where Chota or Ram Charan or someone from the outcastes' colony might recognise him. As time passed and he became conscious of the emptiness around him, he felt that the sympathy he longed for would never come.

But he was mistaken. Colonel Hutchinson, chief of the local Salvation Army, was never very far from the outcastes' colony. To his rather irreligious wife he always made the excuse that he was going out for a walk in the hills where the kingdom of Heaven was waiting to be found, though actually he went out wallowing in the mire for the sake of Jesus Christ, talking to some Untouchable among the rubbish-heaps about divinity and trinity. You couldn't miss him even if you saw him from a mile off, for he was one of the few living members of the band of Christian missionaries in India who had originated the idea that the Salvation Army ought to be dressed in the costume of the natives and live among them, if it was to achieve the true end of proselytising. And he had designed the Colonel's uniform he wore: a pair of white trousers, a scarlet jacket, a white turban with a red band across it. He had been a strong man once, if he wasn't quite the image of Eugene Sandow now. In the old days, he had plenty of hair on his head. Now, unfortunately, he was bald, his wife said, because of the infernal turban he wore, and because he was so fond of study. He also once had a turned-up moustache of the real Colonel kind, bushy and black. Now, though it was bushy, it was grey and drooped, his malicious wife said, in defeat, because she alleged that the proselytising mission of Christianity had, in his hands, been a complete failure. The number of conversions to his credit for the last twenty years being not more than five, and those five mainly from among the dirty, black Untouchables. But in justice to the Colonel's moustache, it must be said that his wife was being catty because she had a personal grievance against him. He had charmed her in his youth with his well-groomed, immaculate bearing, a conspicuous feature of which had been his fine black, upright moustache. She was a barmaid in Cambridge and had developed an aesthetic taste for the gem-like, glistening drops of wine that adorned the hair of Hutchinson's moustache when he had had a drink. She had married him for that. India, however, had embittered her. For not only did she hate the 'nigger' servants in her house, but she discovered that her husband was too studious for her gay card-playing, drinking and love-making tastes. Still, she had borne with him for a great many years, on the strength of whisky, but then Hutchinson's moustache had grown grey and it had begun to droop under the weight of age, the Colonel now being turned sixty-five. Despite all that his wife said, therefore, we must give credit to Colonel Hutchinson for his unflinching devotion to duty and loyalty to the cause which he had taken up.

He was marvellously active for his three-score years and five, laying himself in hiding as of yore in deep pits of filth or behind heaps of dung, to wait for some troubled outcaste who might be tired and hungry and would listen in his despair to the gospel of Christ. He always carried a number of copies of the Hindustani translation of the Bible under his arm, and he stuffed the pockets of his jacket and overcoat with the gospel of St. Luke, to thrust into the hands of any passer-by, be he willing or unwilling. He was a short fellow, pitiably weak and hobbling along on his stick. But the edge of his tongue was like a pair of scissors which cut the pattern of Hindustani into smithereens as a parrot snips his food into bits. The impulse that had made him think of learning Hindustani before he started his mission was a noble one considering that his work lay among the natives; the habit of muddling through the language, and never learning it properly during the thirty years of his stay in India, was most disastrous in its consequences.

'*Tum udas*' (You are sad), said the Colonel, putting his hand on Bakha's shoulder.

The sweeper-boy had the shock of his life to hear the broken Hindustani of a person he presumed to be an Englishman. He looked up with a start. He had expected that Chota or Ram Charan might come and console him, or someone from the outcastes' colony. He had not the foggiest notion that he would be surprised by Colonel Hutchinson, who although he freely mixed with the natives and had thus lost some of the glamour attaching to the superior, remote and reticent Englishmen, was yet a sahib who wore trousers and used a commode. Bakha felt honoured that the sahib had deigned to talk Hindustani to him, even though it was broken Hindustani. He felt flattered that he should be the object of pity and sympathy from a sahib. Of course, he at once recognised the Colonel. Who didn't know the missionary? But it was the first occasion on which he had found himself face to face with him. Being of a very retiring disposition and full of a feeling of inferiority he had never talked to

Hutchinson, although he remembered that the Colonel often visited his father when he (Bakha) was a child. His father, he recalled, also talked of the sahib, sometimes if he saw him in the distance, saying that the old sahib had wanted to convert them to the religion of *Yessuh Messih* and to make them sahibs like himself, but that he had refused to leave the Hindu fold, saying that the religion which was good enough for his forefathers was good enough for him.

'Salaam, Sahib,' said Bakha, putting his hand to his forehead as he got up.

'Salaam, salaam, you sit, don't disturb yourself,' squealed the Colonel in wrong, badly accented Hindustani, patting Bakha affectionately the while.

There was something wonderful in the brave effort the Colonel seemed to make to be natural in this unnatural atmosphere. But he was not self-conscious. He had thrown aside every weight—pride of birth and race and colour in adopting the customs of the natives and in garbing himself in their manner, to build up the Salvation Army in India. And he had swamped the overbearing strain of the upper middle-class Englishman in him by his hackneyed effusions of Christian sentiment, camouflaged the narrow, insular patriotism of his character in the jingo of the white-livered humanitarian.

'What has happened? Are you ill?' the Colonel asked, bending over.

Bakha felt confused, embarrassed by the flood of kindness. 'Charat Singh,' he thought, 'was kind to me this afternoon; the sahib is generosity itself.' And he wondered if he were dreaming. He looked and saw the form of the Colonel real enough before him. And hadn't he heard the strange, squeaky voice of the Englishman speaking Hindustani? good Hindustani, Bakha thought, considering it was spoken by a sahib, for ordinarily he knew the sahibs didn't speak Hindustani at all, only some useful words and swear words: '*Acha* (good); *jao* (go away); *jaidi karo* (be quick); *sur ka bacha* (son of a pig); *kute ka bacha* (son of a dog)!'

'Nothing, Sahib, I was just tired,' said Bakha shyly. 'I am sweeper here, son of Lakha, Jemadar of the sweepers.'

'I know! I know! How is your father?'

'Huzoor, he is well,' replied Bakha.

'Has your father told you who I am?' asked the Colonel, coming to the point in the practical manner of the Englishman.

'Yes, Huzoor. You are a sahib,' said Bakha.

'No, no,' pretended the Colonel. 'I am not a sahib. I am like you. I am padre of the Salvation Army.'

'Yes, Sahib, I know,' said Bakha, without understanding the subtle distinction which the Colonel was trying to institute between himself and the ordinary sahibs in India whose haughtiness and vulgarity was, to his Christian mind, shameful, and from whom, on that account, he took care to distinguish himself, lest their misdeeds reflect on the sincerity of his intentions for the welfare of the souls of the heathen. To Bakha, however, all the sahibs were sahibs, trousered and hatted men, who were generous in the extreme, giving away their cast-off clothes to their servants, also a bit nasty because they abused their servants a great deal. He knew, of course, that the Colonel was a padre sahib, but he did not know what a padre did except that he lived near the *girja ghar* (church) and came to see the people in the outcastes' colony. To him even the padres were of interest because of their European clothes. This padre did not wear a hat like the padre in the barracks of the British regiments. But that was of little account. He wore all the other items of clothes that the sahibs wore. He was a sahib all right. And this sahib had condescended to pat him on the back, to speak kind words to him, even to ask him why he was looking so sad. He could have cried to receive such gracious treatment from a sahib, cried with the joy of being in touch with that rare quality which was to be found in the sahibs. In spite of it all, however,.he seemed to be vaguely aware of the difference the Colonel was trying to define.

'I am a padre and my God is *Yessuh Messih*,' emphasised the Colonel. 'If you are in trouble, come to Jesus in the *girja ghar*.'

He was seeking vainly to paraphrase the promise: 'Come all ye that labour and I will give you rest.'

Bakha was struck with the coincidence. How did the padre know he was in trouble? 'And who is *Yessuh Messih* to whose religion my father told me this padre wanted to convert us? I wonder if he lives in the *girja ghar*?' He recalled that the *girja ghar* had seemed to him a mysterious place whenever he had passed by.

'Who is *Yessuh Messih*, Sahib?' Bakha asked, eager to allay his curiosity.

'Come, I shall tell you,' said Colonel Hutchinson. Come to the church.' And dragging the boy with his arm, babbling, babbling, all vague, in a cloud, and enthusiastic as a mystic, he led him away on the wings of a song:

'Life is found in Jesus,
Only there 'tis offered thee;
Offered without price or money
'Tis the gift of God sent free.'

Bakha was dumb with amazement, carried away by the confusion, feeling flattered, honoured by the invitation which had come from the sahib, however much that sahib looked like a native. He followed willingly, listening to each word that the Colonel spoke, but not understanding a word:

'Life is found in Jesus,'

the Colonel sang again, absorbed in himself, and unconscious that he was in charge of a soul in trquble.

Jesus! Who was Jesus! The same as *Yessuh Messih*? Who was he? The sahib says he is God. Was he a God like Rama, God of the Hindus, whom his father worshipped and his forefathers had worshipped, whom his mother used to mention quite often in her prayers? These thoughts gushed into Bakha's mind, and he would have exploded with them had it not been that the Colonel was absolutely absorbed in his sing-song:

'Life is found alone in Jesus,
Only there 'tis offered thee;
Offered without price or money;
'Tis the gift of God sent free.'

'Huzoor,' said Bakha, breaking in impatiently at the close of the third recitation,' who is Jesus? The same as *Yessuh Messih*? Who is he?'

'He died that we might be forgiven,
He died to make us good,
That we might go at last to heaven,
Saved by His precious blood,'

answered the Colonel quickly, rhythmically, before Bakha knew what he had asked. He was still baffled. The answer, if it was an answer, was like a conundrum to him; words, words. He felt overwhelmed and uncomfortable. But being, of course, too happy to be seen walking with the sahib, he bore all, trying to remember parts of the Colonel's song and asking himself what they meant. But apart from the muffled sound of words he could not catch anything.

'Sahib, who is *Yessuh Messih*?'

'He is the Son of God,' answered Colonel Hutchinson, coming down to earth for a moment. 'He died that we might be forgiven.'

And then he burst into song again:
He died that we might be forgiven,
He died to make us good,
That we might go at last to heaven,
Saved by His precious blood.'

'He died that we might be forgiven,' thought Bakha. 'What does that mean? He is the son of God! How could anybody be the son of God if God, as my mother told me, lives in the sky? How could He have a son? And why did His son die that we should be forgiven? Forgiven for what? And who is this son of God?'

'Who is *Yessuh Messih*, Sahib? Is he the God of the sahibs?' Bakha asked, slightly afraid that he was bothering the white man too much. He knew from experience that Englishmen did not like to talk too much.

'He is the Son of God, my boy,' answered the Colonel, ecstatically revolving his head. 'And He died for us sinners:

He died that we might be forgiven,
He died to make us good,
That we might go at last to heaven,
Saved by His precious blood.'

Bakha was a bit bored by this ecstatic hymn-singing. But the white man had condescended to speak to him, to take notice of him. He was happy and proud to be in touch with a sahib. He suffered the priest and even reiterated his enquiry:

'Do they pray to *Yessuh Messih* in your *girja ghar*, Sahib?'

'Yes, yes,' replied the Colonel, breaking into the rhythm of a new hymn:

Jesus, tender shepherd, hear me.
Let my sins be forgiven!
Let there be light,
Oh, shed Thy light in the heart of this boy.'

Bakha was baffled and bored. He did not understand anything of these songs. He had followed the sahib because the sahib wore trousers. Trousers had been the dream of his life. The kindly interest which the trousered man had shown him when he was downcast had made Bakha conjure up pictures of himself wearing the sahib's clothes, talking the sahib's language and becoming like the guard whom he had seen on the railway station near his village. He did not know who *Yessuh Messih* was. The sahib probably wanted to convert him to his religion. He didn't want to be converted. But he wouldn't mind being converted if he knew who *Yessuh Messih* was. The sahib, however, was singing, singing to himself and saying *Yessuh Messih* was the son of God. How could God have a son? Who is God? If God is like Rama, He has no son, for he had never heard that Rama had a son. It was all so puzzling that he thought of excusing himself by lying to the sahib that he had to go to work and couldn't come with him. The Colonel saw Bakha lagging behind and, realising that his new follower was losing interest, exerted the peculiar obstinacy of the enthusiastic missionary in him and dragging at the boy's sleeve, said, '*Yessuh Messih* is the Son of God, my boy. While we were yet sinners, He died for us. He sacrificed Himself for us.' Then again he became rapt in his devotional songs:

'O Calvary! O Calvary!
It was for me that Jesus died
On the Cross of Calvary!'

He sacrificed himself for us, Bakha reflected. His idea of sacrifice was something very certain and definite. He remembered that when some calamity brooded over the family, such as an epidemic of sickness, or starvation, his mother used to make offerings to the goddess Kali, by sacrificing a goat or some other animal. That sacrifice was supposed to appease the goddess's wrath and the evil passed over. Now, what did this sacrifice of *Yessuh Messih* mean? Why did he sacrifice himself?

'Why did *Yessuh Messih* sacrifice himself, Huzoor?' he asked.

'He died that we might be forgiven,
He died to make us good,
That we might go at last to heaven,
Saved by His precious blood,'

answered the Colonel, forgetting, as he had often done while he had been with Bakha, that the sweeper-boy didn't understand a word of what he was singing. Then in a sane moment he recognised the look of anxious solicitude on the face of the boy and realised he had been babbling too much, and mostly to himself.

'He sacrificed Himself out of love for us,' he said. 'He sacrificed Himself to help us all; for the rich and the poor for Brahmin and the Bhangi.' The last sentence went home. 'He sacrificed himself for us, for the rich and the poor, for the 'Brahmin and the Bhangi.' That meant there was no difference in his eyes between the rich and the poor, between the Brahmins and the Bhangis, between the pundit of the morning, for instance, and himself.

'Yes, yes, Sahib, I understand,' said Bakha eagerly. '*Yessuh Messih* makes no difference between the Brahmin and myself.'

'Yes, yes, my boy, we are all alike in the eyes of Jesus,' the Colonel answered him. But he began garrulously: 'He is our superior. He is the Son of God. We are all sinners. He will intercede with God, His Father, on our behalf.'

'He is superior to us. We are all sinners. Why, why is anyone superior to another? Why are we all sinners? Bakha began to reflect.

'Why are we all sinners, Sahib?' he queried.

'We were all born sinners,' replied the Colonel evasively, the puritan in him shying at an exposition of the doctrine of original sin which seemed called for.

'We must confess our sins. Then alone will He forgive us, otherwise we will have to suffer the eternal torment of hell. You confess your sins to me before I convert you to Christianity.'

'But, Huzoor, I don't know who *Yessuh Messih* is. I know Ram. But I don't know *Yessuh Messih.*'

'Ram is the god of the idolaters,' the Colonel said after a pause, and a bit absent-mindedly. 'Come and confess your sins to me and *Yessuh Messih* will receive you in Heaven when you die.'

Now Bakha was utterly bored. Never mind if it was a sahib who was giving him his company. He was afraid of the thought of conversion. He hadn't understood very much of what the

Salvationist said. He didn't like the idea of being called a sinner. He had committed no sin that he could remember. How could he confess his sins? Odd. What did it mean, confessing sins? 'Does the sahib want some secret knowledge?' he wondered. 'Does he want to perform some magic or get some illegal knowledge?' He didn't want to go to Heaven. As a Hindu he didn't believe in the judgment day. He had never thought of that. He had seen people die. And he just accepted the fact. He had been told that people who died were reborn in some form or other. He dreaded that he should be reborn as a donkey or a dog. But all that didn't disturb him. '*Yessuh Messih* must be a good man,' he thought, 'if he regards a Brahmin and a Bhangi the same.' But who was he? Where did he come from? What did he do? He had heard the story of Ram. He had heard the story of Krishna. But he hadn't heard the story of *Yessuh Messih*. 'This sahib will not tell me the story,' he said to himself. But he still hoped he might give him a pair of his cast-off trousers. And he followed him half unwillingly.

'Look, that is our home,' said the Colonel, reaching the gate of a compound leading to a pile of mud-houses among the neem-trees with thatched and sloping roofs.

'I know, Sahib,' said Bakha, who had often passed by it.

'It was a drug-house once, an opium distillery,' said the Colonel with great pride. 'But five years ago we took it.' He paused for a moment to recall the trouble it had cost him to acquire the piece of land to erect a building, and he burst out piously into an exclamation of his gratitude to Christ. 'O Lord, how great are Thy works, and Thy thoughts how deep! God has indeed brought light into the world!' Then turning from his thoughts to the young man, he said: 'He has cast out the heathen from the place.'

A muffled song proceeded from the tall mud-house in the centre of the compound, which Bakha knew to be the *girja ghar*. The Colonel gave it shape for the benefit of the young man by lifting his finger and reciting:

'Share your blessings, share your blessings,
Share them day by day;
Share your blessings, all life's long way;
Share your blessings, though you've only one,
And it will surprise you how much good you've done.'

'George, George, tea is ready!' came a shrieking, hoarse and hysterical voice, tearing the Colonel's squeaky song to bits.

'Coming, coming!' responded the Colonel automatically, standing where he stood, but with his arms and legs all in a flurry. He had heard his wife's voice. He was afraid of her. He was confused. He didn't know whether to go into the mud-house on the right which was his bungalow, and to take Bakha in there, or to take him to the church. He stood hesitating on the edge of a conflict.

'Where are you? Where have you been all the afternoon?' came the shrieking voice again. And behind it appeared the form of a round-faced, big-bellied, dark-haired, undersized, middle-aged woman, a, long cigarette-holder with a cigarette in her mouth, a gaily-coloured band on her Eton-cropped hair, pince-nez glasses on her rather small eyes, a low-necked printed cotton frock that matched her painted and powdered face and reached barely down to her knees.

'Oh, is that what you've been doing, going to these blackies again!' she shouted, frowning, her heavily-powdered face showing its layers of real, vivid scarlet skin underneath the coating. 'I give you up. Really you're incorrigible. I should have thought you would have learned your lesson from the way those Congress wallahs beat you last week!'

'What is the matter? I am just coming. I am coming,' responded the Colonel, impatient, disturbed and embarrassed.

Bakha was going to slip away in order to save the Colonel the displeasure of his wife, for which, he felt, he was mainly responsible.

'Wait, wait,' said the Colonel, holding the sweeper-boy's hand. 'I'll take you to the church.'

'So that the tea should get cold!' exclaimed Mary Hutchinson. 'I can't keep waiting for you all day while you go messing about with all those dirty *bhangis* and *chamars*,' and saying this, she withdrew into her boudoir.

Bakha had not known the exact reason for her frowns, but when he heard the words *bhangi* and *chamar* he at once associated her anger with the sight of himself.

'Salaam, Sahib,' he said, extricating his hand from the old man's grasp before the missionary realised he had done so. And he showed his heels; such was his fear of the woman.

'Wait, wait, my son, wait,' cried the padre after him.

But in the white haze of the afternoon sun he hurried away as if the Colonel's wife were a witch, with raised arms and crooked feet following him, harassing him.

The old man was piously reciting another hymn as he stood staring at Bakha's receding figure:

'Blessed by Thy love, blessed be Thy name.'

'Everyone thinks us at fault,' Bakha was saying to himself as he walked along. 'He wants me to come and confess my sins. And his mem-sahib! I don't know what she said about *bhangis* and *chamars*. She was angry with the sahib. I am sure I am the cause of the mem-sahib's anger. I didn't ask the padre to come and talk to me. He came of his own accord. I was so happy to talk to him. I would certainly have asked him for a pair of white trousers had the mem-sahib not been angry.'

He walked along, vacantly oppressed by the weight of his heavy cloud of memories. He felt a kind of nausea in his stomach—the spiritual nausea that seemed to rise in him when he was in difficulties. He was unnerved again as in the morning after his unfortunate experiences. Only, he was now too tired to care. He just let himself be carried by his legs towards the edge of the day. There was a faint smell of wetness oozing from the dusty earth which paved his way, a sort of moist warmth that rose to his nostrils. High above the far-distant horizon of the Bulashah dales the sun stood fixed, motionless and undissolved, as if it could not bring itself to go, to move or to melt. In the hills and fields, however, there was a strange quickening. Long rows of birds flew over against the cold blue sky towards their homes. The grasshoppers chirped in an anxious chorus as they fell back into the places where they always lay waiting for food. A lone beetle sent electric waves of sound quivering into the cool clear air. Every blade of grass along the pathway, where Bakha walked, was gilded by the light.

As he went on, striding lightly from his heavy rumps, his head bent, his eyes half closed, his lower lip pressed forward, he felt the blood coursing through his veins. He seemed full of a sort of tired restlessness. The awkwardness of the moment when the missionary's wife emerged from her room on to the veranda of her thatched bungalow and glared at her husband, stirred in his soul the echoes of those memories which had shaken and stirred him during the morning. There was a common quality in the look of hate in the round white face of the Colonel's wife and in the sunken visage of the touched man. The man's protruding lower jaw, with its transparent muscles, shaken in his spluttering speech, came before Bakha's eyes. Also his eyes emerging out of their sockets. The Colonel's wife had also opened her little eyes like that, behind her spectacles. That had frightened Bakha, frightened him much-more than the thrust of the touched man's eyeballs, for she was a mem-sahib, and the frown of a mem-sahib had the strange quality of unknown, uncharted seas of anger behind it. To Bakha, therefore, the few words which she had uttered carried a dread a hundred times more terrible than the fear inspired by the whole tirade of abuse by the touched man. It was probably that the episode of the morning was a matter of history, removed in time and space from the more recent scene, also, perhaps, because the anger of a white person mattered more. The mem-sahib was more important to his slavish mind than the man who was touched, he being one of his many brown countrymen. To displease the mem-sahib was to him a crime for which no punishment was bad enough. And he thought he had got off comparatively lightly. He dared not think unkind thoughts about her. So he unconsciously transferred his protest against her anger to the sum of his reactions against the insulting personages of the morning.

His attention was diverted to a black leper who sat swathed in tattered garments, exposing his raw wounds to the sun and the flies by the wayside, his crumpled hand lifted in beggary, and on his lips the prayer: '*Baba pesa de*' (Oh, man, give me a pice). Bakha had a sudden revulsion of feeling. He looked away from the man. It was the Grand Trunk Road near the railway station of Bulashah. The pavements were crowded with beggars. A woman wailed for food outside one of the many cook-shops which lined one side of the road. She had a little child in her arms, another child in a bag on her back, a third holding on to her skirt. Some boys were running behind the stream of carriages begging for coppers. Bakha felt a queer sadistic delight staring at the beggars moaning for alms but not receiving any. They seemed to him despicable. And the noise they made through their wailings and moanings and blessings oppressed him.

He heard the rumbling thunder of a railway train which passed under the footbridge he was ascending. Almost simultaneously he heard a shout from the golbagh garden rend the still, leafy air. The shadow of the smoke-cloud that the engine had sent up to the bridge choked Bakha's throat and blinded his eyes. Then the fumes of smoke melted like invisible, intangible flakes of snow, leaving a dark trail of soot behind. This too paled in the sunshine. The train had rushed into the cool darkness of the tin roof on Bulashah station.

Two choruses of voices tore through the air this time one charged the sky from the platform where the train had stopped; another rose above the tree-tops of the golbagh, undulating from horizon to horizon.

Bakha stood for a moment on the platform of the footbridge

and stared towards the tin roof. Myriads of faces were jutting out of white clothes. He looked in the direction of the golbagh. A veritable sea of white tunics faced him in the oval, where, ordinarily, he had seen the city gymkhana play cricket. Now there was a profound silence. He waited in the hush and listened. The chorus began again. As a spark of lightning suddenly inumines the sky, the myriad of voices leapt up the curve of the heavens before Bakha and wrote in flaming colours the cry: '*Mahatma Gandhi ki-jai.*' And, in a while, there was a rush of eager feet ascending the footbridge behind him shouting: 'The Mahatma has come! The Mahatma has come!'

Before Bakha had turned round to look at them, they were descending the steps south of the bridge. A passing man answered the questioning look of all the pedestrians by informing them that there was going to be a meeting in the golbagh, where the Mahatma was going to speak.

At once the crowd, and Bakha among them, rushed towards the golbagh. He had not asked himself where he was going. He hadn't paused to think. The word 'Mahatma' was like a magical magnet to which he, like all the other people about him, rushed blindly. The wooden boards of the footbridge creaked under the eager downward rush of his ammunition boots. He began to take several steps at a stride. He was so much in a hurry that he didn't even remember the fact of his being an Untouchable, and actually touched a few people. But not having his broom and basket with him, and the people being all in a flurry, no one noticed that a sweeper-boy had brushed past him. They hurried by.

At the foot of the bridge, by the tonga and motor-lorry stand, the road leading to the fort past the entrance of the golbagh looked like a regular racecourse. Men, women and children of all the different races, colours, castes and creeds, were running towards the oval. There were Hindu lallas from the piece-goods market of Bulashah, smartly dressed in silks; there were Kashmiri Muhammadans from the local carpet factories, immaculately clad in white cotton; there were the rough Sikh rustics from the near-by villages swathed in handspun cloth, staves in their hands and loads of shopping on their backs; there were fierce-looking red cheeked Pathans shirted in red stuff, followers of Abdul Gaffar Khan, the frontier revolutionary; there were the black-faced Indian Christian girls from the Salvation Army colony, in short coloured skirts, blouses and aprons; there were people from the outcastes' colony, whom Bakha recognised in the distance, but whom he was too rushed to greet; there was here and there a stray European—there was everybody going to meet the Mahatma, to pay homage to Mohandas Karam Chand Gandhi. And like Bakha they hadn't stopped to ask themselves why they were going. They were just going; the act of going, of walking, running, hurrying, occupied them. Their present motive was to get there, to get there somehow, as quickly as possible. Bakha wished, as he sped along, that there were a sloping bridge on which he could have rolled down to the oval.

He saw that the fort road was too long and too congested. Suddenly, like a stag at bay, he swerved round to a little marsh made by the overflow of a municipal pipe in a corner of the golbagh, jumped the fence into the garden, much to the consternation of the sweet-peas and the pansies which grew on the edges, but wholly to the satisfaction of the crowd behind him, which, once it had got the lead, followed like sheep. The beautiful garden bowers planted by the ancient Hindu kings and since then neglected were thoroughly damaged as the mob followed behind Bakha. It was as if the crowd had determined to crush everything, however ancient or beautiful, that lay in the way of their achievement of all that Gandhi stood for. It was as if they knew, by an instinct surer than that of conscious knowledge, that the things of the old civilisation must be destroyed in order to make room for those of the new. It seemed as if, in trampling on the blades of green grass, they were deliberately, brutally trampling on a part of themselves which they had begun to abhor, and from which they wanted to escape to Gandhi.

Beyond the bowers, on the oval, was a tumult, and the thronging of the thousands who had come to worship. The eager babble of the crowd, the excited gestures, the flow of emotion, portended one thought and one thought alone in the surging crowd—Gandhi. There was a terror in this devotion, half expressed, half suppressed, of the panting swarms that pressed round. Bakha stopped short as he reached the pavilion end of the cricket ground. He leant by a tree. He wanted to be detached. It wasn't that he had lost grip of the emotion that had brought him swirling on the tide of the rushing stream of people. But he became aware of the fact of being a sweeper by the contrast which his dirty khaki uniform presented to the white garments of most of the crowd. There was an insuperable barrier between himself and the crowd, the barrier of caste. He was part of a consciousness which he could share and yet not understand. He had been lifted from the gutter, through the barriers of space, to partake of a life which was his, and yet not his. He was in the midst of a humanity which included him in its folds and yet debarred him from entering into a sentient, living, quivering contact with it. Gandhi alone united him with them, in the mind, cause Gandhi was in everybody's mind, including Bakha's. Gandhi might unite them really. Bakha waited for Gandhi.

Eager and unconscious, he recalled all that he had heard of this man. People said he was a saint, that he was an *avatar* (incarnation) of the gods Vishnu and Krishna. Only recently he had heard that a spider had woven a web in the house of the *Lat Sahib* (Viceroy) at *Dilli* (Delhi), making a portrait of the sage, and writing his name under it in English. That was said to be a warning to the sahibs to depart from Hindustan, since God Almighty Himself had sent a message to a little insect that Gandhi was to be the Maharajaha of the whole of Hindustan. That the spider's web appeared in the *Lat Sahib's kothi* (Viceroy's residence) was surely significant. And they said that no sword could cut his body, no bullet could pierce his skin, no fire could scorch him!

'The *Sarkar* (Govemmeni) is afraid of him,' said a lalla standing by Bakha. 'The magistrate has withdrawn his order against Gandhiji's entry into Bulashah.'

'That is nothing, they have released him unconditionally from gaol,' chimed in a babu, spitting out a phrase of the *Tribune*, pompously, in order to show off his erudition.

'Will he really overthrow the government?' asked a rustic.

'He has the *shakti* (power) to change the whole world,' replied the babu, and he began to vomit out the whole article about Gandhi that he had crammed from the *Tribune* that morning. 'This British Govemment is nothing. Every country in Europe and America is passing through terrible convulsions, politically, economically and industrially. The people of *Vilayat* (England), the *Angrez log* (the English), are less convulsed on account of their innate conservatism, but very soon every country on earth including *Vilayat* will be faced with problems that cannot be solved without a fundamental change in the mental and moral outlook of the West. Without a radical change from a hankering after sense-gratification, which is the goal of Western civilisation, through a striving after sense-control, whether in individual or in group life, which is the essence of India's *dharmic* (religious) culture! India has been the privileged home of the world's eternal religion, that teaches how every man and woman, according to their birth and environment, must practise *swadharma* (sense-control), how through sense control they must evolve their higher nature, and so realise the bliss of divinity, deep-seated in the hearts of all beings. For this bliss all humanity blindly pants, not knowing that neither cigarettes nor cinemas nor sense-enjoyment can lead to the path of *dharmic* discipline, which alone is the highest bliss to be realised . . . Gandhi will reveal this path to the modern world, he will teach us the true religion of God-love which is the best *swaraj* (self-government). . .'

'How clever you are, Babu,' said the peasant, staring at the lecturer. He was impressed by the babu's speech, but baffled. To him Gandhi was a legend, a tradition, an oracle. He had heard from time to time during the last fourteen years how a saint had arisen as great as Guru Nanak, the incarnation of Krishna-ji-Maharaj, of whom the *Ferungi Sarkar* (English Government) was very afraid. His wife had told him of the miracles which this saint was performing. It was said that he slept in a temple one night with his feet towards the shrine of the god. When the Brahmins had chastised him for deliberately turning his feet towards God, he told them that God was everywhere and asked them to turn his feet in the direction where God was not. Upon this the priests turned his feet in the direction opposite to the one where the image of the god was, and lo the shrine of God moved in the direction of his feet. He had hungered for a sight of the saint since then. His wife wouldn't be content with anything less than a touch of the Holy Man's feet. But it was a good thing she wasn't with him. The peasant reflected that if she had come, the boys would have wished to accompany her, and they might have been crushed to death in the throng. It was a good thing they didn't know. For myself, I am glad I shall see him. It is lucky he is coming on the day that I came out shopping.

Bakha had listened hard to the babu, and, although he couldn't follow every sentence of his rhetorical outburst, he had somehow got the sense of it all.

'Tell me, Babu,' Bakha heard the yokel say to the round, felt-capped, bespectacled man who had made the oration, 'will he look after the canals when the *Ferungis* (British) have gone?' It seemed the peasant had more than a vague idea of what Gandhi was about.

'*Bhai ji* (brother), don't you know,' said the babu, 'that according to Mr. Radha Kumud Muker ji we had canals in ancient India four thousand years before Christ? Who made the Grand Trunk Road? Not the British!'

'But what about the *mukadamas* (lawsuits)?' asked the jat rustic. 'The five elders of my village use the *Panchayat* (committee of five) to wreak vengeance on their enemies, or to bring pressure on the village menials, if they become too independent, and I hear Gandhi says we must not go to the *Sarkari Adalat* (British Courts of Justice), but must take up our suits to the *Panchayat*.'

'A good *Panchayat*,' replied the babu sonorously, 'can get the villagers to do their bit from time to time in preventing damage by erosion and other causes. It may not be a good judicial body now, but it was, and always has been so in the past. So far as affairs of executive action are concemed, however, you know that the *Panchayats* have done much good in the service of this country, in the cause of good administration in general, in making walls, rebuilding roads, etc.'

The peasant didn't understand that. Nor did Bakha. But the mention of village menials by the peasant recalled to Bakha's mind the fact that he had heard that Gandhi was very keen on uplifting the Untouchables. Hadn't it been rumoured in the outcastes' colony, lately, that Gandhi was fasting for the sake of the *bhangis* and *chamars*? Bakha could not quite understand what fasting had to do with helping the low-castes. 'Probably he thinks we are poor and can't get food,' he vaguely surmised, 'so he tries to show that even he doesn't have food for days.'

'We are willing to do all we can,' the lalla disturbed Bakha's cogitations with a dramatic gesture towards the babu. 'We can boycott Manchester cotton and Bradford fancies, if it is going to mean that in the end we will have a monopoly of *swadeshi* cloth. I hear, however, that Gandhi ji is making terms with Japan.'

'You must ask the Mahatma that,' the babu replied, flurried because he heard noises at the gate from which he presumed that Gandhi was approaching. He wanted to work his way to a position from which he could obtain a good view of the great man.

'Mahatma ji is not speaking about *swadeshi*, or on civil disobedience,' put in a Congress volunteer authoritatively. 'The government has allowed him out of gaol only if he will keep strictly within the limits of his propaganda for *harijans* (men of God, as Gandhi chooses to call the Untouchables), for the removal of untouchability.' And he walked away after this declamation, showing a little of the glory that he assumed, on account of his powerful position, as an official appointed to serve the community, during the reception to be given to Gandhi.

'*Harijan!*' Bakha wondered what that meant. He had heard the word before in connection with Gandhi. 'But it has something to do with us, the *bhangis* and *chamars*,' he said to himself. 'We are *harijans*.' He recalled how some Congress men had come to the outcastes' street a month ago and lectured about *harijans*, saying they were no different from the Hindus and their touch did not mean pollution. The phrase, as it dropped from the mouth of the volunteer, had gone through Bakha's soul and body. He knew it applied to him. 'It is good that I came!' he thought. 'Is he really going to talk about the outcastes, about us, about Chota, Ram Charan, my father and me? What will he say, I wonder? Strange that the sahib of the *Mukti* (Salvation Army) said that the rich and the poor, the Brahmins and *bhangis*, are the same. Now Gandhi Mahatma will talk about us! It is good that I came. If only he knew what had happened to me this morning. I would like to get up and tell him.' He imagined himself rising on the platform, when all was still and the meeting had begun, and telling the Mahatma that a man from the city, where he had come to remove untouchability, had abused him for accidentally touching him and had also beaten him. Then the Mahatma would chastise that man perhaps, or, at least, he would chide the citizens here, and they won't treat me again as they did this morning. He seemed to get a thrill imagining himself in this scene. He felt theatrical. Then a queer stirring started in his stomach. He was confused. His face was flushed and his ears reddened. His breath came and went quickly. A chorus of '*Mahatma Gandhi ki-ji*' released his tension, as it came from the distance and chilled the heat of his body with a sudden fear that it brought into his soul.

He looked across and saw that a vast crowd had rushed the gates of the golbagh and surrounded a motor-car in which, presumably, the Mahatma was travelling. He didn't know what to do, stand still or rush. He realised he couldn't rush even though the Mahatma had abolished all caste distinctions for the day. He might touch someone and then there would be a scene. The Mahatma would be too far away to come and help him. He hesitated for a moment, then he looked at the tree overhead. There were some people perched on the branches like eagles waiting for their prey. He made for the trunk. His ammunition boots were an encumbrance but he scrambled up; using his knees as rests against the round trunk. He looked not unlike an ape as he sat commanding a view of the advancing procession along the road.

Behind a screen of flower petals showered by ardent devotees under many-coloured flags, with garlands of marigolds, jasmine and molseri around his neck, amid cries of 'Mahatma Gandhi ki-jai. Hindu—Mussulman—Sikh ki-jai, Harijan ki-jai,' the great little man came into sight. His body was swathed in a milk-white blanket, and only his dark clean-shaven head was visible, with its protruding big ears, its expansive forehead, its long nose, bridged by a pair of glasses which were divided in the lenses in two, the upper for looking, the lower for reading. There was a quixotic smile on his thin lips, something Mephistophelean in the determined little chin immediately under his mouth and the long toothless jaws resting on his small neck. But withal there was something beautiful and saintly in the face, whether it was the well-oiled scalp that glistened round the little tuft of hair on the top, or the aura of the astral self that shone like an aureole about him.

Bakha looked at the Mahatma with a mixed feeling of wonder and fear. The sage seemed to him like a child as he sat huddled up between two women, an Indian and an Englishwoman.

'That's Mrs. Kasturabai Gandhi,' Bakha heard a schoolboy whisper to a friend who sat on a branch of the tree next to him.

'And who is the other lady?' the boy asked.

'Mahatma ji's English disciple, Miss Slade, Miraben. She is the daughter of an English Admiral.'

'He is black like me,' Bakha said to himself. 'But, of course, he must be very educated.' And he waited tensely for the car which was marooned right under his eyes among the throngs of men and women seeking to touch the Mahatma's feet. The Congress volunteers struggled to carve a way through the turbans and fezes and boat-like Gandhi caps, and at last they succeeded in getting the car under way. Half pushed, half towed with the engines shut off, the chauffeur steered the vehicle to the gate, improvised at one end of the oval, with broad-leafed banana-trees decorated with flowers and paper-chains.

Bakha saw a sallow-faced Englishman, whom, he knew to be the District Superintendent of Police, standing by the roadside in a khaki uniform of breeches, polished leather gaiters and blue-puggareed, khaki sun helmet, not as smart as the military officers', but, of course, possessing for Bakha all the qualities of the sahibs' clothes. Somehow, however, at this moment Bakha was not interested in sahibs, probably because in the midst of this enormous crowd of Indians, fired with an enthusiasm for their leader, the foreigner seemed out of place, insignificant, the representative of an order which seemed to have nothing to do with the natives.

'Mahatma Gandhi ki-jai, Mahatma Gandhi ki-jai,' the cry went thundering up into the smoke-scented evening. Even Bakha's attention was switched off the man who held the sceptre of British rule in the form of his formidable truncheon, and turned to the diminutive figure of the Mahatma, now seated in the lotus seat on the Congress *pandal* (platform), surrounded by devotees, who had come soft-footed up the steps, joined hands in obeisance to the master, touched the dust at his feet, and scattered to sit around him.

The Mahatma raised his right arm from the folds of his shawl and blessed the crowd with a gentle benediction. The babble of voices died out, as if he had sent an electric shock through the mass of humanity gathered at his feet. This strange man seemed to have the genius that could, by a single dramatic act, rally multicoloured, multi-tongued India to himself. Someone stood up to chant a hymn. The Mahatma had closed his eyes and was praying. In the stillness of the moment Bakha forgot all the details of his experience during the day, the touched man, the priest, the woman in the alley, his father, Chota, Ram Charan, the walk in the hills, the missionary and his wife. Except for the turbaned, capped and aproned heads of the men and women sitting on the grass before him, his eyes seemed intent on one thing and one thing alone, Gandhi, and he heard each syllable of the Hindu hymn:

'The dawn is here, O traveller, arise;
Past is the night, and yet sleep seals thine eyes.
Lost is the soul that sleeps—dost not thou know?
The sleepless one finds peace beyond all woe.

Oh, waken! Shed thou off thy slumber deep,
Remember him who made thee and oh, weep.
For shame, is this the way of love—to sleep
When he himself doth ceaseless vigil keep?

Repent, O soul, from sin and find release,
O erring one, in sin there is no peace.
What boots it now to mourn on bended knees,
When thou thyself didst thine own load increase?

What thou wouldst do to-morrow do to-day,
Do thou the task that thou must face to-day.
What shall avail thy sorrow and dismay
When thieving birds have borne thy grain away?'

Then his attention began to flag. His mind wandered. He thought of the race he had to run to get here. He noticed how still everyone was. It irked him to see everyone so serious. The silence was getting on his nerves. But a part of him seemed to have flown, to have evaporated. He felt he had lost something of himself and was uneasy on account of it, yet thrilled about it, happy. He felt pleased to be sharing the privilege of being in a crowd gathered before the Mahatma. The hymn seemed so heavy. Yet the other feeling was light. The sage seemed so pure. Yet there was something intimate and warm about him. He smiled like a child. Bakha gazed at him. It was the only way in which he could escape feeling self-conscious. By doing that he forgot himself and everything else, as he felt he ought. The brown and black faces below him were full of a stilled rapture. He sought to feel like them, attentively absorbed. Luckily for him, just then, the Mahatma began his speech. It was a faint whisper at first, the Mahatma's voice, as it came through a loud-speaker:

'I have emerged,' he said slowly, as if he were measuring each word and talking more to himself than to anyone else, 'from the ordeal of a penance, undertaken for a cause which is as dear to me as life itself. The British Government sought to pursue a policy of divide and rule in giving to our brethren of the depressed classes separate electorates in the Councils that will be created under the new constitution. I do not believe that the bureaucracy is sincere in its efforts to elaborate the new constitution. But it is one of the conditions under which I have been released from gaol that I shall not carry on any propaganda against the government. So I shall not refer to that matter. I shall only speak about the so-called "Untouchables," whom the government tried to alienate from Hinduism by giving them a separate legal and political status.

'As you all know, while we are asking for freedom from the grip of a foreign nation, we have ourselves, for centuries, trampled underfoot millions of human beings without feeling the slightest remorse for our iniquity. For me the question of these people is moral and religious. When I undertook to fast unto death for their sake, it was in obedience to the call of my conscience.'

Bakha didn't understand these words. He was restless. He hoped the Mahatma wouldn't go on speaking of things he (Bakha) couldn't understand. He found his wish fulfilled, for a potent word interpreted his thoughts.

'I regard untouchability,' the Mahatma was saying, 'as the greatest blot on Hinduism. This view of mine dates back to the time when I was a child.'

That was getting interesting. Bakha pricked up his ears. 'I was hardly yet twelve when this idea dawned on me. A scavenger named Uka, an Untouchable, used to attend our house for cleaning the latrines. Often I would ask my mother why it was wrong to touch him, and why I was forbidden to do so. If I accidentally touched Uka I was asked to perform ablutions; and though I naturally obeyed, it was not without smilingly protesting that untouchability was not sanctioned by religion and that it was impossible that it should be so. I was a very dutiful and obedient child; but, so far as was consistent with respect for my parents, I often had tussles with them on this matter. I told my mother that she was entirely wrong in considering physical contact with Uka as sinful; it could not be sinful.

'While on my way to school, I used to touch the Untouchables; and, as I never would conceal the fact from my parents, my mother would tell me that the shortest cut to purification after the unholy touch, was to cancel it by touching a Mussulman passing by. Therefore, simply out of reverence and regard for my mother, I often did so, but never did it believing it to be a religious obligation.'

As each part of the story which the Mahatma related about the beginning of his interest in untouchability fell on his ear, Bakha felt as if he were Uka, the scavenger. By feeling like that, he thought, he would be nearer the sage, who seemed a real and genuine sympathiser. 'But the speech, the speech,' he became aware that he was missing the words of the Mahatma's speech. He eagerly returned to attention and caught the narrative at:

'The fact that we address God as "the purifier of the polluted souls" makes it a sin to regard anyone born in Hinduism as polluted—it is satanic to do so. I have never been tired of repeating that it is a great sin. I do not say that this thing crystallised in me at the age of twelve, but I do say that I did then regard untouchability as a sin.

'I was at Nellore on the National Day. I met the Untouchables there, and I prayed as I have done to-day. I do want to attain spiritual deliverance. I do not want to be reborn. But if I have to be reborn, I should wish to be reborn as an Untouchable, so that I may share their sorrows, sufferings and the affronts levelled at them, in order that I may endeavour to free myself and them from their miserable condition. Therefore I prayed that, if I should be born again, I should be so, not as a *Brahmin*, *Kshatriya*, *Vaishya*, *Shudra*, but as an outcaste, as an Untouchable.

'I love scavenging. In my ashram an eighteen-year-old Brahmin lad is doing a scavenger's work, in order to teach the *ashram* scavenger cleanliness. The lad is no reformer. He was born and bred in orthodoxy. He is a regular reader of the *Gita*, and faithfully says his prayers. When he conducts the prayers, his soft melodies melt one in love. But he felt that his accomplishments were incomplete until he had also become a perfect sweeper. He felt that if he wanted the *ashram* sweeper to do his work well he must do it himself and set an example.'

Bakha felt thrilled to the very marrow of his bones. That the Mahatma should want to be born as an outcaste! That he should love scavenging! He loved the man. He felt he could put his life in his hands and ask him to do what he liked with it. For him he would do anything. He would like to go and be a scavenger at his *ashram*. 'Then I could talk to him,' he said to himself. 'But I am not listening, I am not listening; I must listen.'

'If there are any Untouchables here,' he heard the Mahatma say, 'they should realise that they are cleaning Hindu society.' (He felt like shouting to say that he, an Untouchable, was there, but he did not know what the Mahatma meant by 'cleaning Hindu society.') He gave ear to the words with beating heart and heard: 'They have, therefore, to purify their lives. They should cultivate the habits of cleanliness, so that no one shall point his finger at them. Some of them are addicted to habits of drinking and gambling of which they must get rid.

'They claim to be Hindus. They read the scriptures. If,

therefore, the Hindus oppress them, they should understand that the fault does not lie in the Hindu religion, but in those who profess it. In order to emancipate themselves they have to purify themselves. They have to rid themselves of evil habits, like drinking liquor and eating carrion.'

But now, now the Mahatma is blaming us, Bakha felt. 'That is not fair!' He wanted to forget the last passages that he had heard. He turned to the Mahatma.

'They should now cease to accept leavings from the plates of high-caste Hindus, however clean they may be represented to be. They should receive grain only—good, sound grain, not rotten grain—and that too, only if it is courteously offered. If they are able to do all that I have asked them to do, they will secure their emancipation.'

That was more to Bakha's liking. He felt that he wanted to turn round and say to the Mahatma: 'Now, Mahatma ji, now you are talking.' He felt he would like to tell him that that very day, in that very town where he was speaking, he (Bakha) had had to pick up a loaf of bread from near the gutter; that to-day, there, in that very city, his brother had had to accept leavings of food from the plates of the sepoys, and that they had all to eat it. Bakha saw himself pitied by the Mahatma in his mind's eye and consoled by him. It was such a balm, it was so comforting, the great man's sympathy. 'If only he could go and tell my father not to be hard on me! If only he could go and tell him how I have suffered, if only he could go and tell my father he sympathises with me in my sufferings, my father would at once take me back and be kind to me ever afterwards.'

'I am an orthodox Hindu and I know that the Hindus are not sinful by nature,' Bakha heard the Mahatma declaim. 'They are sunk in ignorance. All public wells, temples, roads, schools, sanatoriums, must be declared open to the Untouchables. And, if you all profess to love me, give me a direct proof of your love by carrying on propaganda against the observance of untouchability. Do this, but let there be no compulsion or brute force in securing this end. Peaceful persuasion is the only means. Two of the strongest desires that keep me in the flesh are the emancipation of the Untouchables and the protection of the cow. When these two desires are fulfilled there is *swaraj*, and therein lies my soul's deliverance. May God give you strength to work out your soul's salvation to the end.'

When the crowd scattered irreverently at the end of the Mahatma's speech, Bakha stood on the branch of the tree spellbound. Each word, of the concluding passage seemed to him to echo as deep and intense a feeling of horror and indignation as his own at the distinction which the caste Hindus made between themselves and the Untouchables. The Mahatma seemed to have touched the most intimate corner of his soul. 'Surely he is a good man,' Bakha said.

Muffled cries of 'Mahatma ji ki-jai,' 'Hindu—Mussulman ki-jai,' 'Harijan ki-jai' arose from the middle of the throng again, and Bakha knew that the sage was going from the platform to the gate. He clung to his position on the tree, and was rewarded for his patience by the sight of the Mahatma passing beneath him.

A man seated on a high wooden board, with a bucket beside him, was distributing water in a silver tankard to Muhammadans in red fezes and Hindus in white Gandhi caps.

'He has made Hindu and Mussulman one,' remarked a citizen, surcharged with the glow of brotherliness and humanitarianism which the Mahatma had left in his trail.

'Let's discard foreign cloth. Let's burn it!' the Congress volunteers were shouting. And true enough, Bakha saw people throwing their felt caps, their silk shirts and aprons into the pile, which soon became a blazing bonfire.

'Sister,' said another citizen to a grass-cutter's wife, who struggled in her heavy accordion-pleated skirt to take her two children home, 'let me help you through the crowd. Give me the big boy to hold.'

There was only one queer voice which dissented from all this.

'Gandhi is a humbug,' it was saying. 'He is a fool. He is a hypocrite. In one breath he says he wants to abolish untouchability, in the other he asserts that he is an orthodox Hindu. He is running counter to the spirit of our age, which is democracy. He is in the fourth century B.C. with his *swadeshi* and his spinning-wheel. We live in the twentieth. I have read Rousseau, Hobbes, Bentham and John Stuart Mill and I . . .'

Bakha came down the tree like a black bear, and arrested the democrat's attention by the ridiculous sight he presented. He was going to slink away shyly, but the man, a fair-complexioned Muhammadan dressed in the most smartly-cut English suit he had ever seen, interrupted him:

'Eh, eh, black man, come here. Go and get a bottle of soda-water for the sahib.'

Bakha came back with a start and stood staring at the dignitary who had called him. The man wore a monocle in his left eye and Bakha, who had never seen anything of that kind, wondered how a single glass could remain fixed on the eye without a frame.

'Don't stare at me!' shouted the gentleman, while Bakha was wondering who the man could be, too sallow-faced for an Englishman, too white for an Indian, and clad in such fine clothes, yellow gloves on his hands and white cloth on his buckskin shoes.

'*Ham desi sahib* (I, native sahib), don't stare at me,' said the man deliberately using the wrong Hindustani spoken by the English, but becoming kinder for a moment. 'I have just come from *Vilayat* (England). Is there a sodawater shop near here?'

Bakha had been taken unawares. He couldn't adjust himself to this phenomenon. So he moved his head to indicate that he didn't know. Fortunately for him the man's attention was switched off to his friend, a young man with a delicate feline face, illuminated by sparkling dark eyes and long black curly hair, who stood next to him dressed in flowing Indian robes like a poet's. Bakha's inadequate answer did not, therefore, evoke the insolent flourish of the democrat's cane as it might have done.

'It is very unfair of you to abuse the Mahatma,' Bakha heard the young poet say gently, as he walked a little way away from the two men who were now surrounded by a group of people. 'He is by far the, greatest liberating force of our age. He has his limits, of course. But . . .'

'Precisely,' Bakha heard his companion interrupt. 'That is exactly what I say. And my contention is . . .'

'Yes, but listen, I haven't finished,' the poet was saying. 'He has his limitations but he is fundamentally sound. He may be wrong in wanting to shut India off from the rest of the world by preaching the revival of the spinning-wheel, because, as things are, that can't be done. But even in that regard he is right. For it is not India's fault that it is poor; it is the world's fault that the world is rich! . . .'

'You are talking in paradoxes. You have been reading Shaw,' interrupted,the monocled gentleman.

'Oh, forget Shaw! I am not a decadent Indian like you to be pandering to those European film stars!' exclaimed the poet. 'But you know that it is only in terms of economic theory that India is behind the other countries of the world. In fact, it is one of the richest countries; it has abundant natural resources. Only it has chosen to remain agricultural and has suffered for not accepting the machine. We must, of course, remedy that. I hate the machine. I loathe it. But I shall go against Gandhi there and accept it. And I am sure in time all will learn to love it. And we shall beat our enslavers at their own game . . .'

'They will put you into prison,' someone interrupted from the crowd.

'Never mind that. I am not afraid of prison. I have already been a guest at His Majesty's boarding-house with a hundred thousand others who were imprisoned last year . . .'

'The peasant who believes this world to be *maya* (illusion) will not work the machine,' remarked the supercilious man in spats, as he adjusted his monocle to reflect the cynical glint in his eye.

'It is India's genius to accept all things,' said the poet fiercely. 'We have, throughout our long history, been realists believing in the stuff of this world, in the here and the now, in the flesh and the blood. Man is born, and reborn, according to the *Upanishads*, in this world, and even when he becomes an immortal saint there is no release for him, because he forms the stuff of the cosmos and is born again. We don't believe in the other world, as these Europeans would have you believe we do. There has been only one man in India who believed this world to be illusory—Shankaracharya. But he was a consumptive and that made him neurotic. Early European scholars could not get hold of the original texts of the *Upanishads*. So they kept on interpreting Indian thought from the commentaries of Shankaracharya. The word *maya* does not mean illusion, it means magic. That is the dictum of the latest Hindu translator of the *Vedanta*, Dr. Coomaraswamy. And in that signification the word approximates to the views on the nature of the physical world of your pet scientists, Eddington and Jeans. The Victorians misinterpreted us. It was as if, in order to give a philosophical background to their exploitation of India, they ingeniously concocted a nice little fairy story: "You don't believe in this world; to you all this is *maya*. Let us look after your country for you and you can dedicate yourself to achieving *Nirvana* (release from the trammels of existence)." But that is all over now. Right in the tradition of those who accepted the world and produced the baroque exuberance of Indian architecture and sculpture, with its profound sense of form, its solidity and its mass, we will accept and work the machine. But we will do so consciously. We can see through the idiocy of these Europeans who deified money. They were barbarians and lost their heads in the worship of gold. We can steer clear of the pitfalls, because we have the advantage of a race-consciousness six thousand years old, a race-consciousness which accepted all the visible and invisible values. We know life. We know its secret flow. We have danced to its rhythms. We have loved it, not sentimentally through personal feelings, but pervasively, stretching ourselves from our hearts outwards so far, oh, so far, that life seemed to have no limits, that miracles seemed possible. We can feel new feelings. We can learn to be aware with a new awareness. We can envisage the possibility of creating new races from the latent heat in our dark brown bodies. Life is still an adventure for us. We are still eager to learn. We cannot go wrong. Our enslavers muddle through things. We can see things clearly. We will go the whole hog with regard to machines while they nervously fumble their way with the steam-engine. And we will keep our heads through it all. We will not become slaves to gold. We can be trusted to see life steadily and see it whole.'

The harangue was impressive, with such fire was it delivered. Not only was the crowd moved but the anglicised Indian was silenced. Bakha was too much under the spell of Gandhi to listen intently to anyone else, and he did not follow all that the poet said although he strained to catch his words.

'Who is he?' someone in the crowd queried.

'Iqbal Nath Sarshar, the young poet who edits the *Nawan Jug* (*New Era*). and his companion is Mr. R.N. Bashir, B.A. (Oxon.), Barrister-at-Law,' someone volunteered the information.

There were whispers of consent and appreciation, but Mr. Bashir's voice rose above the others in a derisive little chuckle.

'Ha, ha, ho ho! but what has all this got to do with untouchability? Gandhi's plea is an expression of his inferiority complex. I think . . .'

'I know what you think,' put in the poet fiercely, exciting some amusement with his brisk retort. 'Let me tell you that with regard to untouchability the Mahatma is more sound than he is in his political and economic views. You have swallowed all those cheap phrases about inferiority complex and superiority complex at Oxford without understanding what they mean. You slavishly copy the English in everything . . .'

'That's right!' shouted a Congress volunteer. 'Look at his silk neck-tie and the suit of foreign cloth that he is wearing! Shame!'

'The heredity and the environment of different people varies,' continued the poet with a flourish of his hand to still the rude Congress wallah. 'Some of us are born with big heads, some with small, some with more potential physical strength, some with less. There is one saint to a hundred million people perhaps, one great man to a whole lot of mediocrities. But essentially, that is to say humanly, all men are equal. "Take a ploughman from the plough, wash off his dirt, and he is fit to rule a kingdom" is an old Indian proverb. The civility, the understanding and the gravity of the poorest of our peasants is a proof of that. Go and talk to a yokel and see how kind he is, how full of compliment, and how elegantly he speaks. And the equality of man is no new notion for him. If it had not been for ride the wily Brahmins, the priestcraft, who came in the pride of their white skin, lifted the pure philosophical idea of *Karma*, that deeds and acts are dynamic, that all is in a flux, from the Dravidians, and misinterpreted it vulgarly to mean that birth and rebirth in this universe is governed by good or bad deeds in the past life, India would have offered the best instance of a democracy. As it is, caste is an intellectual aristocracy, based on the conceit of the pundits, being otherwise wholly democratic. The high-caste High Court Judge eats freely with the coolie of his caste. So we can destroy our inequalities easily. The old mechanical formulas of our lives must go, the old stereotyped forms must give place to a new dynamism. We Indians live so deeply in our contacts; we are so acutely aware of our blood-stream . . .'

'I can't understand what you mean,' interrupted Bashir irritatedly.

'Well, we must destroy caste, we must destroy the inequalities of birth and unalterable vocations. We must recognise an equality of rights, privileges and opportunities for everyone. The Mahatma didn't say so, but the legal and sociological basis of caste having been broken down by the British-Indian penal code, which recognises the rights of every man before a court, caste is now mainly governed by profession. When the sweepers change their profession, they will no longer remain Untouchables. And they can do that soon, for the first thing we will do when we accept the machine, will be to introduce the machine which clears dung without anyone having to handle it—the flush system. Then the sweepers can be free from the stigma of untouchability and assume the dignity of status that is their right as useful members of a casteless and classless society.'

'In fact,' mocked Bashir, 'greater efficiency, better salesmanship, more mass-production, standardisation, dictatorship of the sweepers, Marxian materialism and all that!'

'Yes, yes, all that, but no catch-words and cheap phrases. The change will be organic and not mechanical.'

'All right, all right, come, don't let us stand here, I feel suffocated,' said Mr. Bashir, pulling out a silken handkerchief to wipe his face.

The crowd looked, ogled, stared with wonder at the celebrities and followed them at a little distance, till they disappeared in the unending throng of people going out of the golbagh.

Bakha had stood aside, beyond polluting distance, thinking vaguely of the few things he had understood from the poet's outburst. He felt that the poet would have been answering the most intimate questions in his (Bakha's) soul, if he had not used such big words. 'That machine,' he thought, 'which can remove dung without anyone having to handle it, I wonder what it is like? If only that "gentreman" hadn't dragged the poet away, I could have asked him.'

The fires of sunset were blazing on the western horizon. As Bakha looked at the magnificent orb of terrible brightness glowing on the margin of the sky, he felt a burning sensation within him. His face, which had paled and contracted with thoughts a moment ago, reddened in a curious conflict of despair. He didn't know what to do, where to go. He seemed to have been smothered by the misery, the anguish of the morning's memories. He stood for a while where he had landed from the tree, his head bent, as if he were tired and broken. Then the last words of the Mahatma's speech seemed to resound in his ears: 'May God give you the strength to work out your soul's salvation to the end.' 'What did that mean?' Bakha asked himself. The Mahatma's face appeared before him enigmatic, ubiquitous. There was no answer to be found in it. Yet there was a queer kind of strength to be derived from it. Bakha recollected the words of his speech. It all seemed to stand out in his mind, every bit of it. Specially'did the story of Uka come back. The Mahatma had talked of a Brahmin who did the scavenging in his *ashram*. 'Did he mean, then, that I should go on scavenging?' Bakha asked himself.

'Yes,' came the forceful answer. 'Yes,' said Bakha, 'I shall go on doing what Gandhi says.' 'But shall I never be able to leave the latrines? 'came the disturbing thought. But I can. Did not that poet say there is a machine which can do my work?' The prospect of never being able to wear the clothes that the sahibs wore, of never being able to become a sahib, was horrible. 'But it doesn't matter,' he said to console himself, and pictured in his mind the English policeman, whom he had seen before the meeting, standing there, ignored by everybody.

He began to move. His virtues lay in his close-knit sinews and in his long-breathed sense. He was thinking of everything he had heard though he could not understand it all. He was calm as he walked along, though the conflict in his soul was not over, though he was torn between his enthusiasm for Gandhi and the difficulties in his own awkward, naïve self.

The sun descended. The pale, the purple, the mauve of the horizon blended into darkest blue. A handful of stars throbbed in the heart of the sky.

He emerged from the green of the garden into the slight haze of dust that rose from the roads and the paths.

As the brief Indian twilight came and went, a sudden impulse shot through the transformations of space and time, and gathered all the elements that were dispersed in the stream of his soul into a tentative decision: 'I shall go and tell father all that Gandhi said about us,' he whispered to himself, 'and all that that poet said. Perhaps I can find the poet some day and ask him about his machine.' And he proceeded homewards.

Annotations

Page 1. *Outcaste.* Literally refers to people who are regarded as situated beyond the pale of the Hindu *varna vyavastha* or caste structure, comprising of the four *varnas: Brahman, Kshatriya, Vaishya, Shudra*, and hence often referred to as the *panchamas* (the fifth) or outcastes. Note that etymologically, the word caste (first used by Portuguese as *casta*) is derived from the Latin 'chaste', which means 'unmixed', or 'pure'. Outcaste, therefore, literally means someone who is regarded as 'impure' or 'ritually polluted'. In the 1930s, when Anand was writing this novel, several groups of people (often situated at the bottom of the socio-economic scale) in India, were condemned as outcastes for the 'dirty' work they were ordained to perform for caste Hindus, such as scavenging or cleaning of human refuse, handling of dead humans or animals, handling of waste organic products, or washing of dirty clothes.

Page 1. *Outcaste colony.* This description of the outcaste colony was based on Anand's actual experience of outcaste colonies, though he was considerably influenced by Charles Dickens's description of slums in novels such as *Bleak House*. After suggestions from several critics, he toned down the intensity of the squalor described in these pages and deleted several portions which were found repetitive. It is interesting to note Gandhi's reaction to these outcaste colonies after he visited them in Delhi:

> In the 1930s, Gandhi visited a number of *dalit* colonies in Delhi and he found the conditions of life in them to be abhorrent. In 1937, he described the Delhi colonies as 'the worst of any I had seen' and urged the tax payers to wake up and make the city fathers realize their duty. ... Eight hundred people lived in hundred rooms and shared two water taps and thirteen ramshackle latrines. The

tenements looked like 'miniature black holes' with as many as ten people sharing a room.[1]

Page 1. *Jamedar.* A title used to describe the head of the sweepers. To monitor the entire system of sanitary work, the Delhi Municipal Corporation appointed *Jamedars*, or headmen, variously called conservancy Daroga, Safai Daroga, Muquaddam Sardar. Jamedars were notorious for their bullying ways, but in *Untouchable,* the only person Jamedar Lakha seems to be capable of bullying is his eldest son Bakha.

Page 2. *Otherwise, the rest of the outcastes ... parted it like Englishmen on one side, wore a pair of shorts at hockey and smoked cigarettes like them.* There is a great deal of Anand's own fascination for English clothes and the English way of life, in this description of Bakha and the outcaste colony boys' attraction for English 'fashuns.' In his biographical *Seven Summers* (1951), Anand writes how he naively emulated Europeans through an exaggerated respect for hats, top boots, hockey sticks, cricket bats, shorts, trousers, push-bikes, and so forth. Note, however, that though all sections of Indians were influenced by the British way of life, this was particularly true of most *Dalits*, led by Dr. Ambedkar. Their fascination with the European way of life was related to the supposed freedom that colonial modernity seemed to offer; a freedom from the hide-bound, hierarchised Hindu society where they were condemned to a life of permanent humiliation and slavery. Ambedkar was accused of shameless British toadyism and promoting unabashed anti-national Anglophilia among the Dalits, by Hindutva hardliners. For more facts on this subject, read Arun Shourie's *Worshipping False Gods: Ambedkar and the Facts which have been Erased.*[2]

Page 7. *38th Dogra Regiment.* An autobiographical touch as Lal Chand, his father was a head-clerk in the 38th Dogra Regiment of the British Indian Army.

Page 10. *Kala admi zamin par hagne wala.* For more on the great sanitary debate that was raging in Europe as a vital component of the Enlightenment agenda and how it was transported to the colonies to fortify racial divide, see my essay 'Clean book, Dirty book?' in this edition.

Page 12. *The toil of the body had built up for him a very fine physique.* This description of the sweeper (paradoxically confined to the lowest strata of Indian/Hindu society) as a kind of superbly built male god, seems to be a legacy of E.M. Forster who described a low-caste *punkah*-puller in *A Passage to India:*

> When that strange race nears the dust and is condemned as untouchable, then nature remembers the physical perfection that she accomplished elsewhere, and throws out a god—not many, but one here and there, to prove to society how little its categories impress her. This man would have been notable anywhere: among the thin-hammed, flat-chested mediocrities ... he stood out as divine, yet he was of the city, its garbage had nourished him, he would end on its rubbish heaps.[3]

Note that in one the of the latest literary representations of an 'untouchable' man, Arundhati Roy follows the same tradition of portraying him as an epitome of physical perfection, as if to compensate for the ignominy that society has heaped upon him:

> In the dappled sunlight filtering through the dark green trees, Ammu watched Velutha ... She saw the ridges of muscle on Velutha's stomach grow taught and rise under his skin like the divisions on a slab of chocolate. She wondered at how his body had changed—so quietly, from a flat-muscled boy's body into a man's body. Contoured and hard. A swimmer's body. A swimmer-carpenter's body. Polished with a high-wax body polish.[4]

Page 14. *The outcastes were not allowed to mount the platform surrounding the well.* The 'untouchables' were prohibited from using wells, ponds and other public facilities for fear of ritual pollution on the part of caste Hindus, in British India. This was one of the major issues, which triggered off dalit revolt in various parts of the country. Significantly, B.R. Ambedkar led a *satyagraha* in 1927, to establish rights of dalits to draw water from a public tank in Mahad and won the ensuing legal battle in Bombay High Court in 1937. The using of public wells or water sources is the subject of many Indian stories dealing with untouchables or the issue of caste prejudice in general. Refer to Premchand's 'Thakur ka Kua' (1932) where Gangu, wife of Jokhu (an untouchable) attempts to 'steal' a bucket of water from the well reserved for upper-caste thakurs, because the water in their village well is stinking with a rotting dead animal within it. She fails in her quest and comes home to find her husband drinking water drawn from that same stinking well.

Page 22. *And he looked long at her.* Refer to Munshi Premchand's novels for many such examples of upper caste men taking sexual advantage of young 'untouchable' women. In *Godan* the Brahmin priest Matadin, seduces Silia, an 'untouchable' girl. The mother of the girl cries out; 'You will sleep with her but you won't drink water touched by her.'

Page 25. *He lifted his face to the sun.* There is an implicit association between Bakha, a noble and worthy man blighted by the ill-luck of being born into the *panchama* caste which renders him hateful to all, and the epic hero Karna, the illegitimate son of the queen Kunti and Suryadev, the sun-god in the epic *Mahabharata.* Like Karna, Bakha is *bhagyahata* (blighted by fate) from birth, possessing all the qualities of a hero, but condemned to live and die on dung-heaps because of the caste. Like Karna he is naturally attracted towards the sun, the democratic giver of warmth and light to all, irrespective of their caste or class. Anand notes the difference between Bakha's eager absorption of the sun's liberating rays and the other 'untouchables' hesitation to accept its warmth — 'The great life-giver had cut the inscrutable knots that tied them up in themselves. It had melted the innermost parts of their being. And their souls stared at the wonder of it all, the mystery of it, the miracle of it' (*Untouchable,* 27).

Page 34. *For a sweeper, a menial, to be seen smoking constituted an offence.* For the myriad restrictions imposed on 'low castes' in various parts of India, before Independence, refer to J. H. Huton's *Caste in India*[5] For example, 'untouchables' belonging to the Kallar community in Tamil Nadu, were prohibited from wearing gold and silver ornaments, good clothes, using flowers, cooking food in metal vessels, wearing shoes or even using umbrellas. Note the following lines about the position of *paravans,* a group of untouchables in Kerala before Independence, in Roy's *God of Small Things:*

> In Mammachi's time [before Independence] Paravans, like other Untouchables, were not allowed to walk on public roads, not allowed to cover their upper bodies, not allowed to carry umbrellas. They had to cover their mouths when they spoke to divert their polluted breath away from those whom they addressed.[6]

Page 38. *Do you know you have touched me and defiled me ...* On various modes by which an 'untouchable' could pollute a caste Hindu, in various parts of India, refer to Louis Dumont's *Homo Hierarchicus*. I quote Tapan Basu on this subject:

> An overall survey of untouchability practices in different states of India till 1930s reveals that the notion that the upper castes could be 'polluted' through contact with the lower castes was more pervasive and powerful in Western as well as Southern India. In some areas of Maharashtra, in fact, the 'untouchable' castes such as Mahars and Mangs were forced to maintain prescribed distances—varying with the lowliness of the castes—from caste Hindus. There were unwritten and written edicts which forbade these castes from coming into the city of Pune, the capital city of the Chitpavan Peshwas, between 3pm and 9am, because before 9am and after 3pm their bodies caste too long a shadow, and whenever their shadow fell upon a Brahmin, it 'polluted' him so that he dared not take food or water until he had bathed away the 'polluting' effect. Similarly, members of the 'untouchable' castes were made to lie at a distance on their faces when caste Hindus came by lest their shadows fall upon caste Hindus, and were forbidden to speak loudly in their (caste Hindus') presence. A more or less similar edict applied against the 'untouchables' in several areas of Kerala, Tamil Nadu and Karnataka. In certain districts of the South, a Brahmin would not cross even the shadow of an 'untouchable' for fear of getting 'defiled.' Sometimes, 'untouchables' had to ring a bell to announce their 'polluting' arrival, and to wear spittoons around their neck (in the case of the Ande Koragas of Madras) so as to catch any polluting spittle that might drop from their lips. There was even a caste of 'unseeables' (the Purada Vannans of Tinnevelly district) who washed the clothes of other "untouchables" by night and hid their 'polluting' selves by day. 'Pollution' norms such as these were prevalent well into the eve of Indian independence.[7]

However even in the northern part of India where 'pollution norms' were not so strictly maintained, castes of scavengers and sweepers, the Mehtars, Bhangis, Doms and so on were comprehensively shunned in a physical sense.

Page 40. *'I don't know what the kalijugs of this age is coming to!'* In the Hindu consciousness, *Kalijug* is the last of the four cycles of time or age (*yuga*), the other three being *Satya, Treta,* and *Dwapar.* While *Satyayug* is generally considered to represent perfection, *Kaliyug* is the dystrophic age when things fall apart, and 'normal' hierarchies (with the Brahmin male on top and Shudras and women at the bottom) are reversed. This evoking of *kalijug* or *kaliyug,* to describe and lament the topsyturvydom of values, as well as the Hindu Brahmin's submission to *mleccha* (heathen) British rule in India during the colonial period, was common among Hindu gentry. Refer to Sumit Sarkar's essay 'Kaliyug, Chakri and Bhakti' in *Writing Social History*[8] for more on the upper caste Hindu's employment of this concept (*kaliyug*), as a means of negotiating with alien-ness of colonial modernity.

Page 43. *I am an Untouchable!* Bakha's utterance, though born out of extreme personal agony has certain historical ramifications. The term 'untouchable' or *acchut* was pejorative and humiliating, and in the late 1920s and 1930s as a result of Gandhian as well as other reformers' efforts, this appellation was increasingly fading out of fashion. An early effort was made by a Maharashtrian Brahmin reformer, Matre, who proposed calling the lower castes '*aprusha*' (untouched, pure) rather than '*acchut*' or untouchable. M.K. Gandhi first proposed the use of the name *harijan* or children of god, and published a journal with the same name bringing the issue of untouchability to the national forefront. However in his writings he also referred to them as *panchama*, or the fifth and lowest caste, in the Hindu *varna vyavastha* or caste system. Gandhi's term *Harijan* was later rejected by all sections of people for its condescending dimensions. B.R. Ambedkar used the term *dalit* first in his journal *Bahishkrit Bharat*, to indicate the oppressed status of lower castes. Some sections of the lower castes objected to this name and preferred the appellation *bahujan* or the majority.

Page 49. *...who was Hari, Narayan?...He realised that an Untouchable going into a temple polluted it past purification ...* Traditionally, caste Hindus had stopped 'untouchables' from entering their temples, as this was supposed to pollute the temples beyond purification. It is no wonder that Bakha was unaware of Hindu gods as he would never have been allowed to enter a temple or worship them. Significantly, one of the persistent demands of Dalits, apart from the right to use public utilities like wells and ponds, was the right to enter Hindu temples, and six days before the historic signing of the Poona Pact, (which solved differences between Ambedkar and Gandhi) one of the vital issues that the Dalit and Hindu leaders debated was that of temple entry. It is significant that most radical Dalit leaders like Ambedkar ultimately rejected Hinduism, and claimed affiliation to either Buddhism or some original religion pre-dating Hinduism in India. Many Dalits called themselves Adi-Dharmis or the aboriginals of the Indian subcontinent, boasting of a religion pre-dating Aryan invasion. Gandhi, however, repeatedly insisted that Dalits were Hindus and must be brought to the Hindu fold by allowing them entry into temples.

Page 56. *He came of peasant stock.* Most of the scavenger castes in northern India (such as *Bhangis, Mehtars, Chamars* and *Chuhras*) were originally peasants, landless labourers, who performed the most back-breaking and menial jobs in agricultural lands and were forced to migrate to the newly developing cities of Punjab (such as Jalandhar, Amritsar, Lahore), due to famines and inflation, and be inducted as the sanitary work-force by the colonial government at the end of the nineteenth century. Refer to Prashad's *Untouchable Freedom*[9] for more information on this subject.

Page 56. *He could not overstep the barriers which the conventions of his superiors had built up to protect their weakness against him.* Long before Michel Foucault had described modes by which the modern state insidiously 'disciplined' its subjects, the upper-caste Hindus had devised a near perfect system of socialization (*varnashram* or caste hierarchies) that would mentally enslave and 'discipline' millions of oppressed people.

Page 63. *You eater of your masters ... You spoiler of my salt!* Anand used these literal translations of Punjabi colloquialisms in his novels to give them a peculiar flavour. Note how similar expressions are used in *Coolie*. In his essay entitled 'Pigeon-English: Some Notes on Indian Writing', he says he was impressed by his mother's expressions in the local dialect which 'could not have been expressed in any other way except in almost literal translation.' Often, as a result of these translations Anand's language seems to possess a bilingual, bicultural flavour that is unique of Indian-English texts.

Page 111. *Colonel Hutchinson, chief of the local Salvation Army, was never very far from the outcastes' colony.* It is estimated that of the 20 million Christians in India, nearly 70 per cent, that is more than 14 million, are Dalits. They include Pulyans of Kerala, Pariahs of Tamil Nadu, Malas and Madigas of Andhra Pradesh, Tigalas of Karnataka, Chamars of Madhya Pradesh, Uttar Pradesh and Bihar, Churhas of Punjab, Vankars of Gujarat and Mahars from Maharashtra. Conversions in northern India took place during the last 100–150 years, whereas this process of conversion to Christianity has a much older prehistory in southern India. Conversions to Christianity among Dalits, ground to a halt after Independence. Ambedkar noted in the Mahar conference on conversion, in 1946, that: 'to the Untouchables, Hinduism is a veritable chamber of horrors' and any hope of equitable or humane treatment for Dalits within the folds of Hinduism was a virtual impossibility. He, therefore, urged Dalits to 'choose any religion that gives [them] equality of status and treatment' (Zelliot 2001). For most Dalits such as Bakha, condemned to a lifetime of segregation, humiliation and back-breaking menial labour by caste Hindus, conversion to Christianity (or for that matter, Islam or Buddhism) meant hope of a more equitable and human society. Bakha also dimly recognises the democratic possibilities of Christianity when Hutchinson assures him that in the eyes of Christ, Brahmin and Bhangi (scavenger) are the same (p. 120).

Page 127. *It was as if they knew ... that the things of the old civilisation must be destroyed in order to make room for those of the new. It seemed as if ... they were deliberately, brutally trampling on a part* *of themselves which they had begun to abhor, and from which they wanted to escape to Gandhi.* One of the most powerful and moving portions of *Untouchable* where Anand is indicating, through the consciousness of Bakha, the enormous and sweeping change that Gandhi will bring about in the lives of the Indians, enslaved not only by their colonial masters but by age-old superstitions and beliefs.

Page 128. *People said he was a saint, that he was an avatar (incarnation) of the gods Vishnu and Krishna ... And they said no sword could cut his body, no bullet could pierce his skin, no fire could scorch him!* This deification of Gandhi in terms of Hindu mythologies, and this conscious and contemporary use of religion/ mythology for political and temporal ends was part of the Indian National Congress' anti-colonial strategy. Significantly, in the Bardoli Conference, Gandhi was presented as one of the avatars of Vishnu possessing supernatural powers. Raja Rao's *Kanthapura* depicts this interesting process of deification, as Jayaramachar, the *harikatha* man introduces Gandhi as the new god in the Hindu pantheon and reframes the entire anti-colonial movement in terms of an ethical/ eternal struggle between *asuras* (the demons in Hindu mythology, representing evil forces) and Gandhi, the new *avatar* of Vishnu, a god who appears in every age in new forms to protect the good and destroy the evil forces. Ernest Cassirer speaks of this political and contemporary use of myths to make new ideas seem traditional and acceptable, by Nazis in 1930s, in his book. Gandhi contributed to this process of myth-making by using mythological and quasi-religious icons such as *ramrajya* (or utopia under a just ruler like Ram).

Page 129. *India has been the privileged home of the world's eternal religion, that teaches how every man and woman, according to their birth and environment, must practise swadharma.* Most of these ideas (regarding superiority of Indian religion and civilisation) are to be found in Gandhi's *Hind Swaraj*. For Gandhi, *swadharma* meant faithful practising of one's own vocation or calling and realising one's own fullest potential, instead of trying to be something different. An excellent example of this idea may be located in Narayan's *Waiting for the Mahatma.* In an effort to cover up his diffidence and anxiety,

Sriram assures Gandhi (after his first meeting with the great man) that he would now be a different man. Gandhi corrects Sriram saying 'Why do you say "different?" You will be all right if you are fully yourself.' For Gandhi, self-realisation or performance of *swadharma* is both the means as well as the end, as his lifelong endeavour had been to bring India to a realisation of her own traditions and strengths and prevent her people from gazing and mimicking the West in the hope of salvation. Significantly, this is also the conclusion that Bakha arrives at, at the end of the novel. He recognises the dignity of his work, and the importance of doing it well. For the first time in the novel, the picture of the European man in Western clothing does not appear so overwhelmingly attractive. Bakha realises his *swadharma.*

Page 129. *Gandhi ... will teach us the true religion of God-love which is the best swaraj.* The concept of *swaraj* or selfrule, as developed by Gandhi, was an all-encompassing notion of both political and psychological import. Gandhi conceived of *swaraj* very much in the manner of a psycho-ethical utopia, to be achieved by conquering one's baser instincts like hatred, anger and propensity to violence and thus achieving a complete control over self. According to Gandhi, this psychological control over self must precede as well as be the basis of political and economic freedom. For Gandhi, the concept of *swaraj* was far more integral and superior to the European concept of 'independence' or 'nation.' One of the first steps towards achievement of *swaraj* was the recognition of the essential brotherhood of Indians, and a removal of the curse of untouchability, which left a nation divided. In *Young India* he answered S. Srinivasa Iyengar's Congress Presidential address of 1926, which insisted that there was no integral connection between the achievement of Swaraj and removal of untouchability: 'There is, too, confusion regarding *Swaraj* ... Real organic Swaraj is a different question. That freedom which is associated with the term Swaraj in the popular mind is no doubt unattainable without not only the removal of untouchability and the promotion of heart unity between different sections but also without removing many other social evils that can be easily named. ... Swaraj cannot be had so long as the walls of prejudice, passion and superstition continue to stifle the growth of that stately oak.[10]

Page 133. '*That's Mrs. Kasturabai Gandhi...* Mohandas Karam Chand Gandhi was married at the age of thirteen to the daughter of a Porbander merchant named Gokuldas Nakanji, and his bride, also a child of twelve or thirteen, was called Kasturabai. The marriage lasted for sixty-two years.

Page 133. *Mahatma Ji's English disciple, Miss Slade, Miraben ...* Miss Madeline Slade, daughter of Sir Edmund Slade, a British admiral joined the Gandhi ashram in 1925 and lived there for many years, and was one of Gandhi's closest and most ardent followers. Later, Miss Slade founded her own ashram on the banks of the Ganges. According to Louis Fischer, 'her bond with him was one of the remarkable platonic associations of our age. He [Gandhi] often said to her that 'When this body is no more there will not be separation, but I shall be nearer you. The body is a hindrance'.[11]

Page 136. *The British Government sought to pursue a policy of divide and rule in giving our brethren of the depressed classes separate electorates.* B.R. Ambedkar's insistent demands in the Round Table Conference of 1931, that the depressed classes be granted separate electorate as, like the Muslims, they (the untouchables) too could, by no stretch of imagination, be defined as Hindus, and their interests were fundamentally opposed to those of caste Hindus, led to Ramsay Macdonald's granting of a separate electorate for the depressed classes, or what came to be known as the Communal Award of August 1932. Gandhi saw this British move as a further attack on the national unity and in protest, began a fast unto death, till he was able to arm-twist Ambedkar into an agreement, better known as the Poona Pact of 1932. By this pact, the Communal Award was modified and Hindu joint electorate retained, with reservation of seats, and greater representation for the depressed classes.

Page 136. '*while we are asking for freedom from the grip of a foreign nation, we have ourselves, for centuries, trampled underfoot millions of human beings ...* Unlike many other Congressmen, Gandhi felt that there was an integral connection between *swaraj* and the removal of untouchability. In an answer to a query about the nature of *swaraj* in *Young India*, Gandhi replied: '*Swaraj* for me means freedom for the meanest of our countrymen. If the lot of the *panchama* [the fifth caste or untouchables] is not improved when we are all suffering, it is not likely to be better ... I am not interested in freeing India merely from any yoke whatsoever. I have no desire to exchange "king log for king stork." Hence for me the movement of *swaraj* is a movement of self purification'.[12] Elsewhere he underlines this deep connection between the concept of *swaraj* and the removal of untouchability: 'We shall be unfit to gain *swaraj* so long as we would keep in bondage a fifth of the population of Hindustan'.[13]

Page 137. *A scavenger named Uka.* This narrative is to be found in *Young India,* a journal edited by M.K. Gandhi. Significantly, in 1932, Anand was so impressed by this portion of the narrative in *Young India* that he decided to come to India, meet Gandhi, and show him the first draft of his *Untouchable.*

Page 138. *I love scavenging.* For Gandhi, cleaning one's refuse was both a social as well as a spiritual act. Socially speaking, it is only by cleaning one's own dirt that one could appreciate the work done by scavengers and, ultimately rid society of its meaningless prejudices regarding its sanitary work-force. Spiritually speaking, for Gandhi, cleaning of latrines was the first step towards weakening of the ego and spiritual regeneration. In his ashram, Gandhi invited every member to clean his own latrine and Anand joined this regimen for several weeks before he felt spiritually fit to write the final version of *Untouchable.*

Page 138. *If there are any Untouchables here ... they should realise that they are cleaning Hindu society.* Caste Hindus shunned the so-called 'untouchables' because they handled 'dirty' things like human refuse. One of the significant ways in which Gandhi waged war against these irrational beliefs was by re-framing notions of 'cleanliness' versus 'dirt.' The bhangi (sweeper), he said, is performing a valuable service to society by cleaning up its dirt, and should therefore be accorded due respect. In his journal *Harijan* of November 1936, Gandhi notes that 'a Bhangi constitutes the foundation of all services' and that 'a Bhangi does for society what a mother does for her baby. A mother washes her baby of dirt and ensures his health. Even so the

Bhangi protects and safeguards the health of the entire community by maintaining sanitation for it'.[14]

Page 139. *They should now cease to accept leavings from the plates of high-caste Hindus … They should receive grain only … and that too, only if it is courteously offered.* In his essay 'The Ideal Bhangi' in the journal *Harijan,* Gandhi repeatedly stresses the need to give back the sweeper his due respect. Caste Hindus insult sweepers on a daily basis by throwing left-over food at them, and Gandhi exhorts sweepers not to accept such leavings, so discourteously offered; 'Our woebegone Indian society has branded the bhangi as a social pariah, set him at the bottom of the scale … a creature who must subsist on the leavings of the caste-people …'.[15]

Page 139. *Do this but let there be no compulsion or brute force.* One of the major planks of the Gandhian platform was the constant valorisation of love, persuasion and non-violence. Gandhi called this method *satyagraha*, whereas he condemned application of brute force as *duragraha.* As Gandhi notes: 'But as the author of the word [*satyagraha*] I may be allowed to say that it excludes every form of violence, direct or indirect, veiled or unveiled, and whether in thought, word or deed. … It was conceived as a complete substitute to violence.[16] He goes on to outline the difference between *satyagraha* and *duragraha.* 'The man who follows the path of *duragraha* becomes impatient and wants to kill the enemy. … Hatred increases. … The spirit of revenge thus descends from father to son. … The *satyagrahi* and *duragrahi* are both warriors. The latter bereft of arms, acknowledges defeat, the former never does. He does not depend upon the perishable body and its weapons, but fights on with the strength of the unconquerable and immortal *atma.*'[17]

Page 140. '*Let's discard foreign cloth. Let's burn It!*' One of the significant anti-colonial agendas of the Congress Party was the nationwide boycotting of foreign-made goods so that the British would no longer continue the economic drain of India. Gandhi's Dandi march to symbolically make and use Indian salt, is an important milestone in the history of agitations to boycott, foreign-made goods.

For a significant and critical analysis of such boycott see Rabindranath Tagore's *Ghare Baire* (Home and the World).

Page 141. *Gandhi is a humbug ... He is a fool.* One of the important areas where Gandhi was severely criticised was regarding his campaign against untouchability and abolition of caste prejudice. Notable among his critics was Dr. Ambedkar, belonging to the depressed classes, who persistently accused Gandhi of actually being an orthodox Hindu at heart, but advocating hypocritical reforms that preserved all the evils of the caste system. For Ambedkar, *varna* was 'simply a new name for the caste system retaining all its worst features. ... the Untouchables must still hold that the best way to safeguard themselves is to say 'Beware of Mr. Gandhi'.

Most critics of Gandhi (including Ambedkar) accused him of propagating irrational primitivism that would lead India back to the dark ages. The source of such accusations is, primarily, Gandhi's writings in the *Hind Swaraj* where he unequivocally denounces Western civilization and its agents such as railways, automobiles, and almost all big or complicated machinery such as power-looms, or steam engines, as evil and detrimental to human life. For example in *Hind Swaraj* Gandhi says: 'It must be manifest to you that but for railways, the English could not have such a hold on India as they have now. The railways too have spread the bubonic plague. ... Railways have increased the frequency of famines because owing to the means of locomotion people sell out their grain and it is sent out to the dearest markets. People become careless and so the pressure of famine increases. Railways accentuate the evil nature of man.' (40) or 'It is machinery that has impoverished India ... It is due to Manchester that Indian handicraft has all but disappeared ... Machinery is the chief symbol of modern civilization; it represents a great sin' (80). The Anglicised Muslim democrat in *Untouchable* quotes Positivist thinkers like Mill, Bentham and Rousseau and accuses Gandhi of dragging India back to the primitive times. This was precisely the position of Socialist thinkers such as M.N. Roy and Dr. Ambedkar who felt that Gandhi's primitivist ideas would drag India back to the dark ages of superstition, poverty and squalor.

Page 143. *We can see through the idiocy of Europeans who deified money. They were barbarians and lost their heads in the worship of gold.* The author is restating, in his own words, Gandhi's major ideas in the *Hind Swaraj.* Gandhi argued that the Indian civilisation was far superior to the European one and Indians should learn to take pride in their own culture rather than slavishly imitate their conquerors. By turning the colonial discourse of European 'civility' and 'enlightenment' as against Indian 'primitivism' on its head, Gandhi is providing Indians with a sense of self-respect and identity. These ideas have a profound significance for Bakha whose very identity is constructed on the axis of blind mimicry of the Western man. By the end of the novel, Bakha will learn to discover his indigenous self.

Notes

1. *Untouchable Freedom,* p. 137.
2. Arun Shourie, *Worshipping False gods: Ambedkar and the Facts which have been Erased,* New Delhi: Harper Collins India, 1997.
3. E.M. Forster, *A Passage to India,* New York: Harcourt, Brace and World, 1924, p. 217.
4. Arundhati Roy, *The God of Small Things,* New Delhi: IndiaInk, 1997, 175.
5. J.H. Hutton, *Caste in India,* Cambridge, England: Cambridge University Press; New York: Macmillan, 1946.
6. Roy, *The God of Small Things,* p. 74.
7. Tapan Basu (ed.), *Translating Caste,* New Delhi: Katha, 2002, p. xix.
8. Sumit Sarkar, 'Kaliyug, Chakri and Bhakti' in Writing Social History, New Delhi, 2002.
9. See note 1 above.
10. *Collected Works of Mahatma Gandhi (CWMG)* 33, p. 149.
11. Louis Fischer, *The Life of Mahatma Gandhi,* New York: Harper and Row, 1950, p. 440.
12. *CWMG* 24: p. 227.
13. *CWMG* 19: p. 20.
14. M.K. Gandhi, 'The Ideal Bhangi,' *CWMG* 64, p. 86–8.
15. *CWMG* p. 64, 86–8.
16. *CWMG* 54, p. 416–17.
17. *CWMG* 14, p. 63–5.

The Epic Of Misery

SAROS COWASJEE

No Indian writer, writing in English or in one of India's several languages, has had more to say on the theory and writing of fiction than Mr Anand himself.[1] All too often his soaring idealism, as expressed in his essays and articles, clashes with what he has achieved in practice. But it is quite a different matter when he comes to make value judgements in letters to friends and acquaintances while actively engaged in the process of writing: judgements such as those made by Gustave Flaubert to Ivan Turgenev or by Stendhal to Balzac. One of Anand's most telling utterances on the role of the novelist is in a letter written to me while he was revising *Morning Face*:

> The novelist should try to become the great god, Brahma, who creates mankind, but is not responsible for it, that is to say, does not determine their destiny. Distance is very important in art, because art though like life, and reflecting it, is not life. Literature and life are parallel developments.[2]

Here there is a clear echo, perhaps unconscious, of Flaubert's contention that the artist must be in his work as God in his creation, invisible yet powerful. Though Flaubert and Anand have little in common, both novelists in their best writings approximate the goals they set before themselves—Flaubert more than Anand, for he is first and foremost an artist. So objective is Flaubert that it is difficult to say from his novels what he must have thought in private life, while Anand's stories tell us as much about himself as about those of whom he writes. And though he is in his own way a stylist, there is in his writing no conscious attempt at perfection of style nor involvement with the fine details of technique and form which so obsessed Flaubert.

Anand's theories, though unoriginal, have a definite place in the study of his novels. They arise from his concept of literature, which is to reveal life in all its contrarieties and in the process to create awareness in the reader. Conditioned by Marxian dialectics, the social impulse is, as with the writers of the thirties, at the heart of his writing. A work of art, be it a novel or a painting or a play, is first of all a social event. This explains why he gives maximum emphasis to the duties of a novelist (and to what a good novel should be), and very little to the tools at his disposal. In the dozen or so articles concerned with the novel, he has to my knowledge only once commented on the need for a style:

> Of course, it is not enough to want to say something. Everything depends on how one says it—how the imagination of a writer can transform the various realities, interpenetrate characters with insight, and 'connect' the poetry and the prose. And, certainly, there has to be some kind of style.[3]

This is a half-hearted acceptance of the importance of style—almost a concession since there seems to be no way out of it. As to form, he dismisses it as a question of secondary concern. Reviewing Henry Green's *Loving* in *Life and Letters To-Day,* he says: 'And, if I may venture an arbitrary dictum, I should say that the primary condition of art is not form but sensibility.'[4] He insists, and not without reason, that anything could make a novel provided the writer can carry it off and communicate it with some effect. The novel form is loose enough to include both scandal like *Anna Karenina* (1875–76) and history of the Napoleonic period like *War and Peace* (1865–72), so long as the novelist talks in terms of human beings and not puppets. However, Anand seems to leave the impression that neither style nor form is basically fundamental to the novel. 'What is the use', he wrote to me angrily, 'of keeping the form, the kerb and the edge all right and destroying the bloody horse—Roy Campbell's phrase, not mine.'[5] This outburst is not without its irony, for his best novels are not formless nor is he a writer without style.

By far his most lucid and balanced discussion on the functions of a novelist is to be found in his long confessional essay, *Apology for Heroism.* Very much a writer of the thirties himself, he judges the period to be aesthetically a failure: one in which there was little heroism but many heroic gestures. In a characteristic passage he tells us what he firmly disapproves:

> There were the simpletons who believed that an art form like the novel, for instance, was nothing else but reportage about social conditions. There were the subjectivists on the other hand who believed that it was enough skilfully to describe the phantasmagoria of one's psychological states, particularly the subconscious, dream, or clinical experiences. And, of course, there were always the vast bulk of those others, the low pressure artists, the whores of literature, who wrote to provide escape and relaxation to the tired ladies and gentlemen of our suburban civilization. And they all bandied words with each other.[6]

That Anand disapproves of propaganda is no evidence that his writing is free of propaganda or diatribe against those whom he mistrusts. But he is no facile propagandist: he is what George Orwell was—an expositor, a political novelist, one who sees his characters and their actions in relation to the social, economic and political upheavals of his time. The distinction between political literature and propaganda 'is extremely complex and involves the writer's ability to distinguish between his social conscience and his obligation to his art'.[7] Also, the line of demarcation is so fine that it very often is a matter of how one chooses to interpret it. Like Thomas Mann, Anand believes that politics is everybody's business and that the modern writer with a conscience cannot shut himself up in an ivory tower. Discussing his obligation to his fellow men, he quotes Marx: 'Philosophers have so far interpreted the world, the thing is to change it,' and then goes on to ask, 'But where was one to begin?'[8]

He began by recalling the lives of the people he had known, and in his narratives introduced a whole new set of people who had seldom entered the realms of literature. The task was not easy, and with remarkable candour and humility he confesses:

> I could not, of course, sense the suffering of the poor directly because I had always been comparatively better off. No, mine was a secondary humiliation, the humiliation of seeing other people suffer. I do not know to what extent envy of the rich on my part was disguising itself as a hunger for social justice. Perhaps there

> was an element of this. Also the indequacies of our life in India may have contributed something to my preoccupation. But I do not apologize for this because it is not easy in the face of such wretchedness and misery as I had seen in India to believe that material happiness and well-being had no connection with real happiness and the desire for beauty. So I sought to recreate my life through my memories of India in which I grew up, with a view to rediscovering the vanities, the vapidities, the conceits and the perplexities with which I had grown up, indifferent to the lives of the people around me. I felt guilty, for needless suffering was no matter for complacent pride or gratitude.[9]

The fact that most of Anand's novels are concerned with people not of his own caste or class is important, for it provides the necessary detachment. It may be purely coincidental, but in his first nine novels (the only ones to have been first published in England), one notices a gradual progression in the caste and social standing of his hero. His first novel deals with a sweeper, the second with a coolie, the third with an uprooted field labourer, the next three with a sturdy peasant lad, followed by one about a machine-hand, then an autobiographical novel about his childhood, and finally a novel with a prince as its central character. Princes or paupers, all his heroes are victims: some of society's making, others of their own. And he has for them all what Arnold Bennett took to be the most essential gift in a novelist—'a Christ-like, all-embracing compassion'.

UNTOUCHABLE

Untouchable was written over a long weekend in 1930. The author tells us that it 'poured out like hot lava from the volcano of my crazed imagination',[10] and that during its composition he hardly slept for more than six hours in three days. The hero of the novel was his childhood playmate, Bakha, a sweeper lad who excelled in games, and despite the lack of formal education could recite whole cantos of Waris Shah's *Heer-Ranjha.* The contradiction between the inherent qualities of the boy and the degradation to which he had been condemned was no doubt the chief *motif* of the work, but its successful realization proved no easy task.

Anand's wide and desultory reading were to have their bearing on the novel. Rousseau's idea of the 'noble savage' particularly appealed to him and this is not difficult to see; so did Tolstoy's populism. Arthur Rimbaud's *A Season in Hell* (1873) vivified his own preoccupation with the symbolic journey through hell his outcastes had been going through, and Picasso's pictures of the 'Blue and the Pink Periods' dealing with prostitutes, beggars, drunkards, and harlequins seem relevant to his subject. But the works which most influenced him were Gorki's *The Lower Depths* (1902) and *Creatures that Once Were Men* (1901) and Joyce's *Ulysses* (1922). Like Gorki he went to the lowest dregs of humanity in search of his hero, like Joyce he dramatised the events of a single day (in both novels the time covered is about sixteen hours). But the book as it then stood was too amorphous. Joyce had been imitated rather than assimilated, and the reverie sequences were over-written and savoured of self-pity. The author tinkered with it for two years but made no appreciable improvement.

In 1932, while perusing the pages of Gandhiji's magazine *Young India,* he was impressed by Gandhiji's narrative about a sweeper called Uka, and decided to meet the Mahatma and read to him his novel. On the boat, the British passengers treated Anand and the other Indians with contempt, and for the first time he felt what it was like to be an untouchable. Roused, he began revising his book with a new anger. But what the work sought was love, not hate, and this he learnt to feel in Gandhiji's *ashram.*

After taking a vow to clean latrines once a week, not to touch liquor or look with desire at women, Anand settled down in the *ashram* to redraft his novel. Gandhi advised him to give up the novel and to write a tract on untouchability:

> The Mahatma said, 'The straight book is truthful and you can reform people by saying things frankly'.
> I said, 'Though I do want to reform people, I believe in posing the question rather than in answering it.'[11]

The thrice-a-week discussions with Gandhiji, and the symbolic act of cleaning the latrines enriched his perception. He found that he could make the very act of cleaning latrines seem no better or worse than any other work. The love and warmth that emanated from Gandhi found its way into the hero's personality; the charity and forgiveness that Gandhi preached taught Anand to temper his hatred against the caste Hindu oppressors. The work revised, he returned to London to find a publisher.

For the next two years the book made its round of the publishers' desks. It troubled both Anand and his literary friends that no publisher would accept it, and Edward Thompson, who himself had written several books about India, gave the following reasons:

> As to the reasons you give for publishers' rejection of it, it is true that Indian books do not sell. There is such a welter of propaganda and sentimentalism over everything Indian—British die-hard, National Congress journalist, fake poet and mystic, theosophist, Gandhi-adorer, American women's club, all combine to make everything Indian depressing to anyone not half-witted. I seem to find signs that India is beginning to bore even Indians![12]

The trouble with *Untouchable* was that it was quite unlike anything written about India: a book which, without propaganda or sentimentality, destroyed the image of the British and the Indian people built over the years. Naomi Mitchison, sister of J. B. S. Haldane, viewing the novel from the standpoint of the average reader, was right in saying:

> I have just finished reading your book, and found it fascinating and horrible—I think you might find that a good many people just won't read it, because of the dirt and cruelty you have conveyed in it. However, that's what you mean to do, and it is a very able piece of work, for it really conveys the whole thing with the utmost vividness and without any romanticizing.[13]

Bonamy Dobrée must have felt more or less the same, and in his own kind way urged the author to tone down the writing:

> But in view of what has happened to the book, I would advise you if possible to make the beginning a little different if you can without spoiling the artistic effect. It does smell rather strong. Couldn't you give the sense of the utter beastliness of the job without going

> into so much physical detail? I personally don't mind, but then my stomach is strong: and remember that the average reader does not want to be instructed, but amused. I should think that with a little skill you can make your point just as well.[14]

The novel was revised several times. The opening pages, influenced by Dickens's description of London slums, were toned down considerably, and much of the repetition was deleted. (In the original version Bakha was hit three times, in the printed version only once.) Still the publishers felt shy of the work. Jonathan Cape turned it down though Dobrée recommended it in very strong terms, and so did The Bodley Head, and Chatto and Windus. In the case of the latter, Anand had attached to the manuscript a letter he had received from E. M. Forster:

> Dear Mr Anand,
>
> I am just going abroad, and have only had time to read hastily through your MS., but I found it extremely interesting. It recalled to me very vividly the occasion I have walked 'the wrong way' in an Indian city, and it is a way down which no novelist has yet taken us. I can't of course confirm your details, and I didn't know that in the north, where your scene is apparently laid, the prejudice against the sweeper class was still so strong or so elaborately organized. But you present it all very convincingly. You make your sweeper sympathetic yet avoid making him a hero or a martyr, and, by the appearance of Gandhi and the conversation about machinery at the end, you give the whole book a coherence and shape which it would otherwise have lacked. I felt you always knew what you wanted to say, and the firmness of the general handling makes up for minor blemishes.
>
> If you want to try a new publisher, I suggest you send the MS to Messrs Chatto and Windus, St Martin's Lane, and if you care to enclose this letter with it you are welcome to do so. The objection against the MS. from the practical point of view seems to me not in its length but its 'squalor': I put this word in inverted commas as indicating that it doesn't convey my personal opinion, but it may well represent the opinion of the public, which the publishers are bound to consider when making their decision.
>
> Yours sincerely,
>
> E. M. Forster[15]

By September 1934, the novel had been rejected by as many as nineteen publishers and the author contemplated suicide, but was saved by the timely intervention of a young British poet, Oswell Blakeston, who took the manuscript to Wishart Books. The book was accepted on the condition that E. M. Forster should write a preface to protect it against being called 'dirty'. Forster not only quickly supplied the preface, but insisted that Anand should accept the fee:

> I also enclose a cheque for the amount which they [Wishart] sent to me, and beg you to accept the same. I hope that under the circumstances you will consent to do this. It will be a great pleasure to me if I should be of any help in introducing such an interesting and original piece of work to readers in this country.[16]

Anand gratefully accepted the cheque. Though Edgell Rickword, editor of Wishart Books, was greatly impressed by the novel, he did not expect to sell more than a thousand copies—and offered the tired author an advance of only £35 on royalties. But Wishart gave the author an indefinite loan of £100, and Forster got him another £100 from the Royal Literary Fund.

As for the Preface, it delighted both the author and the publisher. Edgell Rickword wrote to Anand:

> I was glad to get your letter, and to find that you admired Forster's introduction as much as I do. I think from every point of view it was just what we wanted. It is a little masterpiece of suggestion and understanding and will be the book's passport through the latent hostility of the ordinary reviewer. We could not have had anything better.[17]

The book was published on 1 May 1935. The 'little masterpiece of suggestion' proved no passport: it only directed some of the 'latent hostility' of the ordinary reviewer towards Mr Forster himself. Though *The Times, London Mercury,* and *Punch* agreed with Mr Forster's appraisal, the *Left Review, News Chronicle, The Observer, Star, The Sunday Referee* and the *Manchester Guardian Weekly* took issue with him. Much of the argument centred on whether the book was 'dirty' or 'indescribably clean', as Mr Forster made it out to be.[18] The book, however, quickly cut its ways through supercilious criticism and established for itself a popularity that remains unrivalled for a work of fiction by an Indian author.

Untouchable opens quietly on an autumn morning, and by the time the evening approaches, the author has been able to build round his hero Bakha (a sweeper lad of eighteen who cleans latrines) a spiritual crisis of such breadth that it seems to embrace the whole of India. 'Get up, ohe you Bakhya, ohe you son of a pig!' calls out his father, and Bakha sheds his reverie of the Tommies' life he wishes to lead and tackles his task of cleaning the public latrines once more. Returning to his hut to quench his thirst for tea, he is soon out again to sweep the market road and the temple courtyard. On the way he buys four annas worth of cheap sweetmeat, after weighing the consequences of doing so in both rational and philosophic terms:

> 'Eight annas in my pocket,' he said to himself, 'dare I buy some sweets? If my father comes to know that I spend all my money on sweets,' he thought and hesitated, 'but come, I have only one life to live,' he said to himself, 'let me taste of the sweets; who knows, tomorrow I may be no more.'[19]

Overjoyed at his possession, he forgets to call out 'posh, posh, sweeper coming' and accidentally touches a caste Hindu. He earns for his transgression much abuse from the public and a slap from the man he has polluted. This incident, along with the attempt of a priest to seduce his sister (when the girl screams, the priest cries out 'polluted'!) poisons everything that happens subsequently, even such pleasant incidents as a hockey match, a country walk and a wedding. The approaching evening presents three solutions: he could become a Christian with the help of the Salvation Army missionary Hutchinson, he could take comfort in Gandhiji's chastisement of the caste Hindus and wait till the social conscience of the people is roused; or better still he could put his faith in the water-closet about which the positivist poet had talked. Bakha returns to his wretched bed with more hope than he had set out with in the morning, but a hope that is nowhere near fulfilment forty years after the novel was written. Though the Indian constitution has made it a crime to practise untouchability, there are untouchables to be found in every corner of India.[20]

E. M. Forster in his Preface calls *Untouchable* a 'remarkable novel' and goes on to say that the author owes his success probably to 'the directness of his attack' and the fact that he has 'the right mixture of insight and detachment' in his hero's character. This is certainly true and worth examining in some detail, but equally remarkable is Anand's handling of the plot and the judicious arrangement of the various episodes that make his sweeper's Indian day.

What immediately strikes the reader is the gentle and balanced writing, which does not at the first impact move us to instant indignation. It is only after we have put the book aside and ruminated on Bakha's fate that the full implications of the tragedy become explicit—a tragedy of a large section of mankind ostracised and condemned to misery. Conscious of the magnitude of his theme, Anand wisely opens in a low key, and the most violent incident in the novel is only a slap that Bakha receives from a passer-by. I have said *only,* for not too long ago three untouchables in a village in Madhya Pradesh were shot by caste Hindus for daring to grow their moustaches upwards, when local custom decrees that persons of low caste grow them downwards.[21] And a young boy in Andhra Pradesh was tied to a pole and burnt alive before a huge crowd—the incident making repeated headlines in the press. Anand could have inflicted any torture he wished to on his hero and remained fully within the bounds of credibility. The temptation, too, must have been strong (I have already mentioned that in the first draft Bakha was slapped three times), for the novel compassed a single day of which most had to be made. But whether he could have moved us more than he does now is extremely doubtful. Let it be said at once that the book gains much of its strength from the author's depiction of the emotional crisis in his hero's life quietly and without hysteria, and from the treatment of a political subject without political jargon.

The story in the conventional sense hardly exists. Bakha's day is made up of a series of incidents, some sad and some happy, which alternate with a measured regularity bringing forth varying responses from him. Early in the novel, Anand piles up hard, one upon another, three humiliating experiences on his hero: a slap from a caste Hindu for polluting him, a priest molesting his sister, and a housewife abusing him and throwing a pancake at him from the top of her house. When Bakha returns home, his father Lakha, 'Jemadar' of the sweepers, roundly berates him, and his cup of frustration and misery is full. From this point onwards, Anand reverts to his technique of alternating pleasant with unpleasant episodes, except that Bakha's few pleasures are contaminated with the memory of previous misfortunes. The novel concludes on an ambivalent note: Bakha is neither happy nor unhappy as he listens to the missionary, sways with the crowd that has asssembled to hear Gandhiji speak, and from a non-polluting distance attempts to follow the harangue of a poet which ranges from nirvana to modern plumbing.

Bakha is an attractive person. His physique is distinctive; he is described as intelligent, able-bodied and strong, with a broad, frank face, glistening high cheek-bones, quivering lips and a graceful torso. He has, we are told, 'a sort of dignity that does not belong to the average scavenger, who is as a rule uncouth and unclean'. Even those who abuse his service feel that he is a 'bit superior to his job'. Though born a child of darkness, he derives his strength from the sun, which in the *Upanishad* is described as the eye of the whole universe, and is untainted by the feculence of the external world of men and matter:

> He lifted his face to the sun, open-eyed for a moment, then with the pupils of his eyes half closed, half open. And he lifted his chin upright. It was pleasing to him. It seemed to give him a thrill, a queer sensation which spread on the surface of his flesh where the tincture of warmth penetrated the numbed skin. He felt vigorous in this bracing atmosphere. Instinctively he rubbed his face in order to make it warm enough to take in the rays of the sun, to open out its pores .... He caught the full force of its glare, and was dazed. He stood lost for a moment, confused in the shimmering rays, feeling as though there were nothing but the sun, the sun, the sun, everywhere, in him, on him, before him, and behind him p. 25).

Bakha is modelled, as mentioned earlier, on a sweeper boy Anand had known in his childhood and adored as a hero, and he is presented with photographic fidelity. There is also in the contrast between his natural possibilities and his present degradation, a strong echo of the *punkah*-puller in E.M. Forster's *A Passage to India:*

> When that strange race nears the dust and is condemned as untouchable, then nature remembers the physical perfection that she accomplished elsewhere, and throws out a god—not many, but one here and there, to prove to society how little its categories impress her. This man would have been notable anywhere: among the thin-hammed, flat-chested mediocrities … he stood out as divine, yet he was of the city, its garbage had nourished him, he would end on its rubbish heaps.[22]

If Bakha is pictured as a male god, his sister Sohini is portrayed as a goddess with 'a sylph-like form', 'full-bodied', 'well-rounded on the hips, with an arched narrow waist' and 'globular breasts'. Her figure could have vied with the sculptured images of Konarak or Khajuraho, but she has been condemned by birth to walk the path of the outcastes and to suffer their mortification. Bakha and Sohini are by no means representative of their class: the true outcaste (if there is such a thing) is Bakha's brother, Rakha, with his grimy flannel shirt and running nose. Living in the midst of dung he is a human being, but one who belongs to a 'world where the day is dark as the night, and the night pitch-dark'. Rakha is a living death as opposed to his brother who is life in death.

Bakha's slavish emulation of the Tommies, though comic, is his first affirmation that the life he is doomed to live is monstrously unjust. Though he may cut a ridiculous figure as he stumps out in artillery boots, wearing discarded trousers, puttees, breeches and regulation overcoat, with a 'Red-Lamp' cigarette smouldering between his lips, it is all the same a manifestation of his tremendous strength and courage. That he should emulate the Tommies is understandable (many urban children in pre-independence India did so, and Anand as a boy himself copied the ways of the Tommies), for they 'treated him as a human being' and scorned the native population for relieving themselves on the ground and for other filthy habits. For Bakha the observation ends here, but it may suggest more to the reader who knows that the British themselves were untouchables to the Brahmins.

Bakha's admiration of the Tommies is used to other good purposes as well. It enables him to establish his identity and, temporarily, to escape from his sordid existence. It affords Anand an opportunity to maintain an ambivalent attitude towards his hero, and to censure him mildly when the occasion demands it. But above all it provides all the humour in the book: there is something laughable about a sweeper who would forgo his few homely comforts for the sake of what he called 'fashun' and who would say to himself: 'I will look like a sahib', 'And I shall walk like them. Just as they do, in twos, with Chota as my companion.' It is pathetic, too, when the fantasy breaks down and he realises that 'except for his English clothes there was nothing English in his life.' But such moments are few, and the sahibs are a vital presence to him. He looks up to the missionary Colonel Hutchinson, even though the latter has degradeed himself in Bakha's eyes by mixing with the natives. After all the Colonel wore trousers and used a commode—what better proof of a sahib! Bakha's admiration of the sahibs persists right through the book and wanes only when he hears the Mahatma speak. The English police officer at the public meeting, though clad in all the trappings that had earlier fired Bakha's imagination, seems to him at last insignificant and out of place, the representative of an order that has nothing to do with the aspirations of the people. This observation is significant. Anand seems to say that Gandhi's appeal to the public was mainly emotional, and that in his presence people dropped their fads and fancies and rallied round him, even though, like Bakha, they did not understand the full implications of his teachings.

Bakha also differs from the general run of sweepers in that he is clean, is a champion at all games, has principles and a sense of duty. In finely chiselled prose, Anand describes the zest with which his hero tackles his unpleasant job:

> He worked away earnestly, quickly, without loss of effort. Brisk, yet steady, his capacity for active application to the task he had in hand seemed to flow like constant water from a natural spring. Each muscle of his body, hard as a rock when it came into play, seemed to shine forth like glass. He must have had immense pent-up resources lying deep in his body, for he rushed along with considerable skill and alacrity from one doorless latrine to another, cleaning, brushing, pouring phenoil … (pp. 7–8).

It is obvious what the author is trying to convey: work is what one makes of it. Anand himself had cleaned latrines in Gandhiji's *Ashram* and had learnt of the Brahmin boy Uka who did scavenging there. It was not the nature of the work, but the spirit in which it was performed that made the difference. What is revolting is not so much the dirty aspect of the profession, but what Anand calls 'the anal-erotic complex of the Hindus through which they condemned a whole caste of people who cleaned their dung pots'.[23] The Hindu religion is responsible for this fiendish segregation of humanity: the waste products of the body are unclean, therefore those who carry them are dirty and obnoxious. How better can this complex of the Hindus be refuted than by the question Gandhi asked with his characteristic brevity; 'If you consider Harijans [children of God] untouchables because they perform sanitary service, what mother has not performed that service?' Place alongside Gandhi's utterance what Bakha has to say of his job; 'They think we are mere dirt, because we clean their dirt,' While Gandhi speaks with the incisiveness and the cool logic of a social reformer, Bakha merely expresses what he has seen in everyday life. It is a triumph on Anand's part that though he wrote the novel with the aim of condemning a barbaric practice, he did not once assume the posture of the propagandist.

In his almost physical inability to revolt, his submission, his habitual subservience to superiors who insult him, he is one with the vast majority of the outcastes. After heredity and two thousand years of oppression have done their work on him, there are few resources left in him. He goes about his job wearing the smile of humility customary among his kind. Charat Singh's promise to give him a hockey stick brings forth that trait of servility which he has inherited from his forefathers, and in his person he reflects 'the passive contentment of the bottom dog suddenly illuminated by the prospect of fulfilment of a secret and long-cherished desire'. On receiving the hockey stick, his gratitude is overwhelming:

> He was grateful, grateful, haltingly grateful, falteringly grateful, stumblingly gratful, so grateful that he didn't know how he could walk the ten yards to the corner to be out of the sight of his benevolent and generous host. The whole atmosphere was charged with embarrassment. He felt uncomfortable as he walked away. 'Strange! strange! wonderful! kind man! I didn't know he was so

> kind. I should have known. He always had such a humorous way about him! Kind, good man! He gave me a new stick, a brand-new stick!' (p.100)

The cup of gratitude spills over, and fear and doubt creep in. Could his benefactor have made a mistake? Was he absent-minded? Would he ask for it back? What unkind thoughts, Bakha ponders : 'I am mad to think that he was forgetful. So kind a person, and I think *this* about him. I am a pig to do that.' M.E. Derrett comments incisively on this scene:

> Notice the analysis of the states of mind of the young boy, overwhelmed by that rare thing, kindness; full of youthful energy, overcome by the joy of possession, afraid as only one with few possessions could be of possible loss or injury to it, incredulous of the whole quick succession of events, and in dread of the fearful possibility of some mistake. The author's identity with his character seems complete, his humanity communicates itself.[24]

Bakha's sense of gratitude for the least kindness shown to him is basically a part of his obsequiousness, and in its effusion it somewhat resembles that of Aziz in *A Passage to India.* When Mrs Moore tells Aziz not to fret over Fielding having missed the train which was taking them to Malabar Caves, Aziz deliberates: 'There was nothing he would not do for her. He would die to make her happy.' Bakha too would give everything for any show of kindness. He could have cried because the missionary had treated him as a human being; he could put his life into the hands of the Mahatma and ask 'him to do what he liked with it', because the Mahatma had said that if he were to be born again he would rather be born an untouchable.

If kindness brings forth gratitude mingled with humility, excessive abuse occasionally helps him to regain his strength and self-respect. Twice he thinks of retaliation: first when he is slapped by a caste Hindu and later when his sister is molested by a priest. At such moments he appears, we are told, a 'superb specimen of humanity, his fine form rising as a tiger at bay'. But he is a tiger in a cage, securely imprisoned by the conventions his superiors have built up to protect themselves against the fury of those whom they exploit. The instinctive anger gives way, and the slave in him asserts itself—

'Untouchable!' Untouchable! That's the word! Untouchable! I am an Untouchable!', he repeats to himself to regain his equilibrium. I have deliberately used the word 'instinctive', for Bakha reacts mostly by instinct, and it is no accident that the author compares him to animals, and draws analogies between him and animals like tigers, lions, elephants, bears and apes. When the Mahatma spoke about untouchability, 'Bakha pricked up his ears'. 'Pricked' indeed is the right word, and few other words could convey the same meaning.

Anand has been able to create a gallery of authentic people who compel attention. His success with Bakha is not solely because the character has been taken from real life (the reader's notion of 'real life' and the novelist's can be hopelessly apart), but because of what Henry James calls 'the power to guess the unseen from the seen'. He has felt, in his role of a novelist, Bakha's helplessness, despair, blighted hopes and agony to a degree that he has become an untouchable himself. So strong indeed is the identification with his hero that for the best part of the novel we forget the presence of the author. Everything that Bakha says or does is in complete accordance with his character and his status in life. Examples abound, and I shall refer the reader to the most dramatic episode of all—Bakha's visit to the temple to sweep the courtyard.

The scene opens with Bakha viewing with awe and respect the twelve-headed and ten-armed gods and goddesses of the Hindu pantheon. His caste has alienated him from his religion, and these deities themselves are subject to defilement. For his kind, the only religion is to keep others pure and clean, and with a sweeper's instinct his gaze falls on the bird-droppings, and the leaves and the dust he has come to clean. As he attacks his job, he hears from inside the temple the names of the various gods, only a few of whom he recognises. As if by magic, he is drawn towards the temple and mounts the first two steps. But the oppressed underdog in him exerts itself, and he retreats to collect the litter. The urge to see his gods becomes overwhelming as the 'temple stood challenging before him', and then 'seemed to advance towards him like a monster'. With a sudden onslaught he gains five of the fifteen steps; another push and he is on the top step, crouched like a dog at the door of a banquet hall. The smell of incense, the ritualistic chanting, the hoarse shouts of triumphant worshippers overpower him, and 'his hands joined unconsciously, and his head hung in the worship of the unknown god.'

Bakha's homage to his gods is answered with the cries of 'polluted! polluted!' raised by the temple priest to extricate himself from the alarm Sohini has raised to ward off his indecent advances towards her. The worshippers rush out to see Bakha cowering on the steps and give vent to their own cry that the temple is being defiled. Completely unnerved in the beginning, Bakha, on learning the truth from his sister, moves in giant strides to take revenge. The crowd takes to its heels. Only the gods remain, secure in their individual niches, rebuking Bakha with their cold, impersonal stares.

Everything in the episode is exact. We have the sweeper's preoccupation with his job, the sinister appeal of the temple to the uninitiated (something akin to Forster's Marabar Caves), his obeisance to the gods, the hypocrisy of the priest, the cowardice of the 'twice-born' Hindus, the hero's immediate impulse to revenge the insult to his sister, and his failure to do so. Bakha's moment of action has come and gone; and it is in his failure to act that the fidelity—if not the strength—of the novel lies.

Since the social impulse is at the heart of Anand's writing, he finds irony—which works largely through contrasting appearance with reality—a particularly useful tool to destroy the myth and romance built around India by the nineteenth-century novelists. Yeats' lines,

> We had fed the heart on fantasies,
> The heart's grown brutal from the fare,

were an admission of the evil accompanying escapist literature, which writers like Hardy, Joyce and Huxley counteracted by taking the reader back to reality by questioning the very basis of romance. The methods employed by the realists were either (a) to examine the individual psyche with the intention of looking for subtle contradictions within the individual sensibility, or (b) to reveal the moral complexities of life as suggested by Hardy's title *Life's Little Ironies* (1894). The second method involves examining not only man's futile struggles against an ominscient and nonchalant God, but man's pretensions in the face of an actuality he prefers to disregard. It is this second kind of irony that suits Anand's purpose as much as his genius. Untouchability, which can have no moral, religious, or even aesthetic sanction, is particularly vulnerable to an ironic treatment. 'Really, it takes the human mind', says Forster in the Preface 'to evolve anything so devilish. No animal could have hit on it.'

Since irony is implicit in the theme, one finds it everywhere and more pervasively than in any other Anand novel. The novel unfolds with a child of modern India shackled by age-old traditions; the Hindus who pride themselves on their cleanliness gargle and spit in the stream and pollute the water, while a person incomparably cleaner than themselves is treated like dirt. There are Muhammadans walking about with hands in their pajamas, purifying themselves in the ritualistic manner preparatory to their visit to a mosque, but infuriated when asked what they are doing; men squatting in the open to relieve themselves, earning from the Tommies well-deserved abuses; the sub-castes among the apparently casteless untouchables and their claim to superiority over one another; the rich Hindu businessmen overfeeding idle priests with sumptuous food, but grudging dry bread to those who sweat for them; betel-leaf shops where lithographs of Hindu deities contend for space with those of beautiful European women; the petty merchant-cum-money lender whose prices rise to meet the needs of the very poor; the sweetmeat-seller who deftly manipulates the scales and cheats the outcastes, knowing that they dare not protest; orthodox Hindus who worship a stinking bull but will not touch a human being; Hindu temples whose doors are closed to those who keep its grounds clean, temples where a murderer can enter but not those who do what every mother does for her child; the queer Hindu notion of 'pollution by touch' and 'pollution from a distance'; women whose idea of keeping their homes clean is to throw the garbage out the front door; the hypocrisy of Hindu women who like the sweepers to call them 'mother' but treat them as pariahs; women who treat lazy sadhus with reverenee, but the man who does their dirtiest job with derision.

The ruling class too comes in for criticism. Englishmen, after years of stay in India, learn only some useful imperatives and swear-words such as '*Acha* (good); *jao* (go away); *jaldi karo* (be quick); *sur ka bacha* (son of a pig); *kute ka bacha* (son of a dog)'.[25] The missionary's wife in *Untouchable* sums up the attitude of most Englishwomen to the natives, an attitude which Orwell predicted would cost England her Indian empire. The missionary himself, for all his genuine efforts, has failed to transplant himself to the Indian soil, and the presence of his irreligious wife right in his house makes a mockery of his attempt at proselytising the heathens. But in this novel it is not the rulers Anand is really concerned with, but the depravity that has infested Indian society since the first Aryan invasions.

Forster, it appears, must have foreseen the criticism the conclusion of the novel would invite, and in his Preface defended it with these words:

> Some readers may find this closing section of the book too voluble and sophisticated, in comparison with the clear observation which has preceded it, but it is an integral part of the author's scheme. It is the necessary climax, and it has mounted up with triple efffect. Bakha returns to his father and his wretched bed, thinking now of the Mahatma, now of the Machine. His Indian day is over and the next day will be like it, but on the surface of the earth if not in the depths of the sky, a change is at hand (p. viii).

Though some reviewers agreed with Forster's remarks, others found the conclusion unsatisfactory for different reasons, and some gave no reasons at all. The *Evening News* simply called the ending 'unconvincing', the *Star* thought it 'so simple as to seem almost comic', and the *Glasgow Herald* said that 'it is an ending that might have been dispensed with'. Some critics, such as Julian Symons, took the solutions offered as those of the author, and wrote : 'Plumbing plus goodswill can destroy caste distinctions. That was Anand's view at the time, but it has proved too simple.'[26] The fact, however, is that Anand has offered neither solutions nor alternatives, but merely suggested a choice of possibilities. If plumbing appeals to Bakha, there are good reasons for it.

After Bakha has been turned out of doors by his father, utterly despondent and longing for sympathy, he is approached by Colonel

Hutchinson of the local Salvation Army. Like Bakha, Hutchinson too in his own way is an outcaste: alienated from the British residents of the city and driven from home by his card-playing and hard-drinking wife. He is known to hide behind rubbish heaps, waiting for some troubled outcaste who would listen in his despair to the gospel of Christ. The Colonel is a lovable but pathetic figure who, in spite of his zeal, has had little luck with conversion, because of his broken Hindustani, his introspective nature, and a total inability to offer in concrete terms the solace of Christianity. The encounter between the missionary and Bakha is highly amusing: one wallowing in ecstatic hymn-singing, the other oblivious of the message but happy to be in contact with a 'sahib' from whom he might get a pair of cast-off trousers.

'Who is Yessuh Messih [Christ] really, Sahib?' Bakha asked, eager to allay his curiosity.

To this straightforward question the missionary answers in three stanzas from devotional songs:

'Life is found in Jesus
Only there 'tis offered thee; . . .'
'He died that we might be forgiven,
he died to make us good, . . .
'Jesus, tender shepherd, hear me.
Let my sins be forgiven! . . .'

All this adds to Bakha's confusion, but a chance sentence from the missionary goes home: Christ sacrificed Himself 'for rich and the poor, for the Brahmin and the Bhangi'. That makes sense, but it is soon lost in the nonsense the missionary creates in Bakha's mind by asking him to confess his sins to him, and God will receive him in heaven.

> He [Bakha] did't like the idea of being called a sinner. He had committed no sin that he could remember. How could he confess his sins? Odd. What did it mean, confessing sins? 'Does the Sahib want some secret knowledge?' he wondered. 'Does he want to perform some magic or get some illegal knowledge?' (p. 121).

Not only are Bakha's responses completely in harmony with his naivette, but there is tremendous irony in it. There is in his innocent questionings an obstinacy which cannot be removed by theological persuasions and which points towards the inherent weaknesses in Christianity.

But to look on the whole piece as a satire on missionary activity in India is to miss the point. The missionaries did succeed in converting thousands of people to their faith, especially from among the untouchables. If heaven remained an elusive proposition to many converts, they still accepted Christianity to ameliorate their life on this earth and to escape from the abominations of their own religion. Of the alternatives offered to Bakha during the course of the evening, this certainly was the one to have produced the quickest result. His reticence to accept it was not, as has often been claimed, owing to his conviction that 'the religion which was good enough for his forefathers was good enough for him', but because the missionary in his contact with God had lost touch with the people.

Perched on a tree, not quite unlike an ape, Bakha gets his first view of Gandhi. With superb skill, Anand fashions the image of Gandhi as we all knew him: the little man swathed in a white shawl, with his big protruding ears, expansive forehead, quixotic smile, and a determined chin. But more than these details is the magic of Gandhi, which Anand has been able to capture in this novel.[27] The raucous cries of 'Mahatma Gandhi ki jai', repeated endlessly, suddenly die out as the Mahatma raises his hand in benediction. In a brief sentence the author has summed up the unique mass appeal of Gandhi: 'This strange man seemed to have the genius that could, by a single dramatic act, rally multi-coloured, multi-tongued India to himself.' The stage is set for Gandhi to speak, but his power lies not so much in his message as in what he has come to signify to the common mind. It is for this reason that Anand devotes twice as many pages to the frenzy of the audience and to the Gandhi legend—'no sword could cut his body, no bullet could pierce his skin, no fire could scorch him!'—as to the speech itself.

Gandhi's speech is carefully drawn from his *Autobiography, Young India,* and other writings. The opening words are unintelligible to Bakha, but when the Mahatma says that he regards untouchability 'as the greatest blot on Hinduism' and elaborates on it in personal terms, pointing out how he reacted to it in childhood, Bakha is thrilled. He can appreciate Gandhi's castigation of the caste Hindus and the plea that 'temples, schools and wells should be thrown open to the outcastes', for the day's memory is fresh in his mind. But when the Mahatma asks the untouchables to improve their lot by giving up such evil habits as drinking and eating carrion, Bakha is confused and fears that the Mahatma is drifting from the main issue. The Mahatma's concluding words, 'Two of the strongest desires that keep me in the flesh are the emancipation of the Untouchables and the protection of the cow', come as a distinct shock: a very serious social evil is equated with something of far less consequence. This is certainly the case, but Gandhi is not appealing to the purely rational in man, rather to his entire self, in which religious taboos play an important part. To bracket a social evil like untouchability with an accepted religious practice like the protection of the cow is to make untouchability a very serious issue. Anand sees that Gandhi's genius lies, not in his doctrines, which are often inconsistent, but in the uncanny way he can feel the pulse of the people and win them over.

Gandhi, and what he stands for, is the second remedy offered to Bakha. But in terms of effectiveness, and despite Bakha's immense enthusiasm for those pious sentiments of the Mahatma that he has been able to follow, it is less than the muddled offering of the missionary. Bakha and his kind are to play only a nominal part in their own release; they must passively wait for a change of heart in the fickle crowd. The cause of the untouchables, one may infer, died for the present with the last reverberation of 'Harijan ki jai' shouted aloud as the Mahatma departed.

Anything following a visit by the Mahatma is bound to come as an anti-climax, and what happens in the novel is no exception. A group of people remain behind arguing over the Mahatma's views. There is much confused talk about *Vedas* and *Upanishads, maya* and *nirvana*, machine versus man, and so on, much of which could have been briefer. For the greater part of the time a young poet dominates the stage, but Bakha is too much under the Mahatma's spell to listen to anyone. But the mention of a 'machine which clears dung' and which would enable a sweeper to change his profession so that be would no longer be thought of as an untouchable, grips his attention. It also catches his fancy. But he doesn't forget the Mahatma. In fact till the machine comes he will take comfort in Gandhi's teachings. If his predilection is for the flush system, it is not because it is the best, but because it is the one that he best understands. It makes no demands on his religion, or on the compassion of others. He goes home wishing he could meet the poet on the way and find out more about the machine.

Notes

1. Anand's comments on the subject are scattered through many essays and articles. Some of the more important ones are: Preface to *The Hindu View of Art* (1933), Introduction to *The Golden Breath* (1933) and Ralph Fox's *The Novel and the People* (1944), *Apology for Heroism* (1946), 'English Novels of the Twentieth Century on India' (1943), 'New Bearings in Indian Literature' (1961), 'The Writer's Role in National Integration' (1962), 'Creative Writing in the Present Crisis' (1963), 'A Note on Modern Indian Fiction' (1965), 'Is Universal Criticism Possible?' (1966), 'The Role of Creative Writers and Artists in the Developing Countries of Afro-Asia' (1966), 'The Story of My Experiment with a White Lie' (1967), 'Old Myths and New Myths: Recital Versus Novel' (1969), 'I Believe' (1969), 'Pigeon-Indian: Some Notes on Indian-English Writing' (1971), 'The Changeling—an Indo-Anglican Novelist's Credo' (1972).
2. Letter dated 22 Nov, 1967. *Author to Critic,* pp. 14–15.
3. 'Creative Writing in the Present Crisis', *Indian Literature,* Vol. 6, No. 1, 1963, p. 74.
4. *Life and Letters To-Day,* Vol. 46, July 1945, p. 55.
5. Letter dated 25 October 1970. See *Author to Critic,* p. 101.
6. *Apology for Heroism,* p. 85.
7. F. R. Benson, *Writers in Arms*, New York: New York University Press, 1967, pp. 51–2.
8. *Apology for Heroism,* pp. 72–3.
9. Ibid., pp. 76–7.
10. 'The Story of My Experiment with a White Lie', *Indian Literature,* Vol. 10, No. 3, 1967, p. 29.
11. Ibid., p. 86.
12. Letter to Anand dated 17 July 1934. By courtesy of Mr. Anand.
13. Letter to Anand (no date). By courtesy of Mr. Anand.

14. Letter to Anand dated 12 June 1934. By courtesy of Mr. Anand.
15. Letter to Anand dated 5 May 1934. By courtesy of Mr. Anand.
16. Letter to Anand dated 9 December 1934. By courtesy of Mr. Anand.
17. Letter to Anand dated 30 November 1934. By courtesy of Mr. Anand.
18. Maurice Brown too spoke of the book's cleanness in a letter to the author dated 24 August 1934: 'The criticism, which you tell me has been made, that the book is obscene and so forth, seems to me utterly puerile: there is not, to my way of thinking, one vulgar sentence in the entire book. There are many exceedingly unpleasant ones but that is, of course, an entirely different matter.' By courtesy of Mr. Anand.
19. *Untouchable,* The Bodley Head, London, 1970, p. 38. Subsequent quotations from *Untouchable* are from the Penguin edition and are indicated by page numbers in parentheses following quotation.
20. See my Afterword to the Bodley Head edition of the novel.
21. For the inhuman treatment of untouchables see 'Plight of Harijans Today', *Link,* 2 February 1969, pp. 17–21; 'Untouchables Forever!', *Blitz,* Bombay, 19 August 1972, p .5; 'Feudal Caste Terror on Hapless Harijans', *Blitz,* Bombay, 16 December 1972, p. 3.
22. *A Passage to India,* Harcourt, Brace & World, New York, 1924, p. 217.
23. 'The Story of My Experiment with a White Lie', p. 37.
24. *The Modern India Novel in English : A Comparative Approach* Bruxelles: Université Libre de Bruxelles, 1966, pp. 66–67.
25. Sir Malcolm Darling records this conversation with his peon: 'Do you know, what "fool" means, Ghulan?' 'No, Huzoor.' 'Do you know what "damned fool" means?' 'Ah!' he exclaimed, 'those are the Sahib's words.' See M. Darling, *Apprentice to Power,* London: Hogarth Press, 1966, p. 56.
26. '*The Evils that Men Do*', *The Sunday Times*, London, 22 November 1970.
27. There is a good discussion of this in C.D. Narasimhaiah's *The Writer's Gandhi,* Patiala, Punjabi University, 1967, pp. 62–70.

Clean Book or Dirty Book? Reading Anand's *Untouchable* in the Light of Enlightenment Sanitary Discourses

NANDINI BHATTACHARYA

'How could she stand the smell? Haven't you noticed? They have a particular smell, these Paravans'[1]

It was E.M. Forster who first suggested that Mulk Raj Anand's novel *Untouchable*[2] was predicated around issues of cleanliness *versus* dirt. For Forster, however, the entire controversy regarding cleanliness and dirt revolved around the artistic feasibility of a subject exploring the life and work of an Indian scavenger. Forster was, of course, engaging with the typical Edwardian queasiness regarding frank exploration of bodily functions (such as the act of sex, or that of human beings relieving themselves), in any artistic work. Could a novelist actually speak of human excreta, and men who handled it, without committing the crime of aesthetic impropriety? Could a novel be written about 'unmentionable' things and yet not be called 'dirty'? Forster's answer to this question is an emphatic 'yes', as he states that Anand has gone straight to the heart of the matter and purified it by his sheer and brutal honesty.

Anand's frank engagement with 'low life' and 'dirty acts' in the year 1935, must be situated within the context of the Modernist agenda of deliberate and systematic breaching/demolishing of so called Victorian/Edwardian aesthetic proprieties. Mulk Raj Anand himself paid homage to James Joyce as one of his artistic masters, and it is to be noted that Joyce's *Ulysses*, which deals with such equally frank depictions of 'dirty acts' as Bloom relieving himself was disparaged as 'literature of the latrines' and denounced for its obscenities. It is these details about the dirt and squalor in an Indian sweeper boy's existence that Anand's friend and critic Bonamee Dobree urged him to tone down, so as not to offend the sensibilities of readers used to more 'clean' subjects:

> It does smell rather strong. Couldn't you give the sense of the utter beastliness of the job without going into so much physical detail? I personally don't mind, but then my stomach is strong[3] ...

Today, however, nearly 70 years after the original writing of the novel, such questions seem entirely irrelevant to a generation brought up on much sterner stuff. However, the time has come to examine this debate about cleanliness and dirt from an entirely different angle.

This particular essay attempts to explore and re-define this discourse of dirt/cleanliness, and hence re-read *Untouchable* as a text written in the crucible of the colonial encounter. *Untouchable* is informed and enriched by the great sanitary debate that was raging all over Europe, and that had been imported to the colonies as one of the major components of Enlightenment, modernity and civilisation. The Enlightenment project of the late eighteenth and early nineteenth centuries is intimately tied up with questions of cleanliness, sanitation, proper waste management and disposal, as well as their obverse, horror of dirt, germ-related disease and death. Significantly, many of the Enlightenment discourses regarding civilisation (and its obverse, barbarism) were predicated upon the sanitary question. The German scientist Justus von Leibzig wrote in the 1850s that the 'preservation of the wealth and welfare of the nations, and advances in culture and civilization depend on how the sewage question is resolved.'[4] This question of sanitation acquired a particular urgency as population growth, industrialisation and urban expansion brought in its wake virulent and recurring outbreak of infectious diseases like cholera, in 1832 and 1848. All these led to major reconstruction of urban and domestic space in Europe and America from the beginning of the nineteenth century. The valorisation of cleanliness including propagation of regular baths and prompt waste removal became an indication of one's civilisational standard.

At the same time the colonies were considered, as originating sources of these infectious diseases, especially those like cholera.

Just as the European coloniser wanted to associate himself with cleanliness, order and health were associated with progress, civilisation and culture, he was quick to identify dirt, ill-health and disease with his subject people. Tropical countries terrified colonial officials who believed that they harboured malevolent diseases and miasmas. The whole question of native 'pollution' was also a real fear of native dirt, disorder and resultant chaos. In the tropics, cleanliness was as important to British as loyalty. In India, the British settled in a zone apart from the city to secure themselves from the inhospitable biological environment of the native city. They were constantly terrorised by their memory of Asiatic choleras, which no amount of segregation would help.

This association of native spaces with 'dirt' and 'disease', and European ones with purity and cleanliness, is one of the persistent themes of Victorian novels, and Susan L. Meyer, among many, identifies the Victorian novelists' persistent fetish with the cleanliness question, and association of cleanliness with issues like progress, liberalism and emancipation. A novel like Charlotte Bronte's *Jane Eyre* (1847) for example, uses consistently, the paradigm of dirt versus cleanliness to explicate and explore some of its most vital concerns. For Bronte, clean and unclean, healthy and unhealthy environments form a central symbolic structure in the novel. In *Jane Eyre* Bronte associates unhealthy, contagious environments with racial otherness or what she calls 'that poisoned exhalation of the East.' The novel poses an opposition between 'oppressive' and 'diseased' Jamaica and 'pure' England in terms of atmosphere, and associates cleanliness with democracy, liberalism and progress.[5] Similar equation of cleanliness with civilisation/progress/ Europe, and dirt/disease with native primitivism is to be found in the enormous number in the domestic manuals of the nineteenth centuries. Even as the lives and practices of Europeans abroad were used to exemplify the civilised habits of daily and family life, the daily habits of indigenous, colonised peoples themselves were seen to demonstrate the opposite. Punctuality, and cleanliness, were seen as inherent characteristics of the European home, just as dirt, disease and disorder characterised the native homes. The march of human civilisation from barbarism, to clean, orderly, healthy living, recapitulates an Enlightenment story of progress. Fighting dirt in the colonies was as important as fighting primitive practices. Flora Annie Steel and Grace Gardiner's (the authors of the domestic manual *The Complete Indian Housekeeper and Cook*) primary intention was to bring English 'cleanliness' and 'order' into the 'dirty' barbaric Indian homes. These English women complain bitterly about the inconceivably dirty habits 'ingrained in native cooks' and the unbelievable 'dirt and slovenliness' which Indian servants were capable of.[6] 'An Indian household' they write 'can no more be governed peacefully without dignity and prestige than an Indian Empire'.[7] It is significant that the entire project of domesticity, which became one of the important components of the coloniser's civilising mission, was predicated upon questions of 'imperial cleanliness' as against 'native dirt'.[8] It is equally significant that in Europe itself, this same discourse of cleanliness equals civilisation is directed towards the working masses.[9] One of the significant acts that Professor Higgins commits (of course, by proxy) before he can undertake the mission of class transformation and upgradating a working-class flower girl, Eliza Doolittle into a lady, is the elaborate act of cleaning up (Bernard Shaw, *Pygmalion* 1916). Not only is Eliza given a thorough scrubbing but also her old working-class clothes are burnt to signify her entry into the higher strata of society. This implicit association of dirt with the lower classes and colonised subject is most potently expressed in Charles Dickens's *Bleak House* (1852–53).

The entire question of sanitation, disease, and public health was further acerbated with the rapid urbanisation, sudden explosion of population, and creation/accumulation of unmanageable waste in the European as well as Indian urban spaces. All these concerns inform and enrich our reading of *Untouchable*. Anand was after all a Westernised liberal intellectual, located for a very long period in the heart of the Western metropolis, and shared with the Western liberal intellectuals (such as Dickens), an abiding concern for sanitation, waste management, and public health of the community, at the juncture of social transition. At the same time, Anand's acute awareness that in a colonised country, the racially 'othered' native subject is overdetermined as 'dirty' and 'polluted' by his colonial masters from the very outset—problematises any simplistic reading of *Untouchable* as a text dealing with sanitation as a civic issue.

By the end of the nineteenth century, most Euro-American governments had inaugurated public health reform movements which foregrounded the importance of cleanliness, regular bathing, and prompt waste removal as civilisational practices. Simultaneously, they invested a great deal of money/effort in modern plumbing systems. Along with this, introduction of mechanical modes of waste removal resulted in the erasure of social stigma associated with the act of scavenging.

In the colonies, however, the whole outlook and approach was different, as the imperial masters had formed a preconceived notion that the natives were essentially 'dirty' and primitive, and lacking the intellectual or emotional capability to learn basic methods of hygiene. Aligning cleanliness and a sense of hygiene with civilisation and progress, William Crooke writes that a

> time will come when they [the natives] will comprehend laws of hygiene, just as at some time or other they will get rid of the abject superstition which leads them now, where they will learn to treat their women properly, to discontinue infant marriage, and emerge from the comparative barbarism in which they are plunged at present.[10]

Paradoxically enough though, it was the native's money that was used to install modern systems of sanitation in the European quarters, and the military barracks (all of which required plentiful supply of fresh water), when all the while, the natives themselves were not destined to enjoy the fruits of modern plumbing and sewerage systems. As Prashad writes, 'the officials ignored the demands of Indians for better sanitary care' ... and most colonial officials felt that 'there was no need to expend finances on those natives until the colonial officials themselves deemed the natives worthy of sanitation and hygiene.'[11] All the natives deserved was some monitoring rather than be provided with modern facilities because as one official wrote: 'the habits of natives are such that unless closely watched, they cover the entire neighbouring surface with filth.'[12]

While *Untouchable* begins with a stomach-churning description of the scavengers' colony, a veritable hell, wallowing in dirt, refuse and organic wastes, it is significant that Anand describes the Cantonment town of Balushah as clearly divided—into the cleaner/organised European Tommies quarters, and the chaotic/filthy native quarters. It is obvious from Bakha's reminiscences during his stay and work in the sahib quarters (pp.1–2) that life in the European quarters is superior, surroundings cleaner and more aesthetic. While even in the European quarters Bakha performs his job as a latrine cleaner, he is treated with greater respect, which also makes his work seem less insulting and irksome. The Tommies share with the rest of the European colonial officials in India, a revulsion for 'dirty' natives who relieve themselves on the grounds, anyhow like animals '*Kaala log, zamin par hagne wala*' and perform all kinds of noisy and disgusting ablutions in public view (pp. 10–11). For all the complex divisions of 'upper' and 'lower' caste among Hindus, it is more than apparent that for the British colonisers, all Indians are equally 'untouchable'. This revulsion of the British for Indian habits is brought out in greater force in Anand's *Coolie* where Munoo, the village boy is brutally castigated for relieving himself on the grounds. The lady of the house Bibi Uttam Kaur feels that this act of Munoo's had permanently lowered the family prestige in the eyes of their British masters, who would now regard them as barbaric savages:

> Vay, shameless, shameless, vulgar, stupid, hill-boy! ...What will the sahibs think who pass by our doors every morning and afternoon! The Babuji has his prestige to keep up with the sahibs. Hai! What a horrible, horrible mess he has made outside my door![13]

Significantly enough, while the town of Balushah does boast of a row of public toilets (serviced by Bakha's family) in the native quarters, they are in all probability used mainly by the Indian soldiers such as *havildar* Charat Ram, or some upper caste gentry like Ramanand. Poorer sections of the town and women have no access to these facilities. Bakha notes that a vast majority of men and women simply relieve themselves on the grounds. He 'recalled the familiar site of all those naked Hindu men and women who could be seen squatting in the open, outside the city, every morning' (p.11). Women are further inconvenienced by impositions of modesty and are therefore forced to use the sides of the brook to relieve themselves very early in the morning when it is half-dark (p. 79). 'Cleanliness' and 'dirt' are civilisational issues, but the advantages of clean water, proper toilets, and regular modes of waste removal are not available to most of the native population, and certainly not to the poorer section of the native population, let alone the outcastes, who are in any case condemned to live and die in filth.

The entire native quarters of Balushah resembles a garbage dump, as amenities are few, and civic responsibility even lesser. People don't think twice about dumping refuse on the corners of roads in markets places, leaving them to putrefy (p. 45), ignoring heaps of dog-shit and refuse in so-called respectable localities (p. 58) or allowing fowl, dung-squirting bulls to roam around the streets and make a mess of them (p. 44–5). Well-to-do matrons encourage children to relieve themselves besides open drains so that sweepers may directly clean them (p. 64), and throw bread to the sweeper near that very drain. It is a picture of a diseased society infected by a complex combination of malaises.

Undoubtedly it is a society whose resources are denuded as a result of imperial control, but it is also a society that suffers from complete civic apathy, along with religious bigotry, so much so that it is content to transfer the entire responsibility of civic sanitation to a community of hapless, ill-paid and marginalised people. Paradoxically (in the name of religious taboos), these very people are denied the minimum respect given even to an animal in the city. The result is a town resembling a putrefying garbage dump of which the outcaste's colony is perhaps only the metonym.

Untouchable opens with a description of the outcastes' colony conveying an overwhelming sense of filth and dirt:

> A brook ran near the lane, once with crystal-clear water now soiled by the dirt and filth of the public latrines situated about it, the odour of the hides and skins of dead carcasses left to dry on its banks, the dung of donkeys, sheep, horses, cows and buffaloes heaped up to be made into fuel cakes, and the biting, choking, pungent fumes that oozed from the sides. The absence of a drainage system had, through the rains of various seasons, made of the quarter a marsh which gave out the most offensive stink. And altogether the ramparts of human and animal refuse that lay on the outskirts

> of this little colony, and the ugliness, the squalor and the misery which lay within it, made it an 'uncongenial' place to live in (p.1).

While describing Bakha's brother Rakha 'a true child of the outcaste colony', Anand once again foregrounds those infernal conditions:

> Where there are no drains, no light, no water; of the marshland where people live among the latrines of the townsmen, and in the stink of their own dung scattered here, there and everywhere; of the world where the day is dark as the night and the night is pitch dark (p.75).

Scavengers like Bakha are condemned to live within dung-heaps, manually handle human refuse, and eat left-over, dirty food that is thrown at them like waste thrown at pariah dogs.

II

But the problems of dirt, death and disease in the sweepers' colony are not simply problems of public apathy, or social irresponsibility towards the poor. The plight of Bakha, unlike say, Jo, the London slum boy in *Bleak House* (also condemned to live in dirt, urban refuse and lingering disease) is particularly distressing because, he is also subject to ideological marginalisation in the Indian Hindu society. As a member of the *panchama* or the fifth and lowest of castes in the Hindu *varna vyavastha* (caste hierarchy), his very being is considered, 'dirty', 'impure' and 'polluted', and hence he is condemned as 'untouchable' by the 'caste Hindus'. It is significant that the very term *caste* (Portuguese/Spanish *casta*), which was the term that Europeans used from about 1800, to describe this Hindu practice of segregating/stratifying social groups, is derived from the Latin term *castus*, 'chaste' which means *pure*, or *unmixed.* Thus inherent to the Hindu caste system is the belief in the essential 'impurity, 'dirt' or 'pollution' of one group of people *vis-à-vis* the inherent 'purity', or 'cleanliness' of the other.

While various kinds of taboos about why a particular group of people in the Hindu society were condemned as 'untouchable' existed in the early twentieth century, almost all over British India, communities who dealt with human refuse (scavengers), organic waste products such as hair, or nail clippings (barbers), handled dead humans/animals (*doms* and *chamars*), or washed dirty clothes (*dhobi*) were shunned as 'dirty', 'polluted', and hence, culturally dysfunctional. The social scientist Louis Dumont aptly sums up the caste system as being predicated upon the issue of *purity* and *impurity:*

> Why, it may be asked, this separation of the Untouchables? May it be supposed, for example, that it is due to the nauseating smells of the skins they are accustomed to treat? Hygiene is often invoked to justify ideas about impurity. In reality, even though the notion may be found to contain hygienic associations, these cannot account for it, as it is a religious notion (p. 47) ... It is clear that the impurity of the Untouchable is conceptually inseparable from the purity of the Brahman.[14]

While the 'pure castes' may be temporarily defiled, or rendered 'polluted' during the excretory act, during menstruation (for women), or while coming in contact with a dead or diseased body, these non-permanent states of ritual pollution or dirt could be cleaned by a purificatory bath or other purificatory rituals. However, the 'untouchable' remained in a perpetual state of 'dirt' or 'pollution' which no amount of *shuddhikaran* (purification) could undo. Going on to enumerate the number of ways in which an 'untouchable' is rendered 'polluted' and 'unclean' perpetually, Dumont goes on to conclude that in the Hindu conception of caste, 'the execution of impure tasks by some is necessary to the maintenance of purity for others'.[15]

As Bakha says, 'They treat us like dirt because we clean their dirt.' This very question of ritual pollution makes caste Hindus relegate these essential service providers to the margins of society and treat them with such inhuman contempt. This is one reason why Bakha is insulted by one and sundry when he accidentally touches a caste Hindu. The 'touched' man bursts out in savage anger; 'Do you know you have touched me and defiled me ... Now I will have to go and take a bath to purify myself ... Don't you know you brute, that you must not touch me!' (p. 38). Here the terms *dirt* and *cleanliness* take on an altogether different, ritualistic, and culture-specific meaning. In an attempt to calm down his rebellious son, Bakha's father Lakha tries to explain away the Hindu society's revulsion for sweepers as mere religious prejudice, which has got nothing to do with real hatred for them that 'it is [their] religion which prevents them from touching us' (p. 74). However, for all of Lakha's Uncle Tom-like spirit of acceptance, it is a difficult argument to buy in the context of the inhuman atrocities that are heaped upon the 'untouchables', all in the name of 'fear of ritual pollution' or 'impurity', throughout Anand's novel.

Even drinking water, which is the basic requirement of life, is not available to these people, as apparently, their 'dirty' touch will 'pollute' the public wells and ponds. Sohini, Bakha's sister, has to wait patiently (while her family is parched with thirst) till a Brahmin pundit offers her water, and that too after an insulting, and implied insinuation of future, sexual dalliance in exchange for this 'favour' (p. 20–2).

Sometimes issues of caste, class, and race combine to produce a virulent brand of prejudice and hatred. The *memsahib* Mary Hutchinson's angry denunciation of Bakha (with whom her husband Colonel Hutchinson has been spending time, while his tea is getting cold), is an excellent example of hatred that is born out of a complex mixture of caste, class, and racial prejudices. Predictably, here again, the controlling discursive paradigm is that of 'cleanliness'/'dirt'—'Oh, is that what you' been doing, going to these blackies again! ... I can't keep waiting for you all day while you go messing about with all those dirty *bhangis* and *chamars*' (pp. 122–23).

The issue of cleanliness/dirt is lifted to an altogether different plane in Mahatma Gandhi's speech at the end of the novel, where he exhorts the caste Hindus to abolish the evil practice of untouchability, using the argument that the dirt and pollution associated with the sanitary workers is temporary and external, rather than permanent and intrinsic. The 'untouchable' cleans dirt, comes in constant contact with dirt, and is therefore considered dirty; however, if he cleans himself, he is no longer 'untouchable.' Here Gandhi is performing a paradigm shift, by relocating the issue of untouchability, to, not any ritualistic or essential impurities, but to concerns of hygiene—that is, to external or ephemeral dirt. By reframing the issue of ritual and religious pollution (which is hereditary and hence intrinsic) as an issue related to sanitation, (that is, external dirt which can be cleaned), Gandhi is, as it were, trying to redefine these age-old issues (of ritual purity/impurity) on the discursive lines of colonial modernity. Dirt is bad because it brings ill-health and disease; so anyone who touches dirt must be shunned till he has cleaned himself. As a panacea for untouchability, he again uses the enlightenment discourse of cleanliness: 'They have, therefore, to purify their lives. They should cultivate the habits of cleanliness, so that no one shall point his fingers at them' (p. 138). Gandhi wants to show that there is nothing inherently 'dirty' about a sweeper, except the circumstances, which he has been thrust into.

Gandhi's argument in Anand's *Untouchable* (which is incidentally taken from many of his actual speeches),[16] must be seen within the context of the propagandist activity of Hindu groups at the turn of the century, who employed enlightenment discourses of cleanliness equals modernity equals progress, while attempting to enlist the support of the Dalit classes. In an attempt to couch the age-old prejudices about ritual pollution, in more modern and 'scientific' language, Dalits were exhorted to lead 'clean' lives, that is, live in clean surroundings, clean their bodies and wear clean clothes, as contact with dirt would lead to pollution and disease. Prashad notes:

> B.S. Moonje of the Hindu Mahasabha, in a speech to the Provincial Balmiki Conference in Amritsar in 1927, declared that the dalits must abandon 'evil habits and customs in the interest of their self purification and ultimate fusion on terms of equality with the so called touchable classes.' Liberation would only come if dalits abandoned a set of 'evil habits.' First 'uncleanliness, because it breeds disease and is against religion and the laws of hygiene.' The laws of hygiene (modernity) and religion (tradition) come together to enjoin cleanliness as they do in much of the reformation's ideology. Second, the 'use of leavings of food' should be avoided 'because it indicates loss of self respect and carries several diseases to the persons eating them.' Third, eating of carrion should be stopped because they are a veritable cause of perpetrating untouchabilty and forbidden from medical standpoint as well.[17]

This fusion of the modern and traditional discourse (regarding cleanliness/dirt) and this rephrasing/reframing and thereby revalidating of the traditional in terms of colonial modernity seems to be the essence of the Hindu (as well as Gandhian) approach to the problems of untouchability as well as the conditions of the Dalit classes. The traditional practice of untouchability is thus given a scientific, and modern basis, shifting the blame of dirt/pollution/lack of hygiene/disease on to the very group of people who are most affected by it.

In addition, Gandhi extended the meaning of the words 'clean' and 'dirty' to include questions of 'ethics'.[18] The Dalits are exhorted to lead 'clean lives' in the sense that they are forbidden to drink alcohol, gamble, and visit houses of prostitutes. In order to emancipate themselves they have to purify themselves. They have to rid themselves of evil habits, like drinking liquor and eating carrion. (p.139). Significantly, a similar rhetoric was directed towards the working poor in Britain, in an effort to create a 'moral' basis for aristocracy. Gandhi wanted to create an ethical and scientific/modern basis for caste hierarchies.

All the while, Gandhi, like other militant Hindu groups was well aware of how the *dalit* colonies had been completely abandoned by municipalities and lacked basic amenities like water or drainage facilities. Gandhi noted that the Dalit colonies in Delhi were 'the worst of any I had seen' and tenements resembled black holes where people were crammed up in small rooms, sharing very few water taps and ramshackle latrines. Rameshwari Nehru's (a Gandhian ideologue) observations sum up the situation:

> As long as sweepers live in their present surroundings, no work can be done amongst them by any reformist organization. It is no use trying to teach them to be clean or to keep their children clean when they are forced to live in filth from which they cannot get away.[19]

I find *Untouchable* so fascinating a text, because I locate, embedded within its texture, an implicit rejection of these attempts on the part of caste Hindus, to blame the sweepers of dirt and pollution, when the society has virtually condemned them to live and work within it. For all his implicit support of Gandhi, Anand registers Bakha's rejection of the Gandhian view that *harijans* must purify their lives to earn acceptability. Reacting to Gandhi's plea about how 'untouchables' should 'purify' their lives, Bakha notes; ' But now the Mahatma is blaming us … That is not fair!' (p. 139).

Throughout the novel, Anand notes that Bakha and his kind do not even have enough water to drink, let alone waste it in washing and appearing clean. Describing their kitchen, the narrator observes:

> Most of the utensils were of clay, darkened by the soot of many fires, and never washed since Bakha's mother had died, for Sohini was young and inexperienced … Besides, there was a scarcity of water. And since, on account of their profession, and the filthy surroundings in which they were forced to live, they needed more than a pitcherful of water, but could not get it, they just did without; till sanitation, cleanliness and hygiene had lost its meaning for them (p. 67).

The term 'pitcherful of water' is particularly significant as early in the novel, the narrator reveals the extent of deprivation these people suffer, owing to lack of this basic amenity. Bakha comes back home after back-breaking labour only to find the pitcher empty, and his throat parched for a drop (p. 13–14). The humiliation and torture of young Sohini for 'a pitcherful of water' is one of the poignant highlights of the novel (pp. 20–22). Even when water is available, the untouchables are stopped from touching it because according to the Manichean logic of caste Hindus that the dirty touch of untouchables will pollute the water, and render it unfit to be drunk/used only by the 'pure' castes.[20]

The food available for the untouchables is the soft and rotting leftovers of higher castes, which even Bakha, at times finds nauseating (p. 76). Surely, the narrator is being deliciously ironic when he comments, watching the 'untouchable' family sit down to have dinner; 'They all ate from the same basket and the same bowl, not apportioning the food in different plates as the Hindus do, for the original Hindu instinct for cleanliness had disappeared long ago' (p. 76).

In another significant passage, the narrator describes the dirty, lousy appearances of the untouchables as they come out to enjoy the purity of the winter sun, as if the 'taint of the dark, narrow, dingy little prison cells of their one-roomed homes lurked them, however, even in the outdoor air' (p. 27).

I see *Untouchable* as Anand's way of redefining (and rephrasing) the terms 'cleanliness'/'dirt' or 'purity'/'impurity', locating the 'dirt' amidst 'pure' castes, who take advantage of these so called 'dirty' hapless people, at every step, denying them even the minimum respect that is granted to an animal. In a telling incident, the narrator goes on to show how caste Hindus do not mind 'touching' a disgusting, onion-belching, liquid-dung-squirting bull, but do not hesitate to publicly humiliate and assault a human being (Bakha) because he has accidentally touched, and 'polluted' them (p. 38).

'Cleanliness' and 'dirt' take on another meaning, when the reader witnesses the 'pure' Brahmin priest (who has both sex, and excretion on his mind) leering at the sweeper girl Sohini, and giving her a pitcher of water in exchange for promise that she would come to sweep his house so that he could take sexual advantage of her. He goes on shamelessly to molest Bakha's sister, and then cover up his crime by claiming he has been polluted by the scavenger-girl's touch.

Anand's protagonist Bakha (sometimes acting as the mouth-piece of his liberal creator) shares his creator's horror of the complete lack of hygiene and civic sense among caste Hindus. The incident of the woman encouraging her son to defecate near the open drains so that the sweeperboy could clean it up shows a lack of decency, and civic sense which even animals possess to a degree. The British Tommies' disgust of native habits of defecation ('*Kala admi, zamin par hagne wala*') is shared by Anand as well as his sensitive protagonist.

The most significant protest so far as caste Hindu condemnation of untouchables as 'dirty' comes in the figure of Bakha who is surprisingly 'clean' in body and mind, despite of the dirty job he performs, and despite the filthy environment he inhabits. Even the high-caste *havildar* Charat Singh admits unwittingly, 'Here was a low-caste man who seemed clean!' (p. 8), and that too after Bakha has emerged from the disgusting job of manually cleaning human excreta from the box-pit latrines. As the narrator notes with admiration, 'And though his job was dirty he remained comparatively clean. He didn't even soil his sleeves, handling the commodes, sweeping and scrubbing them' (p. 8).

Bakha's exotic dress-sense comprising of a British soldier's uniform of shirt, boots and puttees, gives him an odd air of distinction.

His deliberate wearing of sahib's clothes is a mode of defiance, a protest that somehow 'removed him above his odorous world' (p. 8).

His inherent sense of self-respect and desire to overcome his circumstances is expressed in his disgust directed at his brother Rakha's appearance and animal-like habits (p. 75); his family's habits of eating left-over, dirty food, thrown at them as if they were dogs (pp. 75–76); his attempts to excel in sports such as hockey, and his burning desire to read like the babu's sons, and enjoy epics such as *Heer Ranjha*. Added to this is his fascination for the sahib's way of life, which of course implies a longing for modernity, an alternative mode of existence where he would be free from caste-prejudices, and other age-old superstitions. All these instincts render Bakha as one of the cleanest characters in the novel.

While many have condemned the ending of *Untouchable* as simplistic,[21] Bakha's fascination for the water closet, the machine that handles dung, is an expression of his desire for a cleaner, a more human and dignified life, where a set of people will not be condemned to handle other people's 'dirt'.

Like Forster, the reader is forced to admit that *Untouchable* is a profoundly 'clean' novel 'because it has gone straight to the heart of its subject and purified it'.[22]

NOTES

1. Arundhati Roy, *The God of Small Things,* New Delhi: IndiaInk, 1997: 257.
2. The 1935 edition; all subsequent quotations are from the Penguin edition of 2001.
3. 'Letter to Anand' dated 12 June 1934, in S. Cowasjee, *So Many Freedoms: A Study of the Major Fiction of Mulk Raj Anand,* New Delhi: OUP, 1977, p. 43.
4. Karl Kautsky, *The Agrarian Question,* New York: Harper Collins p. 54.
5. See Susan Meyer's 'Colonialism and Figurative Strategy of *Jane Eyre'* in *Post-Colonial theory and English Literature: A Reader, ed.* Peter Childs, Endinburgh: Edinburgh, 1999.
6. F.A. Steel, and G. Gardiner. *The Complete Indian Housekeeper and Cook.* 1888, London: Heinemann, 1902, p. 9.
7. Ibid., p. 9.
8. Refer to Jean Comaroff, and John Comaroff 'Home-Made Hegemony'

in *African Encounters with Domesticity*, ed. K. Hansen, New Brunswick: Rutgers University Press, 1992. Also see Vijay Prashad 'Native Dirt/ Imperial Ordure: The Cholera of 1832 and the Morbid Resolutions of Modernity,' *Journal of Historical Sociology,* Vol. 7, No. 3, September 1994, 252–57. Refer to Dipesh Chakraborty's 'The Difference–Deferral of Colonial Modernity: Public debates on Domesticity in Colonial Bengal' in *Tensions of Empire: Colonial Cultures in a Bourgeois World,* eds, Fredrick Cooper and Anne L. Stoler, Berkely: University of California Press, 1997, for information about how colonial discourse of cleanliness and order were internalised by upper-class Bengalis in British India.

9. For associations of dirt/disorder with the lower classes, see Lenore Davidoff and Catherine Hall's *Family Fortunes: Men and Women of the English Middle Class, 1780–1850*, Chicago: University of Chicago Press, 1987.
10. Prashad, *Untouchable Freedom: A Social History of the Dalit Community,* New Delhi: Oxford University Press, 2000, pp. 47–48.
11. Ibid., p. 47.
12. Ibid.
13. Anand, *Coolie,* p.28.
14. Louis Dumont, *Homo Hiearchichus: Caste and its Implications,* 1970. Tr. Sainsbury, Dumont and Gulati. New Delhi: Oxford University Press, 1998, p. 54.
15. Ibid., p. 55.
16. In *Navajivan*, 17 July 1921, Gandhi wrote 'If a Bhangi has been engaged in sanitary work, to take a bath [after contact with him] is simple hygiene and is absolutely necessary, but failure to do so does not threaten one with spiritual ruin.'
17. Prashad, *Untouchable Freedom,* p. 82.
18. In *Navajivan,* 17 July 1921, and *Harijan,* 11 February 1933, Gandhi states that Dalits must abandon 'bad and filthy habits to which they may be addicted' such as 'beef carrion and liquor' and lead 'clean lives'.
19. Rameshwari Nehru 'Harijan Bastis in Delhi,' *Harijan,* 24 April 1937.
20. Using of public facilities such as wells and ponds was a recurrent bone of contention between militant Dalits and caste Hindus. Significantly, in 1927, Dr. B.R. Ambedkar led a *satyagraha* to establish the right of the untouchables to draw water from a public tank at Mahad in Maharashtra, and won the ensuing legal battle in the Bombay High Court in 1937.
21. E.M. Forster was the first to suggest that the ending might be a little inconclusive but many other reviewers such as those belonging to *The*

Evening News, Star, and the *Glasgow Herald* criticised the endings as 'simplistic' or even 'comic.' Refer to Saros Cowasjee's *So Many Freedoms: A Study of the Major Fictions of Mulk Raj Anand,* Delhi: OUP, for more on this subject.

22. E.M. Forster, 'Preface' *Untouchable*, p. *v*.

'The Great Little Man': The Body as a Structural Motif in Mulk Raj Anand's *Untouchable*

NILADRI RANJAN CHATTERJEE

Early in Mulk Raj Anand's *Untouchable* (1935), when the protagonist Bakha is shown at work, Anand comments, 'It seemed as if burning or *destruction* was for him a form of *physical* culture[1] (italics mine).' Towards the end of the novel there is a scene where a crowd, eager to find quick access to a public meeting that Gandhi is scheduled to address, tramples across a garden. The author glosses the incident: 'It was as if they knew, by an instinct surer than that of conscious knowledge, that the things of old civilisation must be *destroyed* in order to make room for those of the new'. (italics mine, p.127). In these two quotations I find a compressed figuration of a structure that may be discerned in the novel. The Poundian dictum to 'make it new' looms unmistakably behind the lines, as does the egomaniacal modernists' confidence in themselves to beat a new path, even if it meant riding roughshod over whatever preceded them. While this analysis of the structure of the *Untouchable* will not be exclusively an attempt to establish its modernist credentials, it will be based on the supposition that Mulk Raj Anand effects an organic synthesis of form and content in the novel. He ekphrastically reproduces in the structure what he tries to communicate in the content. Anand builds up a binary form in the narrative—in replication of the touchable/untouchable binary in the narrative—and 'destroys' it towards the end. In so doing he performs in writing what he urges the untouchable to do as political activism: the old order must change yielding place to the new. He performs social writing as a correctivist activity—and advocates 'social righting'. The form seems clearly inspired by a nineteenth-century equation of physical ugliness with mental pollution[2] and then that form is demolished mostly by the introduction of one figure in whose personality the equation is rendered invalid. Indeed, the historical figure that is used to do the demolition is well-known to have taken actual pride in his physical unprepossessiveness. What I shall try to do in this essay initially is to show how the body can be a site of social performance, resistance, and aspiration while reifying notions of morality. I shall then show how Anand complicates the site by introducing a moral disjunction between what lies on the surface and what lies beneath.

Informing this analysis will be the concepts of alterity, of binary opposition and of the body as a social construction (borrowing from the disability studies inaugurated by Lennard J. Davis[3])—concepts that are post-modernist. This may apparently seem anachronistic to a novel written when modernism had just reached its apogee. However, the widely-acknowledged amorphosity of post-modernism should counter any such anxiety. The term 'alterity' may be defined as the 'otherness' of people, events, ideas that are radically different from those or of those who are in a position of power and has been used by theorists, especially those who are post-colonial, such as Gayatri Chakraborty Spivak and Homi K. Bhabha.[4] The idea of the binary opposition is a corollary of alterity because the cleaving of any narrative into two sides, one in opposition to the other, is the way in which the nature of alterity in that narrative can be detected. It is such a binary, such a detection of alterity that operates in the disability studies of Lennard J. Davis. He suggests that human bodies have been binarised into normal and abnormal, ideal and less-than-ideal by forces starting from the eighteenth-century eugenics to today's Hollywood movies. The disabled body is therefore marginalised, just as the able-bodied is centred. Mulk Raj Anand may be continuing this binarised valorisation of the ideal body at the cost of the less-than-ideal, but he effects a twist in the binary by situating the able-bodied protagonist in the margins and the 'little' people in the centre. He disrupts the stereotypical conjunction between the ideal body and socio-economic centrality. It is this disjunction which gives the binary oppositions in the novel a complexity it would not have had otherwise.

The Intra-Personal Binary

Eighteen-year-old Bakha, the character whose point of view organises the narrative, has a body that is valorised consistently as noble and masculine—'Here is a *man*' (italics mine, p.12). He is a 'superb specimen of humanity' (p. 56) with a 'lithe, active frame' (p. 57). At several points in the narrative we are told about his hefty shoulders (p. 39). He is seen as a young and healthy animal with close-knit sinews (p. 74). He is a big, strong man, 'broad-shouldered, heavy-hipped, supple-armed' (p. 111). His face is not only 'exquisitely well-defined crowning a 'very fine physique' (p. 12) but he has 'glistening high cheek-bones' (p. 45) and a 'fine, full quivering underlip' (p. 46). He is also shown to be obviously sensual, thereby underscoring the aura of masculine sexuality that the author clearly wants the reader to be aware of. The raw unharnessed sexuality that the descriptions are aglow with is furthered by descriptions of his incestuous feelings, albeit transient, towards his sister (p. 55–6) and his desire to rape a young woman he pictures naked at bath (p.79). This sensual and physically powerful being is, however, circumscribed. His cage is the social space he has been assigned, one which he has no socio-political agency to break out of. Bakha's space, be it physical, sexual or geographical, is marked by a sense of indiscipline and formlessness. Just as his sexual feelings are directed at his own sister as easily as it is directed towards a friend's sister, the Indian costume he is supposed to wear is 'shapeless'. The colony where he lives is a miasma of filth and disorderly planning, inducing claustrophobia: a claustrophobia which is dramatised by his difficulty to breathe in the 'congested climate' of the corner of the room where he sleeps (p. 6). The kitchen of Bakha's home is a space where an empty trash basket, a can, two earthen pitchers and a chipped enamelled jug lie 'scattered about' (p. 67).

Bakha resists this general lack of order by cultivating a taste for the opposite. He organises his clothes along the sparse lines of the European silhouette, organises his sexual feelings by reprimanding himself for having lustful thoughts about his sister, organises his colonial gender by forcing himself to develop a distaste for jewellery (p. 47). Thus, just as his body performs the task of cleaning latrines and bears the sartorial mark of his status by always keeping the turban on, it also performs social resistance by garbing itself in the dress of a 'sahib'. Bakha is at the receiving end of dual oppression. He is a British subject and an untouchable, and therefore twice removed from the centre, twice marginalised. His act of resistance is therefore to adopt sartorial markers of power and of a centred social identity. Although the sight of Bakha in shabby European clothes may appear as ridiculous as Dr. Stockmann strutting about in his brother Mayor's hat and with the mace of office in Ibsen's *An Enemy of the People*, both are performances of social aspiration and resistance to the status quo. In his desire to dress like a sahib, Bakha is ably assisted by his body. As noted above, the physiognomy of Bakha's body is constantly valorised in terms of visual beauty. The author's anxiety that the reader should notice Bakha's mesomorphic body is driven by a need to establish the protagonist's physicality as one which is at odds with the position of disempowerment in which it finds itself.

While every reference to Bakha's body is fed with connotations of power, it is shown to operate in a sphere designated for the *dis*empowered. Bakha's determined espousal of English sartorial rules is his way of minimising the humiliation of being subjected to Indian caste rules. His body also seems particularly resistant to the identity-fixing item of the turban. There are at least two occasions in the narrative where his turban comes undone (pp. 9, 44). (That the turban functions as an objective correlative of humble status is underscored later when Col. Hutchinson of the Salvation Army adopts it as part of his patronising attempt to Indianise his appearance and thus, hopefully, endear himself to the natives, p. 112.) Here it should be mentioned that in his sartorial act of (conscious or unconscious) resistance, Bakha is not alone. His two cohorts Ram Charan and Chota share his taste for all things English (p. 87) and are therefore such close companions of his. They get to share a space that Bakha has denied even his own now-departed mother (p. 6). However, Ram Charan does not possess the striking masculinity of Bakha's form. He is, on the contrary, a 'very bony, thin little figure', a stereotype requirement of an 'untouchable'. Bakha's father is also given the stereotypical body of 'a putrefying corpse' (p. 74).

Bakha's self-empowering interest in all things English also lies behind his smoking, albeit furtive (p. 34), his acquisition of a 'broken cane chair' (p. 14), and his desire to speak the empowering language of English (p. 30). The broken cane chair emblematises Bakha's reception of the colonial master's culture. It is second-hand, imperfect, unstable and yet reifying power. The emblematic function of the cane chair is also performed by the solar topee which hangs at the barracks of the 38th Dogras. Stories and legends swirl around the piece of headgear, thereby mythologising it and thus investing it with a power irresistible to Bakha, among other 'natives'. Although he longs to know the true story behind the hat, he has not the courage to ask the sepoys standing guard outside. He even considers stealing the topee. In fact he had asked the sepoys about the hat when he was a child but now as an adult he has lost that wild, careless, dauntless freedom of the child'(p. 93). Here I would like to dwell on the contradictory function that the Englishing of his personality is performing on Bakha. His 'English-apeing mind' (p. 46) gives him a sense of liberation as well as works as an insidious strategy of containment. It has given him a sense of empowerment at the cost of his child-like 'wild, careless, dauntless freedom'. Bakha embodies a palimpsest of contradictions. He is an 'untouchable' who is physically beautiful. He is an Indian who aspires to dress like an Englishman. He espouses the visual/behavioral makers of power, and yet performs his socially-marginalising work of cleaning toilets with ease and grace. This contradictory aspect extends also to his mind, in the sense, on the one hand he accepts his inferior position in society and on the other, feels a superior 'queer sadistic delight staring at the beggars moaning for alms but not receiving any' (p. 125).

The Inter-Personal Binary

Bakha's powerful physicality and yet its restricted field of play is contrasted in the novel by the opposite side of the binary. Here, upper-caste Hindus are consistently represented as physically unimposing. Their position of social puissance is shown to be at comic odds with their physical weakness. Pundit Kali Nath has a 'bony, hollow-cheeked, deeply-furrowed face' (p.18) and 'lanky little limbs' (p.

19). The author informs us that 'one push from his [Bakha's] hefty shoulders would have been enough to unbalance the skeleton-like bodies of the Hindu merchants' (p. 39). The man Bakha accidentally touches in the crowded market has a 'little body' (p. 42). A 'wrinkled old Hindu' touches a bull's feet (p. 44–5). The priest who is 'defiled' by Bakha in the temple is 'lanky' and 'little' (p. 52). It is interesting that the closer one gets to the centre of power, the weaker one's body gets! Col. Hutchinson's physiognomy leaves us in no doubt as to his centrality. He is a 'short fellow, pitiably weak and hobbling along on his stick' (p. 113). This description follows two pages after Bakha is described as 'a big, strong man, broad-shouldered, heavy-hipped, supple-armed ...' in spite of the 'poor nourishment he got' (p. 111), thereby making the contrast as stark as possible.

There is however a further level of sophistication in the positing of this binary. Those Indians who do not adversely impact on Bakha's day are spared the Hogarthian caricature of an unattractive appearance. The priest who blows a conch-shell inside the temple is entirely unaware of Bakha's existence and is therefore guiltlessly eroticised, deploying almost the same descriptive devices used unfailingly for the latter. He is 'tall ... naked, save for a loin-cloth, darkhaired and supple, with a sacred thread throwing into relief the beautiful curves of his graceful body...' (p. 51). So, the physical confrontations or encounters that take place between Bakha and representatives of the Hindu upper-class or the ruling race are marked by incongruities on both sides, favourable on the side of Bakha, unfavourable on the side of his interlocuter or adversary.

The Hindu who impacts on Bakha's day favourably is shown to be Bakha's physical equal: Havildar Charat Singh. He is a hockey player and therefore a strong and sturdy sportsman. His humane, even affectionate behaviour towards Bakha is clearly supported by the author and thus made to exemplify the handsome-is-as-handsome-does correlation between physical beauty and mental health. The fact that the Havildar does not think twice about sending Bakha into his kitchen to get some burning coal for his hookah or that he offers Bakha tea or that he gifts Bakha a new hockey stick is valorised and clearly held as examples of an enlightened attitude towards the 'untouchables'.

COLLAPSING THE BINARIES

Having constructed such a sophisticated binary on two levels: intra- and inter-personal, Mulk Raj Anand collapses the binaries with a non-fictional entrant in the narrative: the 'great little man' Mahatma Gandhi, the man with the little body but 'great soul'. The appearance of Gandhi in the novel not only dissolves both the binaries but also dilutes the fictionality of the narrative. The narrative takes on the discursive features of reportage and yet blends Bakha's subjectivity into it in order to blur the differentiating line between fact and fiction, just as the author blurs the binarising lines discussed above. Gandhi is Winston Churchill's 'half-naked fakir'; his garb does not have any markers of power. He does not wear a solar topee, which could have bestowed on him a sense of power. His head is known for its bareness. In Anand's words, Gandhi's head is 'dark', 'clean-shaven', and 'well-oiled' (p. 133). And yet he is mythologised in the same way that the solar topee is. He is the '*avatar* (incarnation) of the gods Vishnu and Krishna', spiders weave his portraits, 'no sword could cut his body, no bullet could pierce his skin, no fire could scorch him!' (p. 128).

The discursive strategy deployed for Gandhi consists of several other features, one such feature being attempts to suggest his centrality and power. This is done by invoking earlier incidents where power and centrality are represented. Just as the solar topee is encrusted with mythologies that lift it from a mere item of headgear to an icon, commanding reverence and awe, Gandhi generates his own mythologies that work as a counter-narrative to mythologies surrounding the solar topee. Mythologies underscoring British power are countered by mythologies of Indian resistance being funnelled through the personality of Gandhi. He becomes as indestructible as the aura of power that surrounds a sahib. Gandhi's dress consisted of a dhoti which he wore like a loin-cloth and went otherwise bare-bodied. This should remind us of the handsome priest inside the temple who is also naked except for a loin-cloth. The solar-topee's mythology-generating capacity and the loin-cloth are both associated with power. Gandhi generates mythology and wears a loin-cloth made out of a dhoti. The irony here is that Gandhi had decided to espouse the dhoti tied like a loin-cloth not to align himself to power but to signal his solidarity with the powerless. As Ved Mehta quotes one of Gandhi's apostles, 'He wanted to wear or use only what was within the means of any peasant, however poor.'[5] There is a nebulosity, an amorphosity about the personality of Gandhi which resists not only any kind of binarist or identity labelling or fixing, but also continually frustrates physiognomic deductions. It is interesting that in the course of a single paragraph Anand detects 'something Mephistophelean in [Gandhi's] determined little chin' and yet finds 'something beautiful and saintly in the face ...'(p. 133). This echoes a perception of Gandhi quoted by Ved Mehta. Says a follower of Gandhi, 'Sometimes I remember him as small and unimpressive-looking, other times as a tall silhouette. Sometimes I think he must have had rickets as a child, because in my mind I picture him as crooked ... But at other times I remember him as having perfect posture.'[6] Just as a good actor can never have two roles that are ever exactly alike, Gandhi also resists being fixed with any one personality in the public imagination—yet another way in which Gandhi proves disruptive in the novel.

Here is a 'little' man who centres himself in the discourse that is shaping and is being shaped by a nation's constitution of her own identity through difference (Indians are all things that the British are *not*) and overtly advocates the inclusion of those marginalised by the difference of caste and profession. Unlike the other 'little' men in the novel, Gandhi speaks on behalf of Bakha and his 'untouchable' brethren. Gandhi invalidates the qualification of a binary argued earlier, namely that those who impact Bakha negatively are shown to be 'little'. He impacts Bakha *positively* and *yet* is 'little'.

Once this collapsing of binaries has been effected, Anand continues the collapsing by introducing two new characters into the narrative—both Muslim, but one Westernised and the other not so. One is a barrister like Gandhi but has fashioned himself as a 'desi sahib' (p. 141), as Bakha would ideally like to constitute himself. The other wears his 'desi' identity in the form of 'flowing ... robes' (p. 141). Mr. R.N. Bashir has all the sartorial markers of westernisation and the verbal markers to match—because he is imperiously critical of Gandhi calling him 'a humbug'—but these markers are undercut by the fact that he is 'too sallow-faced for an Englishman' (p. 141). So his body functions as a counter-narrative to his clothes and political stance, thereby frustrating his aspirations to centrality. His 'flowing robed' friend, Iqbal Nath Sarshar, has no desire to be a 'desi sahib' and is attributed with 'a delicate feline face, illuminated by sparkling dark eyes and long black curly hair' (p. 141)—physical attributes that are more attractive that a 'sallow face'. By doing this, Anand is clearly valorising one identity formation over another. The fact that the Indian subjects, in the political sense, must attain confidence in their own sartorial markers and appearance, and not attempt to acquire a sense of empowerment and confidence by espousing the cultural markers of their colonial masters, is being communicated. Whereas Mr. Bashir is reduced to a Dickensian caricature, Sarshar is projected as the poet who unwittingly beckons Bakha towards a future of respect and dignity. Bakha decides to tell his father 'all that Gandhi said about us and all that that poet said' (p. 148). By giving Gandhi and Sarshar equal status in this sentence Anand is effecting the recommendation of a way of social progress. It is not a coincidence that both these figures—one historial, the other fictional—have constructed for themselves an identity through a conscious process of othering. If identity exists through difference, then the sanctioned and preferred identity of the colonised created by the author is clearly one which is built on its difference from that of the coloniser. Anand seems to be saying that just as the water-closet looms in the distance as 'the machine' which will rid Bakha and other 'untouchables' of the social taint of uncleanliness and menality, constituting a visually identifiable Indian identity will rid Bakha and indeed Mr. Bashir of the cultural subservience to their colonial masters.

The body and clothes, therefore, function not only as binarising tools in Mulk Raj Anand's *Untouchable* but also underscore the socio-political imperative that lies behind the narrative. The clothed or unclothed human body operates as a site for the performance of power or lack of it, be it social, political or physical. Through the text we find examples of clothes and the body in semiotic conflict with each other or in harmony with each other, performing resistance or subservience, marking centrality or marginality, carrying authorial approval or opprobrium, but always reifying the central concern of the narrative—marking difference, marking binaries, signalling the need for social change.

NOTES

1. Mulk Raj Anand, *Untouchable*. All subsequent quotations are from the Penguin edition of 2001.
2. The novels of Charles Dickens are prime examples of the handsome-is-as-handsome-does school of thought, but only in reverse. Which is to say, handsome-does-as-handsome-is. Characters who are meant to be perceived in a favourable light are hardly ever ugly, whereas the rogue's gallery of Dickensian villians is populated with ugly people, be it Fagin or Uriah Heep. Steerforth is the exception that proves the rule.
3. I refer to his book *Enforcing Normalcy: Disability, Deafness and the Body* published in 1995.
4. My definition of 'alterity' is partially taken from Vircent B. Leitch (Gen. ed.), *The Norton Anthology of Theory and Criticism*, New York and London, 2001, p. 2193.
5. Ved Mehta. *Mahatma Gandhi and His Apostles*, Middlesex: Penguin. 1977, p. 3. All subsequent references in the text as MG.
6. Ibid., P.3.

Annotated Bibliography

This bibliography is divided into two sections, A and B. Section A provides information about the caste system in the Indian subcontinent, the nature of its evolution, and the modes of its flourishing in contemporary India; and lists the protest literature against the menace of caste segregation. Section B deals with books/book chapters/review articles explicating Mulk Raj Anand's writings, especially *Untouchable*.

A

Berreman, Gerald. *Caste and other Inequities*. Meerut: Folklore Institute, 1979. This book is an important critique of Dumont's thesis and notes that caste systems in India are based on unequal and differential access to the most valuable things of life such as land and water. The real difference between upper and lower castes is not purity of the former and impurity of the latter but power, plenty and security of one and vulnerability, want and anxiety of the other.

Dumont, Louis. *Homo Hiearchicus: The Caste System and its Implications*. Trans. M. Sainsbury. Chicago: University of Chicago Press, 1970. This book is a classic for any one interested in caste studies in India. It is remarkable for its scope, density, and wealth of scholarship. Dumont's thesis that caste system is predicated on the binary of purity versus impurity has remained the starting point for most modern critiques and debates on this subject.

Omvelt, Gail. *Dalits and the Democratic Revolution: Dr. Ambedkar and the Dalit Movement in Colonial India*. New Delhi: Sage, 1994. Again, this is a classic text for anyone interested in problems of untouchability and the Dalit movements under the leadership of Dr. Ambedkar. Another important book by the same author is *Dalit Visions*, Hyderabad: Orient Longman, 1995. A useful book on Dalit identity is Ghanshyam Shah's *Dalit Identity and Politics*, New Delhi: Sage, 2001.

Protest literature against caste segregation includes Mulk Raj Anand and Zelliot (eds), *An Anthology of Dalit Literature*, New Delhi: Gyan Publishers,

1992; Arjun Dangle, *Poisoned Bread: Translations from Modern Marathi Dalit Literature*, Hyderabad: Orient Longman, 1992; and Barbara Joshi (eds), *Untouchable Voices of Dalit Liberation Movement*, London: Zed Books, 1986.

B

Margaret Berry's *Mulk Raj Anand: The Man and the Novelist*, Amsterdam: Oriental Press, 1971, is an early examination of Mulk Raj's works along with a great deal of autobiographical material written in the structuralist mode. The book appears somewhat dated. Saros Cowasjee's *So Many Freedoms: A Study of the Major Fiction of Mulk Raj Anand*, New Delhi: Oxford University Press, 1977, still remains the best book for Anand studies, beautifully fusing autobiographical information with acute critical insights. K.R. Srinivasa Iyengar's *Indian writing in English*, Bombay: Asia Publishing House, 1962, is an excellent book for understanding of the general context of Indian English literature and Anand's position within that literary tradition.

M.K. Naik's *Mulk Raj Anand*, New Delhi: Arnold Heinemann, 1973, like most of his books, is extremely competent, detailed and well informed, with a wealth of critical material. This is a good book to begin Anand studies with.

Alastair Niven's *The Yoke of Pity: A Study of the Fictional Writings of Mulk Raj Anand*, New Delhi: Arnold–Heinemann, 1978, is more in the nature of a study guide for the undergraduate-level students. Marlene Fisher, *The Wisdom of the Heart: A Study of the Works of Mulk Raj Anand*, New Delhi: Sterling Publishers, 1985, is a competent critical work discussing the early novels of Mulk Raj Anand from the perspective of his location as a socialist and humanist.

T.M.J Indra Mohan (ed.), *The Novels of Mulk Raj Anand: A New Critical Spectrum*, New Delhi: Atlantic, 2005, is a new collection of essays on novels of Mulk Raj Anand on various topics such as Anand's use of the Indian English language.

Other important books include: Jack Lindsay, *The Elephant and the Lotus: A Study of the Novels of Mulk Raj Anand*, Bombay: Kutub Popular, 1965; K.N. Sinha, *Mulk Raj Anand*, New York: Twayne Publishers, 1972; R.K. Dhawan, *The Novels of Mulk Raj Anand*, New Delhi: Atlantic Publishers, 1992; and P. Rajan, *Mulk Raj Anand: A Revaluation*, New Delhi, 1994.

Some useful reviews and articles are M. Tarinayya, 'Untouchable: An analysis,' *Journal of the Mysore University*, Vol. 26. March 1969; and R.T. Robertson, 'Untouchable as an Archetypal Novel', *World Literatures Written in English*. Vol. 14, No. 2. Nov. 1975.